# THE THICKET'S
# PRODIGY

# THE THICKET'S PRODIGY

## Reflections of an Improbable Life

*From Texas's Big Thicket to Los Alamos, the Atomic Bomb, NASA, and the World Wide Web*

### Ronald G. Brock

Galt/Mirrin Publishing, LLC

Edited by Celene T, Chrissy W and Nikki T of Write My Wrongs, LLC
Final edit and interior design by Scott Amonson
Cover by James Longmore of Write My Wrongs, LLC

Printed and distributed under the Auspices of Galt/Mirrin Publishing, LLC.
Printed by Lightning Source, LLC

## Galt/Mirrin Publishing, LLC

12421 N. 57th way
Scottsdale, AZ 85254
e-mail: ron@galtmirrin.com

ISBN (*Paperback*): 979-8-9865144-0-6
ISBN (*Hardcover*): 979-8-9865144-2-0
ISBN (*Ebook*): 979-8-9865144-1-3

Library of Congress Control Number: 2022912213

*To Carolyn*

# Contents

# Preface

*The Thicket's Prodigy* began as a simple project composed of my personal recollections of life growing up in East Texas and spending a few years in Los Alamos New Mexico.

But it became much more. And so did the research.

Dad's story required a factual accounting of three, highly complex topics, each constituting a story on its own: Texas' Big Thicket, Los Alamos and the atomic bomb, high-powered computation, and NASA's trip to the moon. Added to those was my insider's experience with a World Wide Web business startup, and what we have come to know today as the Internet.

For Los Alamos and the Manhattan Project's making of the atomic bomb, followed by the bomb's remaking, much has been written. Many of the Manhattan Project participants described their association with the Manhattan Project from their perspective. Primarily, those autobiographies were content with the citing of mostly narrow factual descriptions of their experiences.

These facts are important, and interesting of course, but hundreds of publications deal more specifically with various elements of the topic of the bomb and its evolution. Most important among reference sources were: The Atomic Heritage Foundation, National Museum of Nuclear Science and History, Los Alamos National Laboratory, Constitution Daily's blog, The United States Nuclear Regulatory Commission, Global

Security.org, Denver Post, Arms Control Wonk, United States Army Ordinance Department, Lecture Notes of Robert Serber, distributed to Manhattan Project participants, Irvine World News (online edition), 3 Quarks Daily, Atomic Archives, NOVA Online, George Washington University dissertation: Owen Pagano, Famous Scientists.org, U.S. Department of Energy, Legacy Management, and The Nuclear Secrecy Blog.

Two individuals were near single handedly responsible for orchestrating much of the history of Los Alamos and the Manhattan Project: Edith Truslow, serving as a WAC during the time of the Manhattan Project was instrumental in developing documentation memorializing Manhattan Project goings-on. Cynthia Kelly took on the equally daunting responsibility of assembling the writings of many Manhattan Project participants.

Rebecca Collinsworth, Los Alamos Historical Society Archives' Archivist, graciously made information from the archives available to me. Ms. Collinsworth acknowledged need for a narrative describing life during the period shortly after the Manhattan Project, as written by a witness to the transition from an army post to a modern city during the mid-to-late 1940s period. I was able to get down to the heart of that question.

My father's, Eugene H. Brock's, written anecdotal recollections of life as a fifth-generation member of an extended Big Thicket family numbering in the hundreds were supplemented by *The Handbook of Texas Online* which made available an extensive array of academic research conducted through the University of North Texas Press. A rich, multigenerational source of family history was additionally made available through Ancestry.com, providing an excellent source of connections among the several clans important to our family's history in the Thicket.

Houston's El Alacran District required extensive help from several library sources. Among these, the Houston Chronicle proved to be an excellent source as did the University of Houston libraries, and the Houston Historic archives.

## Acknowledgements

What materialized as a book was sufficient need to acknowledge an array of sources instrumental to filling in details among topics requiring written proof. I am grateful to *Write My Wrongs* editors, Celene, Chrissy, and Nicole, all of whom provided excellent recommendations throughout a several months editing period. Then, swooping in for closure, Scott Amonson's exhaustive final review, and edit, iced the proverbial cake.

No amount of thanks is sufficient to express my gratitude to authors Paul Perry and Dr. Howard DeWitt, for their inspiration related to book title development, and bibliography format, and, the two very creative individuals responsible for providing The Thicket's Prodigy's finished appearance. Scott Amonson's, book interior design, combined with a very attractive cover design by James Longmore, *Write My Wrongs*' Creative Director of Self-Publishing.

# Introduction

True genius, the extraordinary intellect that few possess, occurs as randomly as lightning strikes. And it's more rarely encountered in remote, obscure surroundings.

Stories of overcoming impossibly difficult circumstances to achieve colossal accomplishments most often describe pioneers of science and industry. In extremely rare incidents, such stories may have extended beyond probability to have strained disbelief in even the least skeptical.

One such story describes the life of Eugene H. "Gene" Brock, who was this type of individual. He was also my father.

But *The Thicket's Prodigy* didn't begin that way. The story started as an autobiography describing my own life experience, ending with my role as the founder of a pioneering internet company following the World Wide Web's introduction in 1995. In my first cut at an outline, the process resulted in an awakening, and I started to examine the reality of my father's accomplishments. The result triggered an awakened admiration of my Dad. He was, in short, a phenomenon.

During a lifetime of achievement extending well beyond what anyone could reasonably have expected, he participated in and mastered the early stages of two highly complex subjects: atomic bomb technology and high-performance computer technology. But it was how he arrived there that shifted the narrative's autobiographical focus to include Dad's biographical story. My part was played as an observer during my early years, then became a separate story as both of us continued in our individual careers.

As a fifth-generation progeny of an East Texas family whose members had inhabited Polk County, Texas's Big Thicket since the early 1850s, nearly everyone was related among several hundred members, and most were extremely poor, relying near-uniformly on subsistence farms, supplemented by work in oil fields and lumber mills.

In the midst of this, an individual "of great and varied excellence" was born. Dad was brilliant—and interested in just about everything—making him frequently the most interesting person in the room. From very early childhood, he knew he would one day become, in his words, "an educated man." It was a commitment, preempting any possibility of assuming the legacy of an East Texas subsistence farmer or inheriting a position in the family general store.

But his ambition was limited by access to education. Grades one through nine were taught in a two-room schoolhouse by a single teacher. And Polk County's only high school was located in Livingston, a town eight miles in distance by a roadway little better than a mule path. In a necessary accommodation to conditions, Dad's high school years were spent living in a Livingston boardinghouse during the week before traveling home by horseback on weekends.

Following high school graduation, he was accepted at Rice Institute, Texas's highest-rated educational facility, before health reasons required turning to Texas Technological College and the dry climate of West Texas. But after only a single semester, even that option turned out to be a near-impossible challenge; he was informed that the Depression had ended any further family monetary support.

What would be a crushing end to most ambitions prompted what was probably the first of several courageous decisions that were to drive him through a lifetime of career achievements: he would not give in to what most would have seen as an insurmountable obstruction.

He saw it as an inconvenience, but one leaving no choice. He lived homeless for much of the next three and a half years, at the end earning a degree in mathematics. Through a series of menial tasks—babysitting, cutting grass, sweeping floors—any pay earned was applied first to books and classroom expenses; what was left went to food.

Throughout his career, a staggering intellect drove him to explore and, with seemingly little effort, conquer the cutting-edge technologies that were understood by a limited few at the time. The advantage led first to his participation in redesigning the Manhattan Project's atomic bomb, later to his status as chief of the Computation and Analysis Division of NASA's Manned Spacecraft Center in Houston, Texas, and finally to his becoming an internationally acknowledged expert on high-powered computing systems.

Our positions—mine as the son of a polymath and his as the country boy born with an excessively robust IQ coupled with a desire to become someone other than what he was born to be—took some turbulent turns for both of us.

And that's what this story is about.

## CHAPTER ONE

# The Big Thicket

Folklore is full of stories containing forests so foreboding, even the bravest of story participants are hesitant to challenge them. Texas's Big Thicket was like that.

Spanish missionaries traveling through it in the late 1600s described it as "an impenetrable wilderness." When the first pioneers arrived in the early 1800s, Texas's Big Thicket was a vast expanse of woods, reported to have covered as much as 3.5 million acres, a 5,000 square mile geographic area approximately 50 miles wide by 100 miles long.

Early explorers described the Thicket's boundaries as "South of the old San Antonio Road; east of the Brazos River; north of the Coastal Prairies and the La Bahia Road, and west of the Sabine River." Others, more simply, referred to the Big Thicket as "somewhere close to Louisiana, including swamps big enough to be called swamps, or small enough to be called Baygalls, thick with cane breaks, and palmettos."

The notably swampy environment was sustained by several small streams with names like Menard, Mill, Meetinghouse Branch, Beaver, Little Pine Island, Union Wells, Bad Luck, and Big Sandy. The Thicket's most important body of water was

Pine Island Bayou, but one other, Sour Lake, stood out for its foul smell and perceived healing powers.

As one of the most densely vegetated areas found in North America, scientists sometimes referred to the Big Thicket as the "biological crossroads of North America." It was said foliage densities were so extreme that "there were places in the woods that you had to get down on your hands and knees to crawl through, so tight that if you ran into a snake there was no place to go except to back out."

Water moccasins, cane break rattlesnakes, copperheads, coral snakes, and pygmy rattlers crawled the Thicket in unavoidable numbers. If one was looking for the experience, not paying attention to where their foot was placed made for a good chance to get snake-bitten.[1]

An abundance of wild game—panthers, black bears, deer, turkeys, wildcats, wolves, squirrels, skunks, raccoons, rabbits, and possums—served as an important meat source for at least three Native American tribes—Atakapan, Caddo, and Alabama-Coushatta—many years before the 1820s when White settlers began to arrive.

While the earliest settlers stayed away from the interior— "too dark, too thick, and too swampy"—those who came in the 1830s and 1840s began to move into the Thicket's interior, carving out small clearings just large enough to support a subsistence farm for themselves. They were looking for privacy and were people who lived off the land through whatever crops they could raise and whatever game they could hunt. Deer and bears were dominant staples, with venison most favored—

roasted, fried in bear fat, or jerked and hung in the smokehouse. On occasion when venison or bear meat were short squirrels, possums, and raccoons were satisfactory substitutes to the supper table.

Thanks to the early Spanish explorer presence, beef and pork had also made their way onto the list of preferred edibles. Cattle, brought to the new world by Cortez in 1519, had escaped to live wild in the Thicket. And wild hogs, descendants of Hernando de Soto's 1538 expedition's pigs, had extended their territory from Florida into East Texas to become among the Thicket's favorite food sources.[2] Impressively, the Thicket's versions of both these once-domesticated animals had become as wary and tough as any other wild animal stalking the Thicket.

But as wily as the cattle had become in keeping to the Thicket's protection during daylight hours, attractive grazing availability outside the Thicket's perimeter occasionally enticed them to foolishly leave its protection at night, a mistake in their instincts frequently leading to a place on the supper table.

Supplementing game sources, the swamps, bayous, and creeks had bass, catfish, frog legs, and, among the sloughs, crawfish. The woods had pecans, hickory nuts, and black walnuts, and berries grew in the occasional clearing where the sun could reach the ground. Possum grapes grew along the creek banks, and muscadine vines climbed through the top branches to drop their grapes in the fall. Mayhaws dropped their fruit into the rising waters in the spring, making it easy to collect all that was needed for making the winter's supply of jelly.

Conditions in principally the Southern states of Alabama, North Carolina, Mississippi, South Carolina, and Louisiana enticed immigration to the Thicket. Land grants had been awarded to several families in 1834, but few took advantage until 1835 when seven families, including that of James and Matilda Brock, were recorded to have been in residence in Smithfield. In May 1841, Drew's Landing and the settlement of Smithfield were busy shipping points on the Trinity River. But Smithfield failed to survive. Today, the town's specific location is uncertain.

By 1850, thirteen thousand people lived in the nine Thicket counties. What had begun as a few had turned into an influx, and settler encroachment on prior Native American territory had reached such a volume that it attracted sufficient government attention to result in a 1,110.7-acre Alabama-Coushatta reservation being dedicated by Congress in 1854. An additional 3,071 acres were added in 1928, increasing the total reservation size to 4,181.7 acres.

Early settlers—composed mostly of English, Scots, Irish, and Welsh—were described as a "group not strongly attached to government, either of the royal, or proprietary, kind." Most exhibited a calculated wisdom, some, a certain meanness, and all, a kind of toughness. "Philosophically they were Southerners by sympathy, conservative politically, and socially; in religion they were Methodists, Baptists, and Presbyterians by name; Calvinists in practice."

The Thicket was an attractive option for many leaving unpleasant circumstances. "Gone to Texas" was the term applied to people who needed to get out of town and be lost. Reflective of the areas they left, the Thicket's speech, accents, and ways of doing things were Southern. The population that evolved was uniformly independent, wary of strangers, and generally law-abiding, although the law, in a strict sense, was a while in coming. Stories warned of the people who lived in the Thicket.

The seclusion they were looking for was readily available; most found a refuge in which they could live their lives the way they wanted. But some unattractive conditions accompanied that benefit.

Summertime temperatures in that part of Texas exceed 90°F about 110 days annually, and days with temperatures above 95°, even above 100°, are not uncommon. The average annual rainfall of fifty inches assures that humidity exceeds 60 percent most of the time and, with some frequency, more than 90 percent.[3]

When the mosquito hatch was particularly robust, clouds of mosquitoes became more than just a pesky insect, and nighttime discomfort could be made epic. On occasion, one particular variety, the big Trinity River Bottom mosquito, was known to have assumed swarm sizes of dangerous proportions. One story told of mosquitoes that invaded in such numbers they were killing cattle, explaining that "they got up in their noses and smothered them."

When winter came, nighttime lows typically averaged 38° to 48°; daytime temperatures ranged from 55° to 65°. And when the occasional cold front came through, temperatures would drop below freezing.

One can reasonably conclude that those who came and stayed were the most rugged of pioneers.

### The Brock Clan's Participation in the Thicket's Polk County

The Brock and Peebles clans' introductions began sometime prior to 1850 in Alabama.

James Brock and the former Matilda Jowers had married on August 11, 1827, in Henry County. Their arrival at Smithfield was followed, sometime prior to the Civil War, by a move to Polk County's Moscow settlement. Polk was one of nine counties composing the Big Thicket.

Consistent with the times, James and Matilda had a family of fourteen children: William Riley, John J., Green McKinnis, James Levi, Alexander, George, Bevert "Robert," Mary Ann, Henry W., Barbery "Amanda," Calvin "Dick," twins Emaline N. and Eveline N., and Barbara Ann "Poosie."

The Peebles clan began their Polk County immigration in 1853 when twin brothers Wiley and Riley Peebles and older brother Isham, along with their families and several individuals and connected families, arrived to form the "Henry County Settlement" four miles north of Livingston. Five years later, the Henry County Settlement became the settlement of Providence.

The Peebles, for the most part composed of direct descendants of William "Billy" and Elizabeth Peebles and James and Matilda Brock, were responsible for initiating the move to the Big Thicket. Several marriages between the two families had begun prior to leaving Henry County: William Riley Brock and Susanna Peebles married on October 24, 1851, and John Jowers

Brock and Louvina Peebles married on June 20, 1850. A third marriage between Alexander Lowe and Mahala Peebles occurred on June 7, 1852.

Wiley and Elizabeth Peebles brought seven children with them; Riley and Sarah Peebles arrived with nine children, then added another four during the following ten years. Isham Peebles and his wife, Winnaford, known as "Winnie," arrived with seven children. Harvey Galloway married Missouri Ann Peebles in 1854, shortly after their Polk County arrival.

Continuing the Brock-Peebles clan's collaboration, Green McKinnis Brock married Mary Ann Peebles on April 4, 1859, and, keeping with an apparent family tradition, proceeded to add fourteen children to Polk County's population.

Dad recalled family history passed down to him:

*The migrations of family groups to the Big Thicket and Polk County area can be traced back to Tennessee, Virginia, North Carolina, Alabama, and Mississippi. Migrations were stimulated by pre-Civil War unrest and the urge to have more and better land. One quality that was noticed throughout this history—through my time—was the closeness of the family groups. This closeness was woven like a thread among the lives of the families and individuals.*

*These generations, for the most part, were born and raised in the United States. The time spanned is approximately 150 years. Polk County seems to have been the place to go in the early 1800s, but for what reason, no one has established. Grandpa Johnny Brock used to laughingly say "it was the easiest place to get lost." Regardless of reasons, the area now called the Big Thicket had all the characteristics they were searching for.*

*Family locations were defined, insofar as possible, by community, settlement, or village names. Some early family members were located as far as possible from the nearest settlement. However, one must recognize that in the early 1800s, settlements were scarce, and it was difficult to find a community or village. Many of the small settlements are no longer in existence.*

*Several clans were more closely associated over an extended period and, regardless of migration directions, seemed to get back together in the long run. The result of this togetherness was an association of very strong ties. Everyone knew and respected other segments of the several family groups.*

*The immediate family unit was surrounded by relatives at all levels—aunts, uncles, and cousins. The latter group started at the first-cousin level and extended as far as the tenth cousin. Everyone in any of the three categories was close kin. Some cousins-by-marriage connections were just as important a part of the whole clan as those identified by bloodlines. These close ties were the foundation of the total strength of the family groups.*

*Family surnames like Adams, Turners, Holders, Peebles, Nicholsons, Williamsons, Morrisons, McCaghrens, McCraneys, Brocks, and many others . . . Two of our closest families, Peebles and Holders, trace their histories back to the early 1600s.*

My grandmother's Holder clan arrived at the Polk County settlement of Leggett about the same time, as had most clans who settled in Polk County. Clan patriarch William Holder had married Elizabeth Nicholson on January 18, 1852, in Neshoba County, Mississippi, before moving to Polk County sometime in the 1850s.

Between 1835 and 1860, Southern states settlers' dominance led to plantations becoming important to Polk County's economy. At the 1860 Thicket population count, Polk County's population was 8,300, of which a slave count of 4,198 was dominant. Within the Thicket's nine counties, the total population had grown to 87,000.[4]

The Civil War's declaration on April 12, 1861, resulted in eight Confederate Army companies being raised from the Thicket to serve under Major Alexander Hamilton Washington.[5] Five members of the Green Brock family served, along with another few hundred Polk County draftees. Among them, William Riley Brock died on October 25, 1863, at Pine Bluff, Arkansas. Susanna, widowed with four children, remarried Wisemon McCaghren and had five more children.

Not all Thicket residents felt the same patriotic fervor. In April 1862, a group of seventy or so "Jayhawkers," Confederate Army draftees, who opted to disappear into the Thicket, felt the Civil War was a "rich man's war, and a poor man's fight."[6] Only wealthy people owned slaves, and Thicket people felt it made no sense to get involved, instead saying, "We'll just go out here in the woods and stay."

Ignoring Confederate Army harassment, the Jayhawkers found no problem surviving on the Thicket's availability of fish, small game, honey, and wild berries, holding out nearly untouched near the Honey Island settlement in Hardin County until the war ended.

The Civil War's termination also ended Polk County's plantation exports. Only those hardy souls who scratched out their living on small subsistence farms remained. But by 1869, Polk County families supported by subsistence farms had doubled in number,[7] in the process becoming a close-knit society. The typical subsistence farm consisted of a vegetable garden, a few fruit trees, chickens, a milk cow, and sometimes a pig captured from the Thicket for fattening.

The county population had reduced from an 1870 census count of 8,707 to 7,189 in 1880.[8]

The settlement of Moscow, eight miles north of Leggett, was founded in 1847 as a center for farm trade. But the condition changed with a transition from plantation-grown cotton at the Civil War's end. Sawmills assumed a place of prominence in the Thicket's and Moscow settlement's economies.[9]

The Thicket's composition—a lot of attractive woods— had made it inevitable that progress would aggressively find its way there. Great stands of red oak, sweetgum, pin oaks, black gum, dogwood, redbud, magnolia, holly, elm, cypress, loblolly pines, and saw briers were now for the taking.[10]

Gigantic trees of every kind were in abundance—Hickory, Beach, Sycamore, Ash, Buckeye, White Oaks, and Yellow Pine—all six feet in diameter, reaching 50 feet before breaking out in branches. The king of the forest; their monstrous growth, towering height, and extended branches really filled the beholder with awe.

Lumber production had begun quietly in 1856, with relatively small quantities exported by a single Liberty County sawmill. That changed with the Civil War's ending; an explosive proliferation of sawmills became formidable overnight.[11]

By the 1870s, sawmills were gnawing their way through the Thicket like locusts through a cornfield. The 1900 *Texas Handbook* stated: "The Big Thicket includes all, or part of, Hardin, Polk, Jasper, Newton, Sabine, San Augustine, Angelina, Trinity, Montgomery, and Liberty counties."[12] And the Thicket's pine and hardwood forests had been reduced to 300,000 acres, less than 10 percent of their original size. But, at 469 square miles, it was still formidable.

To serve Thicket sawmills, the narrow-gauge Houston East and West Railway reached Moscow in 1880, prompting the ultramodern addition of a horse-drawn streetcar linking Moscow's business district with the train depot.[13] In 1883, the railroad extended farther into the Thicket, adding a Leggett stop along the way.

Railroad service wasn't much. One description stated, "the track was narrow, and crooked, and the engines had only two drive wheels and only pulled a couple of cars." But the logging industry had turned the Thicket on its ear. The railroad was much needed, and Moscow's population growth was stimulated by its addition.[14]

The railway's inclusion of Leggett spurred the construction of a few buildings, initially a cotton gin, saloon, and general store; a sawmill was added in 1889. When the sawmill caught fire and burned eight years later, so did much of the town.[15]

The 7.2 miles separating Leggett and Moscow included two other settlements—Seven Oaks, 3.4 miles northeast of Leggett, and Walda, 2 miles beyond Seven Oaks. Walda no longer exists; Seven Oaks's population today remains about Leggett-size. Farther northeast, 6.4 miles beyond Moscow, was Camden.[16]

These were just a few of the settlements serving Thicket residents during the 1800s. Some survived to continue; many are only memories, even their locations forgotten. But 1895's estimated population of 563 made Moscow and its collection of sawmills Polk County's largest town.[17]

The Brocks and Holders connected when James Andrew Holder (born October 30, 1854, in Polk County) married Louise Morrison on October 22, 1874. Their daughter, Elizabeth Ann "Lizzie" Holder, my grandmother, was born on September 26, 1882, in Leggett. Lizzie was the Leggett Methodist Church's organist when she met Henry Wyatt, one of the Moscow Brocks. Lizzie and Wyatt were married on October 28, 1900.

The Brock-Williamson clan's relationship began when John "Johnny" James Brock, born April 26, 1855, in Henry County, Alabama, married Anna "Matilda" Williamson on September 4, 1877. Shortly after, Anna's brother, Marion Nathaniel Williamson, married Susan "Susie" Ann Brock, John's sister.

**From Left Back:** (Viola Holder, Elizabeth Ann "Lizzie" Holder, Bama Holder) **From Left Front:** (James Holder, Louise Holder, James Andrew Holder, Bertha Holder)

Dad's memories of Thicket relatives were consistent:

> *Most of our ancestors were farmers and, for the most part, needed but little assistance from the outside. Most raised some sugarcane, corn, cotton, watermelons, peas, beans, and had fruit trees of various kinds. This renewable supply source was supplemented with fruit from the forests, sporadic hunting and fishing, wild pig butchering, and gathering nuts.*

It would probably not be regarded as unusual that a few eccentricities, universal to Big Thicket dwellers, made for some fascinating relatives. Most were notably unpretentious people who put on few airs. I never heard an explanation for what seemed a universal lust for individuality, but the tendency was more probably a character trait that was with them when they arrived. A self-reliant breed, almost entirely dependent on the land as a provider, they fished the creeks, bayous, and rivers; hunted the woods for wild game; and gathered a variety of nuts and fruits.

For five generations, clans intermarried, assuring that most Thicket residents were, at some level, kin and had become their own society with their own ways. Customs, manners, speech, and diet all took on great similarity. And in the process, some distinct inherited physical characteristics developed. Sandy-colored hair, chiseled features, and high cheekbones be- came recognizable "of the Thicket" characteristics passed down from one generation to the next.

Prior to the lumber industry hitting its stride, there had been a period beginning around 1850 and extending until 1900 when health-seekers had also made somewhat of an industry around Sour Lake, Hardin County's oldest town.[18]

Supplementing health seekers, an early 1900s industry included black bear hunts within a forty-by-twenty-mile area known as the Bear Hunter's Thicket.[19] The Bear Hunter's Thicket began in the southern part of Polk and Tyler counties and ended below Sour Lake. It was there where the Big Thicket remained not much different than it had been a hundred years before. And Big Thicket Bear hunts were famous, attracting hunters from all parts of the world.

Before the arrival of White settlers, Native Americans had made use of Sour Lake's mineral waters and the pitch found around oil seepages near the lakeshore. Originally known as Sour Lake Springs for the mineral springs that fed the nearby lake, Sour Lake Springs had been settled in 1835 by Stephen Jackson.[20]

The Sour Lake Spring's name was shortened to Sour Lake for promotional reasons, and it became a minor health resort with a couple of hotels, cottages, and campsites to serve visitors by 1850. Early entrepreneurs sold the lake's water for its health benefits; by 1885, the town had two general stores, two hotels, and a population of 150. But the venture failed to last. By 1896, Sour Lake's population had declined to 50 and was reduced to a single hotel.[21]

Relatively nearby, J. F. Cotton discovered a spring at the site of the similarly named town of New Sour Lake. And by the 1880s, another entrepreneur, P. S. Watts, was capitalizing on the foul-smelling water, which, due to the sulfur-enhanced content, was perceived to hold unique health properties.[22] It was a time when the health-conscious had considerable confidence in the healing powers of such "medicinal waters." Toward promoting the area's waters, Watts renamed New Sour Lake to Saratoga, expecting to cash in on New York's famous spa of the same name.[25]

"The Springs," a luxurious antebellum-style hotel and health spa, attracted people seeking its healing capabilities from all parts of the country and Europe. Nestled in the shadows of old-growth, moss-draped oaks, bathhouse facilities extended along the edge of a mineral springs-fed lake. Adding cachet, a pavilion in the lake's center was connected to the shore by an ornamental footbridge.[23]

## Pattillo Higgins Discovers Oil

As early as 1865, it had been speculated that oil was in the Sour Lake area. An 1887 attempt at drilling resulted in a small producing well; similar activity occurred four miles north of the town of Beaumont in 1890.[24]

Beaumont, located eighty-five miles east of Houston, was adjacent to the Big Thicket's Pine Island Bayou and twenty miles north of Sour Lake. The Port of Beaumont had been an important Neches River lumber distribution center since the Beaumont Riverport was activated during the 1880s. But that was about to change; thoughts of oil were raising interest in the area.[25]

In 1892, Pattillo Higgins, along with four others, formed the Gladys City Oil, Gas, and Manufacturing Company to do exploratory drilling in an area known for its gas seeps. The group's attempts were unsuccessful, but Higgins remained convinced there was oil under the salt dome located barely a mile outside of town.[26]

In 1899, Higgins teamed up again—this time with Captain Anthony F. Lucas, the US's leading expert on salt dome formations. Lucas entered into a lease agreement with the Gladys City Manufacturing Company and, separately, struck an agreement with Higgins.[27]

But Lucas's attempts also ran out of money, requiring raising more funds. This time, backing came from Pittsburgh's

Andrew Mellon and a couple of other investors, forming the Guffey Petroleum Company. Negotiations with the new investors left Lucas with a one-eighth share; Higgins was elbowed out of the new partnership.[28]

Drilling continuation encountered one seemingly impossible-to-overcome difficulty after another, each different and each requiring innovative correction. But Lucas was nothing if not persistent. His perseverance paid off on January 10, 1901. At a depth of 1,139 feet, the Texas oil industry was officially born when the Lucas Gusher blasted onto the scene, blowing the drill bit—then six tons of oil pipe—into the air.[29]

Designated "Spindletop," it was the largest gusher the world had seen. A 150-foot geyser of oil was to flow at a rate of 100,000 barrels per day, drowning the drilling rig in a lake of oil before the well could be capped nine days later.[30]

Beaumont's population of 9,000 more than tripled in three months to 30,000. Overnight, a forest of A-frame derricks, serviced by thousands of roughnecks, were drilling every nearby available square foot of soil.[31]

By the end of 1902, more than 500 companies, among them Texaco, Gulf Oil, and Hughes Tool Company, were operating in the area, and 285 wells were pumping oil. The volume of petroleum made available was so extreme that, for a time, the wellhead price of oil was reduced to ten cents per barrel.[32]

Higgins's contention that a large pool of oil was located under a salt dome south of Beaumont had been correct. And things were just beginning. Any freshwater with a smell of rotten eggs meant there was a pocket of oil—maybe a whole sea of it—trapped inside a salt dome somewhere below.

The Lucas gusher's success drove the search for oil farther into the Thicket. And twenty miles northwest of Beaumont in southern Hardin County, the Great Western Oil Company, later to become known as Texaco, struck a gusher of their own at a depth of 683 feet. And Sour Lake transformed from a resort town into a boomtown with a population of 10,000.[33]

A peak oil production of 50,000 barrels daily caused depletion sufficient to result in half the 150 original Sour Lake wells being abandoned by 1903. But the oil frenzy's momentum carried on.

Financed by Beaumont backers, oil was discovered in October 1903 near Pine Bayou, one mile north of Batson's post office, peculiarly named "Otto." The village of Batson was moved adjacent to Otto, Otto was renamed Batson, and Batson became another town of 10,000 workers, camp followers, and curiosity seekers overnight. And it just as suddenly earned a reputation as one of the wildest boomtowns in oil history.[34]

Not to be ignored, Saratoga, thirty-eight miles northwest of Beaumont in west-central Hardin County, experienced speculation of its own. Despite the small producing well in 1897, significant drilling did not begin until 1901. Sandwiched in time between the Spindletop and Batson oil field discoveries, Saratoga's oil discoveries were not as dramatic but still resulted in the stimulation of a similar 10,000 population increase in a period of weeks.[35]

Batson, Saratoga, and Sour Lake, three formerly sleepy settlements, had transformed into the three wildest boom towns in Texas. Every possible facility for feeding and housing, ranging from boarding houses to tents to makeshift shelters fashioned out of cardboard, sprang up overnight. And some just camped out under the pine trees. No inconvenience was too great.[36]

The oil fields attracted a kind of individual even more inclined to hard living than the group who had originally made the Thicket their home. And violence was an everyday part of life.

Saratoga and Sour Lake were rough, but neither rose to Batson's rampant lawlessness. Known for its borderline depravity, it was said, "if violence could have been gauged then on the Richter scale of 1 to 10, Batson would surely have rated an 11."[37]

In Saratoga alone, fifty-two rowdy saloons provided a place for a roustabout working on the drilling platforms to stop off at the end of the day for his usuals. The fierce thirst brought on by the oil rig's heat and humidity left him with a need to clear the crude from his throat.[38]

The saloon was his club to relax with a schooner of beer or a shot and maybe participate in a recreational fight. He was welcome there. Shave or change of clothes? Not needed! Saloons were also notorious for fights. On most days, somebody was killed.

The time between the discovery of Spindletop on January 10, 1901, and the Batson field's discovery in October 1903 was thirty-two months. And there was more coming.

Another new oil source was identified on January 7, 1905, just over one mile northeast of the town of Humble in northeastern Harris County. My grandfather, Wyatt Brock, and great uncle, Pete McDent, were both employed as roustabouts at the Humble oil field.[39]

But before the lumber and oil industries were to make their mark in the Thicket, one extended family member made an impression of his own, earning a reputation for meanness at a more personal extreme. John Wesley Hardin, born October 12, 1853, in the North Texas town of Bonham, was raised in the Big Thicket's Trinity County settlement of Sumpter.[40]

John was killed by a bullet to the head on August 19, 1895, in El Paso. My grandmother, Lizzie Brock, was thirteen at the time and knew plenty about John Wesley, who would drop back to his roots in the Thicket from time to time while he was making his reputation.

John was fifteen when he first killed a man in Sumpter. At the time my grandmother told me about him, I didn't know who he was but learned later that John Wesley had a reputation for a violent disposition and held prejudices toward the Black population and Yankees. But an even more particularly fiery intolerance was reserved for individuals responsible for Civil War resettlement.

He wasn't having any part of forced resettlement or the enforcers who had been sent to the Thicket to see to it. As a result, he had found it necessary to kill a few who had arrived, bent on correcting Thicket resettlement malfeasance.[41]

From there, he developed notoriety as one of the West's most notorious gunfighters. He was best known for having once shot a man snoring in an adjacent boardinghouse room by shooting through the wall, killing the offending sleeper.

Like most who spent their formative years in the Thicket, John Wesley combined strict religious views with moralism, supported by a committed personal view that he "never killed a man who didn't need it."

Lizzie was eighteen when John Wesley's granddaughter, Blanche Elizabeth Billings (born October 12, 1900), married Edward McCaghran, an immediate Brock family relative. The result caused quite a stir among the clan; Lizzie was not happy with that particular family connection and spoke to me of John Wesley only once.

And with that, Gene Brock's story can begin.

**The Early Life of Eugene H. Brock**

Dad was born on September 18, 1912, in Leggett, a settlement like any one of a half dozen extending along the Thicket's Polk County boundaries. The third of four siblings, his oldest brother, Hermes, was nine years his senior, his sister Louise was four years older, and his brother Carl was four years younger. All four siblings shared unusual intellect.

A fifth-generation backwoods country boy, Dad dreamed of one day achieving status as an "educated man," leaving behind the life of an East Texas farmer, as had been every previous generation's lot:

*As a boy, I dreamed of the many things I wanted to be—an artist, violinist, or perhaps an archaeologist. But most of all, I wanted to be someone other than the head of a small farm, East Texas family. The bad parts I remember of that life seem to stem from cold fingers during the milking of our cows and the woodpile required for cooking and heating. I developed a real dislike for both activities. And every step I would take in the future would be away from that latter responsibility.*

Dad's earliest memories began when he was three during a trip one Sunday to the Humble, Texas oilfield where my grandfather, Wyatt Brock, had been working:

*The very first few years of my childhood were spent in the small towns built up around oil exploration, drilling, and production. These towns provided only the worst of shelter and social activities. The only thing that I remember of this early period (other than what others have told me) is related to an accident that happened one Sunday afternoon.*

*My dad had taken my brother, Hermes, and me to a drilling rig he was helping build. Then, while we were there, one of those accidents that happened so often in oil field construction struck; one of the workers fell from the drill rig's top and was killed. Drilling rigs in those early days were constructed of wood, and accidents were frequent. This accident occurred at Humble, Texas (the birthplace of the Humble oil company), which is also the place where Uncle Pete McDent was injured fatally.*

Typical of Thicket residents of the time, my grandfather and many extended family members supplemented their small farm's subsistence with work in sawmills or the oil fields.

Until the 1880s, Thicket inhabitants had been mostly scattered throughout the woods, surviving on what they could raise. Some ran wild hogs on a relatively free-range farm, fattening them for fall slaughter and meat for the smokehouse. Suppertime for the typical Thicket table was not a probable inspiration to the epicurean. But a mess of collards, bacon, potatoes, wild game of some sort, and always cornbread gave them perfect satisfaction.[42]

Cornbread was the early settlers' only bread, but it was "good enough." And it remained a staple even when Wyatt and Lizzie left the Big Thicket for Houston, then, later, College Station. Wyatt made a skillet of cornbread every morning of every day I could remember.

Dad had great affection for his kin. They were self-sufficient and poor by even then-current standards, but they didn't necessarily know it. Farmhouses were noisy with big families, and relatives would often gather from a few miles around. There was a vitality to life that they would miss in later years when their reasons for being there in the first place had long since passed.

When Lizzie and Wyatt married, most Thicket occupants were at least distant kin. The Williamsons, Morrisons, Brocks, Peebles, McCaghrens, McCranys, Adams, Turners,

Holders, and others had intermarried with seemingly wild abandon since the 1850s. It seems probable that at least some marriages were among cousins who, while possibly distant, were
related.

In 1917, Wyatt became co-owner of the Leggett general
store with his brother-in-law, Charles McCraney, Lizzie's sister
Viola's husband. Other than Olidge Morrison, a cousin who
owned the drugstore in Livingston, Wyatt was one of the first
family members to have a means of employment other than a
farmer, sawyer, or oil field laborer. The task of managing the
store's merchandise fell to Lizzie, who began making regular
150-mile round trips to Houston by wagon, returning several
days later with goods to sell.

My first memories of my grandmother were several years
after they had sold the Brock and McCraney general store and
moved to a farm located on the outskirts of Houston. But in my
earliest impressions of her, Lizzie's appearance was straightforward and intelligent. A set to her mouth suggested that she knew
what she was up to and knew what she needed to know. That
look didn't seem to change as she grew older. And even into her
late seventies, a head of light-brown hair showed almost no gray.

Lizzie's formal education had ended with grade school,
but books continued to educate her in the knowledge she needed
to contribute her part to Brock and McCraney's operations serving the population of Leggett and the surrounding area.

And Leggett was where Dad grew up:

*Memories that can be chronicled began in Leggett, Texas, Polk County. Leggett is located just a few miles from the center of the Brock clan as well as being the center of the clan mother came from, the Holders. Everything that can be related to all elements of the history of the family from the early 1800s happened within 25 miles of this small crossroads community.*

The Brock and McCraney general store served families along the Thicket's fringes with every need—from food and household sundries to farming supplies, feed, grain and tack, home and garden general hardware, fabrics and crafts, ladies' and men's apparel, and more. In winter and summer, it was a place for men to gather around the store's potbelly stove to share a plug of Brown Mule and swap stories about anything that came to mind, but more particularly, gossip:

*A small village like Leggett has its interesting things. There was always some juicy gossip to spread around. There was one such time that kept the town busy for several months when the Methodist preacher left his family of redheads for a home-wrecker in the person of the most attractive Cajun filly to ever hit the area.*

*Ongoing feuds among families within a five-mile radius were always worth a few moments of conversation. And the many incidents related to some of the hardier types living in the backcountry were always good to be tossed around, sometimes for months at a time.*

Basic education—grades one through nine—was taught in a two-room schoolhouse. Dad's recollections of his grade school days could just as well have been described in a Steinbeck novel:

> *I was homeschooled by my mother until I was nine years of age. She was my only teacher during those years. I have no doubt my ambition to become a professional man rather than an East Texas farmer first began with my mother's ambition.*

When it became necessary for him to use Leggett's public educational facilities, there was little to support "excellence in educational prospects":

> *The public school system consisted of a two-room building, and, if it was a good year, one could attend classes in the first grade and up through the ninth grade. The classroom was like a three-ring circus, with all sorts of material being covered in several grades simultaneously. And, during the course of an average hour, someone was being disciplined. But one was compelled to learn reading, writing, arithmetic, history (civics), and how to study. The whole act of learning was, from necessity, scheduled like a bus line.*
>
> *Principals came and went like the seasons. It took a very strong individual to last more than even one semester in the Leggett school. He, or she, was fair game for the various groups of students and parents. Nothing was sacred, and anything short of actual murder was acceptable. If the teacher*

*was a good disciplinarian, he would have to fight and whip
at least a part of the student body and often more than one at
a time. And parents joined in the battle as often as the students. But regardless of this instability, the learning process
was good.*

*Other small disturbances made the life of the principal
exciting. You might find a cow or perhaps some other animal
in the classroom Monday morning. Snakes and skunks were
frequently used to get attention. And small pieces of rubber
placed on top of the heater during the cold season would occasionally clear the room in short time. One principal, NDB
Bailey, an athletic type, lasted more than two years and
gained enough strength of character to become district attorney of one of the more populated East Texas counties.*

While life in the Thicket was simple and its pleasures
even simpler, it wasn't as unpleasant as one might imagine. The
Thicket had its own vitality. There were no hideous slums like
the larger cities had incurred. No one went hungry or begging;
if a neighbor was in need, help was available:

*Sundays were great days for everyone, time for big din-
ners and company of some kind. This was most particularly
true when we had a visiting, or circuit, preacher for Sunday
supper. We always had chicken, either fried or dumplings;
mashed potatoes; potato or egg; custard pie; and beans or
greens.*

*One of the more enjoyable evenings I ever had was during one of these dinners when we had a suitably pious circuit preacher as a guest. Ora, a Black lady who helped out at our home occasionally, had cooked the dinner but didn't quite finish cleaning the turnip greens. I watched the preacher trying to discreetly dispose of a reasonably large, now cooked, cabbage worm for at least five minutes. When mother caught me concentrating on his plate, she went to the kitchen and called me in for a short session. When we got back, the worm had disappeared. I still wonder in which coat pocket the worm had been deposited.*

Families and friends made their own entertainment at locations involving family get-togethers. And, more often, Saturday nights were for making music. Music, whether with family or friends, was always provided by whoever showed up with a guitar, fiddle, harmonica, or washboard. Songs like "Digging Taters in Sandy Land," "Shooting Buffalo in the Canebrake," and "Steamboat River" could just as well be sung alone. However a Saturday night sing-along was done, it provided an excuse to get together:

*Any young lady who stayed out later than 10:00 o'clock, for any reason, was "up to no good." But the most fun times were the Saturday night singing sessions that East Texas was noted for in the early 1900s. Here was the most opportune time, under the guise of getting together to sing, for girls and boys to spend some time together and for the boys to have a*

*few snorts of "cane drippings." Singing sessions were recog-*
*nized, at that particular time, that it was perfectly alright to*
*have a good time.*

The Thicket itself was a lonely sort of place, one of vague forms and dark mysteries sustained by an overpowering pungency of decaying vegetation. Dad found the time he spent there alone sometimes felt as though he had entered into another world:

> *If you weren't in a hurry, there were many things in and*
> *around Leggett that one could find were both worthwhile*
> *and exciting. Ten minutes from anyplace, and you were in a*
> *type of wilderness where one could experience the deep silences*
> *of the pine thickets or the spine-tingling environment of the*
> *lowlands and their swampy lagoons and creeks. Unless you*
> *have seen an East Texas Thicket, it would be difficult for me*
> *to find words to describe them in such a way as to make you*
> *feel the solitude as I did.*
>
> *Covered by dense, jungle-like growth of pines, chinqua-*
> *pins, dogwoods, hardwoods of all types, and small under-*
> *growth, the woodlands were impossible to penetrate except on*
> *trails made by animal life. The silence of these areas always*
> *felt so strong and oppressive that I had to fight the urge to get*
> *up and run like I had never run before. But then the woods*
> *were so beautiful and tranquil that you soon forgot the feeling*
> *of oppression and felt as though you had found a real home.*

*As a youngster, I spent many hours in the woods, watching the constant change in the environment and many times enjoying some type of wildlife that seemed to be abundant. One of my most rewarding experiences was watching a mother coon teaching her brood how to hunt on the edge of a slough and how to eat what was found.*

*Another time I watched two large male snapping turtles fight it out in a small slough. It was a fascinating battle, ending only when one got the other by the neck and tore its head off.*

Beyond meditative moments, Dad also viewed the Thicket as a source for the supper table. A lifelong enthusiastic outdoorsman, hunter, and fisherman, as were most Thicket dwellers, he described his experiences:

*Hunting and fishing were popular pastimes for everyone. I personally liked squirrel hunting best in the spring when the mulberries were ripe. Just find a big tree with ripe fruit, and you were on a good stand for every squirrel in the area. I liked to hunt both squirrel and ducks in the fall and spent many good days hunting—but more often just looking and listening.*

*The changing seasons provided a certain amount of stimulation to the hardy souls of the community. After a hot, dry summer, the fall was probably the most rewarding time of the year. Most crops had been harvested, and there was a feeling of festivity everywhere. If you lived in certain areas, such as*

*Midway, you were looking forward to the first real cold days when the semi-wild hogs would be rounded up by the dogs, and hog-killing time was underway, making them ready for the smokehouse, pork chops, and sausage. Razorback hogs were very wild animals and required great expertise to manage, but they were an excellent source of meat.*

Dad's observation of the hog killing was that "*everything about the hog was used except the squeal.*" It made sense, but even though my early years were spent in small-town East Texas, some of those delicacies were, for me, stomach-turners. A cousin preferred a head cheese sandwich in the same manner I enjoyed roast beef. And an uncle found brains and eggs to be particularly desirable when available. I had plenty of other down-home East Texas delicacies to satisfy my taste without those two.

The Thicket had plenty more to offer if one was paying attention:

*The beauty of fall in East Texas is something to remember—the colors of the sweetgum, the smoky haze that covered the land in the late afternoon, and the sweet odor of the cane being crushed at the small mill grandfather had are all part of the glue that holds my memories together.*

*Spring was a good time too. We had so many different types of trees that bloomed, and many had good odors along with their blooms. Several types of fruits came to our table from the woods, mostly in the form of jellies or jams. My favorite was the Mayhaw; it was an easy fruit to preserve since it had an excessive amount of pectin, like an apple.*

In a moment of later-in-life introspection, Dad recalled when, as a young man, he was considering his future. Four prior generations of family had been satisfied with life as day laborers and what their small farms could produce since settling in Polk County in the 1850s. But life in the Thicket meant hard work for just about everybody.

There had been no more grudging way to make a living than as an East Texas farmer.

Dad had seen enough of it.

He wanted out of there:

*The less attractive memories were of cold fingers experienced during early mornings, milking the cows, and working the woodpile for cooking and heating. I developed a real dislike for both activities.*

It seems reasonably certain that the influence such conditions may have had on a commitment to leaving his life in the Thicket was considerable. He had not expressed a lack of appreciation for his Big Thicket childhood; he just knew that he'd had enough of that life. And that became the fuel for a drive that bordered on the nearly superhuman.

It was likely that Lizzie's belief in her children's potential created a quiet but fiercely driving force within him that remained throughout his life. Dad's memoirs reflected his appreciation for his mother's considerable selflessness:

> *My mother did everything within her power to help me do those things that I have mentioned. No one could have done more under the circumstances and in an environment in which she survived without visible complaint.*

What seemed like an easy decision for my dad to leave the Thicket may also have had its emotional ties. Dad mentioned the social composition of the relationships among clans and extended family members that applied through several generations, extending even to a reverence given to maintaining cemeteries:

> *The family cemetery was laid out in such a pattern that the special burial plots indicated seniority of family heads in the family bloodlines.*
>
> *Until recent years, it was a practice to have a reunion at the cemetery with lunch and then have a general cleanup of the cemetery area. It was a good practice in that it brought people together, and old associations were renewed. Every funeral was an excellent opportunity to meet relatives and old friends that you hadn't seen since the last funeral. The whole affair was more joyous than sad.*

The historic quality to family ties reverted some generations back to a time when several decided, near-simultaneously, to make the trek to the Big Thicket. Their reasons and the outcomes created a nucleus of families ultimately so insular they took on near-tribal characteristics.

Livingston had been a settlement of 135 in 1883, the year the Houston East and West Texas Railway was extended through the town. The result stimulated numerous sawmills setting up shop in the area, and the population size increased to 1,024. In 1900, Livingston, already the county seat, had assumed its place as Polk County's largest town.[43]

From the 1900 peak, Livingston's population reduced slightly until 1925, when a new population count was reported. Livingston had the county's only high school, and Dad needed to attend high school if he was going to realize his—and his mother's—ambitions. But there was a problem.

The roadway between Leggett and Livingston was little better than a dusty mule path when dry; when wet, it was a rutted nightmare of sticky mud. Livingston may just as well have been a hundred miles away. Given the time's roads and transportation limitations, a sixteen-mile round-trip daily commute to and from school was impractical to the extreme.

With options limited, it was decided he would stay over in a Livingston boardinghouse during the week. Transportation to and from home for the weekends was by horseback; he would be home on Fridays, then reverse the process Sunday afternoons to return to start a new week at the boardinghouse. As he described it:

*I graduated from the Leggett school in six years and man-*
*aged, through various means, to finish high school in Living-*
*ston at eight miles away, the closest town with a high school.*
*It was all very challenging to a person with my disposition.*

He was seventeen when he completed high school and
had done well. Having satisfied the stringent admission requirements of Texas's most selective institute of higher learning,
Houston's Rice Institute, he was planning for fall enrollment.

His parents had made considerable sacrifices in support
of his education. He had already been the fortunate recipient of
their brainpower. Evidence of that inherited competence was
passed along to Dad's older brother, Hermes, and sister, Louise,
as both also left the Thicket to achieve significant successes in
activities not soil-related. Dad's younger brother, Carl, was a
World War II draftee who, consequently, was deprived of an
education that may possibly have suited the highest IQ of the
siblings.

Dad's high school graduation was on May 23, 1930.
That summer, plans for Rice Institute took a turn:

My entrance to the college scene was colored by a number of naive decisions and incidents that made the whole thing
seem to be an accident rather than a worthwhile activity. I first
planned to enter Rice Institute and had been accepted (very difficult in those days), but then things began to happen.

Most of the time, most creeks feeding the Big Thicket
were of little consequence. Currents could be fast-running or
slow-moving normally. But the spring's rainy season meant

some, like Menard Creek, could change their personality to running wild and dangerous, turning into a threatening yellow-brown color and carrying logs and big pieces of timber that would pile up against bridge abutments, forming a dam that threatened to take out the bridge. Such times could last until summer when creeks might revert to being not much more than ankle-deep during the hottest months.[44]

Dad's late-spring job was on a work crew dealing with the problem. The work paid well, and he would use the funds to help pay for his first year of college. Then:

> *Late in the spring, I was working with a bridge gang pulling logs to prevent jams on the bridge abutments and succeeded in falling in the swollen stream. The rest of that day was spent cold and miserable, resulting in (contracting) a severe cold.*

The illness incurred because of that accident turned out to be more than a simple cold. A high-intensity type of illness, it more probably was some form of pneumonia. Fever near-constantly drained him of strength and left him at the end of the day exhausted and numb. For the rest of the summer, he was so weak and listless he could walk only a few steps without becoming exhausted. In its aftermath, he was left with a significant and permanent hearing loss:

> *By midsummer, I was no better, so the family doctor advised Mother to send me to a high, dry climate.*

*A cousin in Houston had suggested I investigate a rela-
tively new school out west, in Lubbock, called Texas Technological College. None of the family had heard of the place, but
I was ready to go somewhere, so Texas Tech is where I went.
It was also decided (since I seemed to bend in a mechanical
direction) that I would study mechanical engineering. So the
course of study was determined more by instinct than by any
other means.*

Texas Technological College had opened in the fall of
1925 with four separate colleges: the School of Liberal Arts, the
School of Household Economics (later called Home Economics), the School of Agriculture, and the School of Engineering.[47]
Texas Technological College's location in the town of Lubbock
was a prime consideration for where Dad would go, considering
his condition. Lubbock, with a population of just under 20,000,
was Texas's second-largest city to Houston and nearly 700 miles
from Leggett.

Dad had grown up close to home, seldom venturing farther than the eight miles to Livingston. He had never been farther than a single seventy-five-mile trip to Houston. The fact
that he'd had no prior experience in such a venture and was
heading off alone far from the Thicket appears to have been of
little concern. He knew what had to be done, and he was going
to do it.

On the morning of September 2, 1930, he left home for
Livingston to catch a train bound for Lubbock.

## CHAPTER TWO

# Texas Tech, Marriage, and the Depression

A sleepless night before had inspired his early arrival at the Livingston depot. He would confirm once more that all was in order for the transfer required in Dallas for the midnight train to Lubbock.

At 3:15, the wait was over; the weekly Houston East and West Texas train to Dallas left Livingston. The startling lurch as the train began leaving the station triggered a wave of nostalgia as the thought occurred that he was actually leaving home. It was an adventure about which he knew little of what to expect.

His first time as a train passenger, combined with a fascination for the passing landscape, inspiring an exhilaration he had not known before. The stop in Huntsville to allow passengers to disembark and new ones to board raised some questions: Who lived in those houses by the tracks? And what did they do?

One small town after another passed—Bryan, Waco, Brownwood—every stop inspired the same questions. After a few hours, the excitement of train travel settled down, and he was reminded that the last time he had eaten was the day before. The wrapped cornbread and cold chicken Lizzie had packed for him solved the problem as he ravenously finished off all of what was to have lasted him through his arrival at Lubbock.

As he sat back to reflect, previous feelings of excitement for what lay ahead had become tempered. An initial mixture of anticipation and excitement had given way to the feelings of anxiety that unknown circumstances are inclined to bring. What was Texas Technological College going to be like? What if he didn't like it? What would it be like to live in a big city? How would someone with East Texas's country ways fit in?

With nightfall and the passing landscape features no longer visible, the train car's gentle rocking did its work. Around midnight he awoke to make what turned out to be an uneventful transfer to the train to Lubbock. He was awakened again at dawn by the train's slowing as it pulled into Abilene and a strikingly unfamiliar countryside.

Stops were made at Sweetwater and Snyder before the afternoon arrival in Lubbock. The leafy-green East Texas landscape he had left behind had given way to a stark appearance more consistent with bare dirt and sagebrush. This was West Texas? Yes. This really was West Texas. And this was Lubbock.

The school had provided information regarding registration, but it was Thursday, and registration wasn't scheduled until the next day, September 4. The first question of "Where is the school?" was followed by "How am I supposed to get there?" He wasn't prepared for any of this:

*Having left Polk County behind, I was embarking on an entirely new experience, one which I was ill-prepared to take on. This second period of my life began as a college student trying to find myself. Then there was a time following college graduation I spent in attempting to achieve adult status. Both periods I felt as being persistently on the brink of failure.*

His failure of nerve resulted entirely from the fear of changes he expected to encounter while adapting from the unpretentious backcountry East Texas life he had known—no electricity, no running water (water was by a hand-pumped well), bathroom facilities "out back," no radio, and no phonographs—now to be replaced by modern "big city" conveniences.

He never spoke of having felt deprived by life's simplicity back home; that was just the way country folk lived. But it was not so for his soon-to-be classmates, the city-raised sort more likely to be found in a college environment. He was aware of the limitations associated with his naive country style when he began taking classes at Texas Tech:

*Most of everything I did during my early college days was determined and executed in the same ignorant manner. Looking back, I've never ceased to marvel at the fact that I managed to get enrolled and started in the right direction with all the Piney Woods handicaps that I had inherited and cultivated over the beginning years.*

His first college semester had its challenges, but the challenges were more related to social adjustments than classroom stress. Overall, college life was agreeable. No mention was made of any musical instrument he played other than the violin, but, taking advantage of everything available, he somehow found a

way to participate in the school's band. Then, at the end of the
semester came news of a most-unwelcome-surprise variety. The
pleasurable experience that had begun only four months before
took on a new dimension—monetary support from home had to
end:

> *I had $500 [about $7,500 today] when I enrolled at
> Texas Tech and managed, by one means or other, to spend
> most of it during the first semester. Then, the big crash of the
> Great Depression happened, and I was notified that there
> was no additional money available.*

Black Friday, the Great Depression's beginning, had occurred in August 1929. Several months before, the Brock and
McCraney general store had been sold to the Finger Brothers, a
successful family whose investments in Houston retail had expanded into acquiring a few general stores serving the Thicket.
My grandfather, Wyatt, had invested his share of sale funds into
Beaumont-area land speculation. But land speculation, like
many things associated with the Great Depression, had gone
sour.

Dad's graduation from Livingston High in May 1930
had been supported when his September Texas Tech enrollment
required funding. Now, the money that would otherwise have
been available for education was swallowed by the Depression's
tsunami. It was a bewildering blow; he wasn't prepared. Immediate implications were apparent.

But then, was there any reason to pay so grievously for such an aggressively destructive condition over which he had no control? Crushing regrets swept over him:

*The initial $500 was a lot of money in the mid-1900s, more so for someone who came from an area as poor as East Texas farm country. The money could have very well lasted me the full year with better management on my part.*

*And it seemed that most of the students had ended up as I had—without money to continue. My immediate fortunes went from riches to rags in a matter of a few weeks. Depression aside, at least a part of the problem was entirely my fault.*

He had known hard work and hardship. But now, he faced what seemed two impossible alternatives: survive with no money or pack up and go home. The avalanche of thoughts triggered by such a shocking reality kept coming back to one seemingly unavoidable issue: Was pursuing a degree in mathematics and physics under such conditions even plausible?

But then, why did plausibility even enter into the discussion? A variety of factors frame how we see things and how we go about life. In Dad's life, there was only one goal—to become educated.

Whether the decision was spontaneous or carefully considered, he absolutely was not giving up:

*Now, with that ended, everything came to one final head—I had to discover how I was going to be able to stay in*

*school. That began a period of endless frustrations and diffi-*
*cult times.*

The problem of meeting classwork expectations now was replaced by one of determining *how* to measure up to what was required to pay for tuition and books, attend classes, study, and still find a way to survive.

His future was going to be under hard, brutal conditions, at times leaving him homeless and always flat broke. Single-mindedness drove him; he would do whatever was necessary:

*All manners of rinky-dink jobs paying practically noth-*
*ing—babysitting, yard mowing, sweeping floors at a Red*
*and White store, and so on, and on—were the only answers*
*available. I no longer had the money to afford school-spon-*
*sored housing, so I slept anyplace it was legal to sleep. That is*
*until the last two weeks of my second year, when I slept in the*
*backyard of an exclusive home not too far from the campus.*
*Their patio couch proved to be the best thing I could find at*
*the time. I don't know what would have happened if I had*
*been caught; fortunately, it never became necessary for me to*
*find out.*

His definite advantage was an agreeable manner. A congenial likability of the old-style country-type combined with experienced familiarity with the ax handle and the shovel. Both qualities combined well with a brilliance of mind and a fierce determination of effort. It drew people to him:

*There were a number of good people at the college who had decided—along with me—that I was going to remain in school. Just when everything seemed to be falling apart, someone would grab the pieces and put them back together again. One couple, Doctor and Mrs. W.C. Holden, more or less adopted me. They did everything possible to encourage me to stay with it and often stood behind me to push me forward when I really wanted to go backward. I owed a very large debt of gratitude to the Holdens.*

Parents, peers, teachers, and religious beliefs all played a part in his determined mindset of "I *will* become an educated man." Moving through seemingly impossible circumstances with stoic acceptance in the same single-minded manner he applied to the difficult curriculum of college mathematics and physics courses he had chosen, he gained his professors' support:

*Luck plays a big part in everyone's life. I am sure of that and recognize that it was with me most of the time. Even when I was hitchhiking or riding freight trains during those moneyless days, luck seemed to make its appearance just at the right time. When I was hungry, I was invited to go to dinner with someone, or food made its way to me one way or another.*

When the desire is sufficiently powerful, human will becomes a force near-impossible to resist, trumping comfort and all other inconveniences. And luck is more often a function of what is made of the hand dealt than having waited for the right cards before playing the hand.

Trips home were restricted, requiring knowledge of freight train schedules between Lubbock and Livingston. Hard times meant traveling with people of similar means and having to avoid the railroad bulls who found pleasure in forcefully removing unauthorized freight car riders, often at the most inopportune times and locations.

Dad's sister, my aunt Louise, once told me of having agreed to meet the freight train Dad had written he was to arrive on for the 1931 Christmas holiday. But when the train arrived, he wasn't on it. She decided to wait to see if he might have caught the next train, due three hours later. Then, when three hours had nearly passed, she saw him trudging along the tracks. Several miles out of town, he had been thrown off the boxcar in which he had been riding.

In October, midway into his junior year's first semester, serendipity struck; Dad met the girl who was to become his wife. Virginia Wood was from a family of nine siblings from the West Texas town of Childress:

> It was at a party at the Holdens' home that I met Virginia. We seemed to fit together, and, after that, it was a lot easier. We had a lot of fun together, and we did it without the benefit of money.

Prior to the Depression, Virginia's father, Edward Wood, a tough Irishman, had been a prosperous farmer and businessman with over one thousand acres of cotton under cultivation and two cotton gins in operation.

For a small-town West Texas family, Edward and Lena Wood and their nine children had lived well. The family home was the largest in Childress. The family automobile was a Model T touring car, and they had occasionally taken family vacation trips. By the time Dad met the family, there was no indication of their having lived a life of luxury to the extent that the kids were overindulged. Rather, as Mom often stated, their Christmas gift could just as well have been an orange wrapped in tissue.

When the Great Depression began on August 27, 1929, it became impossible to step aside from the wave that swept over the countryside, leaving ginning customers unable to sell their cotton and incapable of paying their ginning bills.

The Depression's reality was clear; financial ruin was going to destroy everything Edward had worked for, and with that, his will to live was taken. On October 3, 1930, he drove his car into the family home's garage, closed the door, and was asphyxiated. His body was found by Arlene, the family's oldest sister. Through assistance from Lena's brother, Wirt Bowman, a prosperous businessman on his own, the family managed to carry on.

Virginia was able to continue school with some help from her uncle, but even that assistance dried up as my grandmother struggled to keep some semblance of holding the family together. The stress of it all was too much for Lena. She descended into an emotional decline, ultimately resulting in a breakdown and commitment to the North Texas State Hospital for the mentally ill at Wichita Falls, where she spent the remainder of her life.

It was midway through Virginia's senior year when the family's devastated finances, no longer able to support the luxury of school, required her to drop out. At the same time, no money was available for Dad to go home for the holiday season. Prospects for traveling by freight car had been greatly reduced as railroads fiercely clamped down on nonpaying passengers. But a silver lining ended up in that cloud—an invitation to spend Christmas with the Wood family was extended to Dad. And he gratefully accepted:

> *I spent Christmas 1932 with Virginia and her family. It was a very happy one and particularly so since I had given up the idea of trying to get home in the middle of winter without travel funds. Also, Virginia was not going to be able to return to school the next semester, so I wanted to be with her as much as possible.*
>
> *The Depression had such a grip on everyone that any means of keeping one's good spirit was a big help. We had a wonderful time, and I enjoyed the stay with the Wood family. It was during this period that Virginia and I decided to get married but to keep it secret until I finished my degree.*
>
> *We were married December 28, 1932, in Hollis, Oklahoma. Perhaps a bit foolish to get married at such a difficult time, but it seemed to be the natural thing to do. And, too, things couldn't possibly get any worse than they already were.*

*We also felt that it was a tie that could perhaps make us both stronger in our efforts to get ahead.*

Dad returned to school in January for his final semester and graduated with a degree in mathematics. He had overcome what seemed impossible circumstances to achieve his dream: he was educated. The next step was to find a job. But a honeymoon took priority:

> *At the end of the semester, my degree completed in mathematics, we decided to take a honeymoon trip to see New Mexico and Colorado. And we could tie it in with a visit with my cousin Cecil Morrison, who had moved to Dolores, Colorado. I went to Leggett in the first part of June 1933 to find some sort of transportation. Scouring the countryside turned up a Model T serving as a chicken roost. I bought it for $13 with an agreement that the farmer would pull it to my grandfather's place.*

Reflecting on more convivial, pre-Depression times, Dad recalled memories of his earlier Model T encounters:

> *When the automobile became a reality in Polk County, Grandpa John Brock saw quickly the potential of the contraption and bought one. He first used it as a taxi for the country drummers who served the product needs of the backward communities. Before this time, drummers were forced to go by*

*buggy or horseback, so they were willing to pay him well for this faster, more comfortable transportation.*

*Dad (Wyatt) soon saw that it was fashionable to own one, so he bought one for the family. But the car was not the answer for everything. The problem was the lack of roads. Those early roads were a continuing stream of dirt, sand, or mud, depending on the season and the rain. Sunday afternoon rides visiting relatives were something to be proud of, and it was easy to become the center of conversation if you were the proud owner of a Dodge or Ford. Then, we decided to drive to Houston.*

*Houston was 75 miles from Leggett. We left at 4:00 a.m. and spent the entire day negotiating the sand, mud, the ferry across the Trinity (no bridges in those days), and getting directions to the next community. Twice along the way, we had to get a team of horses to tow the car out of the mud; not a trip for the modern commuter.*

Since that experience, roadways had improved between major cities. But that isn't what their honeymoon plan was to include. Dad's prior experience with challenging roadway conditions would prove useful:

*After overhauling the T, and with a little assist from everyone, I headed back to Childress to gather up Virginia. That began an adventure that—in retrospect—was so fantastic as to be unreal. Our assets were a Model T worth about $30, about five dollars in cash, and some miscellaneous* *camping gear which included two cots that fell apart before the trip was completed. Then, Virginia pawned her ring for $30, and we were as ready to go as we ever would be.*

This wasn't the sort of honeymoon most would consider conventional. Rather, this honeymoon was a campout focused on crawling over an extensive array of cliff dwellings and other forms of Native American ruins around the town of Dolores, Colorado. One of Dad's favorite cousins, Cecil Morrison, lived in Dolores and had, along with Dad, developed a fascination with Native American culture through their interaction with Polk County's Alabama-Coushatta reservation. Now, they both wanted to explore Colorado's ruins.

Understandably, exploration had required some inconvenient car repairs, including three flats, but it was an unrepairable splintering of the wooden spokes on one of the Model T's wheels that abruptly ended the search for Native American artifacts. Dad was okay with the six weeks required to send for a wheel replacement. By a stroke of luck, the breakdown had occurred on the Navajo reservation, and Dad, in his congenial manner, won over their hosts: *The Navajos took us in as one of their own.*

Then, with the wheel repaired, they found their way to Houston:

*After hocking most of our clothes, etc., we made it to Houston with five cents left in our pockets. What a way to end such a fabulous honeymoon!*

It was September 1933. The Depression was generally acknowledged to have ended in March 1933, but, statistical thought aside, job circumstances were still no friendlier to the unemployed. In no position to be choosy, they needed a place, any place, to catch their breath:

> *When we finally arrived in Houston, we had no money and no prospects. But then, neither did anyone else. It was 1933, jobs were sparse, and I discovered soon that the Depression had resulted in considerably limiting job availability in the field of mathematics. Worse, the competition for work, any work, from a lot of well-qualified people made the job search even more discouraging.*

Dad had struggled for the previous four years with a constant need of finding some way to survive while at Texas Technological College. During that time, a willingness to perform whatever work was available, at just about any price offered, had served him well. Now, with that mindset, he found a job. But not just any job; this was employment that would have turned away anyone but the hardiest:

> *I jumped at the first opportunity: counselor in a Houston settlement house, serving mostly illiterate, all poor to the extreme, Mexican immigrants. Settlement houses, the forerunners of neighborhood centers, were established to "provide educational and social programs for immigrants, the working class, and poor people."*

Chicago's Hull House was the settlement house forerunner and the best known among a series of settlement houses in major cities extending across the country. Settlement houses functioned to serve the most poverty-stricken; consequently, settlement housing facilities always established the lowest common denominator in both accommodations and location.[1]

Houston's Rusk House was consistent with other cities' settlement houses. The City of Houston identified six East Houston Wards as composing the worst slums. Three Wards—one, two, and six—were principally occupied by Mexican American households;[2] the other three were populated by mostly Black households. Rusk House's location held the further distinction as one of the worst slums in North America. To Mexican American residents, the area was known as "El Alacrán." And El Alacrán was home to Mom and Dad:[3]

*Rusk House required that Virginia and I live in the house, but that was okay. Low pay did not allow for a roof over our heads and, at the same time, allow us to buy groceries. Located in the worst part of Houston, Rusk House depended entirely on the surrounding population for its existence. Our job functions were day and night—teaching, counseling, and providing support to the area's poor in any way possible. That often included serving as cook in the kitchen, a talent I put to good use later when an occasional Mexican food craving resurrected those skills. Most could not speak English so, in the process of teaching English to these new immigrants, improvement of my Spanish was a positive benefit.*

Rusk House wasn't the sort of place where one would invite the family to drop by when they were in town, but now Rusk House was exactly what they needed. And the Rusk House provided a useful experience in dealing with students from frequently difficult households. Dad's classroom experience with Leggett grade school students and parents likely played a part in understanding how to best deal with potentially rowdy circumstances:

> *It was through our work at Rusk that I secured a position teaching in a junior high school at an improved salary. The school was located in the same disadvantaged area of Houston, so the work was never dull. I probably did more juvenile police work than teaching. And, because I had initially been part of the band while at Tech, I became the school bandleader.*

Demographically, Ward Two was populated almost entirely by Mexican Americans. In this usage, the word "disadvantaged" is understated. El Alacrán was Houston's worst slum. A degree in mathematics was less the reason he had been offered a teaching job in such an area, more that the Rusk House experience was on his resume.

That Dad had been a part of Texas Tech's band was news to me. I had never known Dad to play a musical instrument

other than the violin. But the disclosure was also no real surprise—he had never let the inconvenience of not having done
something prior get in his way:

> *It was during that period that Shirley Jean, our first*
> *child, was born March 18, 1935. Tragically, she died of*
> *pneumonia two months later on June 12, 1935, in Virginia's*
> *hometown of Childress, Texas. It was emotionally wrenching*
> *for both of us.*

Shirley Jean contracted a cold shortly after she was born.
When the cold developed into pneumonia, Mom took her to
Childress, where the climate was drier. But despite Mom's ef-
forts, Shirley Jean was unable to recover; she died in June. In
Dad's memoir notes, the incident was minimized, most probably
due to the emotional devastation it caused for both of them.

The Depression raged on, and the job market showed no
improvement:

> *The salary with that first teaching assignment was so*
> *low that we had to find other work during summer months*
> *to keep our ship afloat, so I worked as a checker in an A&P*
> *market and took other odd jobs—anything that paid. Three*
> *years later, I transferred to one of Houston's larger high*
> *schools at an increased salary, and life was beginning to take*
> *on a more responsive pattern.*

But just when life seemed ready to cut them some slack, tragedy wasn't through:

*A son, Eugene Harry, was born on July 24, 1938, in Houston. Once again, we suffered an agonizing loss when Eugene Harry died three days later of a congenital intestinal obstruction.*

A relentless string of setbacks and tragedies, extending back to Dad's loss of funding for three and a half of the four years at Texas Technological College; the death of Mom's father, Edward Wood, in October 1930; and Lena Wood's institutionalization, had been serious enough. Now, the loss of two children within a thirty-six-month period capped eight years of near-constant struggle with little relief:

*But with these two near-devastating setbacks, we were able to build our first home in 1939, and life continued to improve. On May 18, 1940, we became parents for the third time; this time was considerably more positive.*

Tragedy could cause some to simply give up, saying "it wasn't meant to be." But that was a mindset Dad had not subscribed to. He had seen family members, both his and Mom's, slide into hopelessness, as what had been their decent life was broken.

The Depression years had blurred. Despite devastating personal losses, Dad and Mom had gone through them as they might have survived a driving, at times near-unendurable, storm. Heads down, jaws locked, their minds fixed on whatever the next step was to bring, they carried on.

Despite the hard times and deep sorrow, life had its sweet moments. Friendships were being made, and social life had begun, including acquaintances with two couples who remained lifetime friends: the Vardens and the Spears:

> *The radio's arrival was a great means for broadening communications and expanding previously limited horizons. Many nights our Houston neighbors came to our house to spend evenings with all of us grouped around the speaker. Trying to hear Will Rogers above the static, squeals, and other types of interference that came through the air was always a real chore.*
>
> *And, when a program was tuned in properly, and the channel became clear, a big hand would be given to the person responsible. The radio made long winter evenings more bearable, and everything was put aside when a good program was scheduled. The laughs Will Rogers and other comedians brought were always good for an evening.*

Dad was a high school teacher when I was born on May 18, 1940, at Houston's Methodist Hospital. My first year was spent in Pasadena, Texas, when opportunity brought the next fateful step—an invitation that began an escalation of life-changing events of a positive nature:

*Ronald Gene was a healthy one-year-old when, in the summer of 1941, Texas A&M College's Dean of Engineering offered a teaching fellowship that would allow me to complete undergraduate and graduate degrees in mechanical engineering. Since it was necessary for me to complete my engineering degrees (my degree at Texas Tech was in mathematics and physics), I felt it imperative that I accept.*

The offer from Texas A&M had come with no strings. The school needed teachers, and they wanted Dad to be one of them. It had been ten arduous years since he had taken the train that September day in 1930 on his way to fulfilling his destiny.

The move to College Station was in the summer—in time for Dad to begin life as a college instructor of engineering drawing and to start classwork toward a degree in mechanical engineering. Things were looking up considerably.

## CHAPTER THREE

# College Station 1941-1948

College Station's 1941 population of 2,184 was sufficient in size to be included with four other Brazos County towns— Navasota, Millican, Wixon Valley, and Kurten. Bryan, College Station's immediate neighbor, with 11,842 residents, included almost half the county's population of 26,997. Texas A&M's student population was 6,679. [1]

Soon after our College Station arrival, Imperial Japanese forces bombed the United States' Pacific fleet at Pearl Harbor, and World War II was declared. In his memoirs, Dad remarked on the turn his fortunes had taken:

> *A strange turn of events had come about as a result of the respiratory infection I had incurred during the summer prior to my entering Texas Tech. The infection had settled into my lungs and sinuses, resulting in chronic ear infections and, ultimately, in permanent hearing loss, rendering my draft rating as 4F when war was declared following Japan's December 7, 1941, attack on Pearl Harbor.*

The next seven years were spent in satisfaction with the coursework required for bachelor's and master's degrees in

mechanical engineering. And Mom and Dad settled in with local social life:

*We all loved the community and found ourselves deeply*
*involved in such activities as scouting, church, and the social*
*activities of the faculty. It was a very happy period.*

Our home on unpaved Foster Street combined a two-
bedroom, one-bath house with a separate building located just
behind containing a studio apartment and washhouse. The
apartment was a 125-square-foot-or-so room with a bathroom
and rudimentary kitchen facilities, which included an icebox requiring regular delivery of blocks of ice to function.

Wednesdays were washdays and the source of one of my
favorite memories—the crisp smell of dried sheets from the
clothesline after a day in the sunshine. Mom's washhouse was a
four- by eight-foot space with a dirt floor and a two-tub, ringer-
type washing machine, which would send thoroughly washed
laundry items from an agitator tub to be fed by Mom through a
wringer to the rinse tub. But occasionally, the wringer would
grab Mom's fingers along with the washed item being transferred, initiating howls of protest as fingers were pulled into the
wringer's rollers before she could stop the process and rescue the
bruised digits.

The most frightening component of our house was a gas
kitchen stove that threatened to blow up each time the broiler
was lit. It was never a happy "I can do this" response when Mom
asked me to light the broiler for her while she was busy.

Thermostatically controlled central heat was showcased in *Popular Mechanics* magazine's "home of the future," [2] but the concept was yet to come. Heat for our whole house was provided by a small gas floor stove set on a living room hearth and turned off during the night.

The effect of this meant mornings were frigid; that little stove never warmed the house before afternoon. At bedtime, the process was repeated. Both Mom and Dad had experienced an absence of nighttime heat during their own childhoods, so the condition was simply one carried forward.

Behind our house, a wide-open field bounded by the Hempstead Highway produced an impressive knee-high-to-an-adult stand of weeds. But to me, the "long weeds" were above waist-high and among my most frequent play areas.

Conscious memories begin sometime in early childhood. There is disagreement among types who study this sort of thing about how early this is likely to happen, but a traumatic event resulted in my first conscious memory when I was two. Floors at the time were typically hardwood, requiring regular maintenance in the form of liberal applications of Johnson's floor wax.

Mom was clearing dinner dishes from the dining room table when she slipped and fell, resulting in an excruciating scream. I recalled having watched her vigorously waxing the floors on her hands and knees the day prior. My panicked reaction was to run for help to Dot, who, along with her husband, Fred, a Texas A&M student, rented the studio apartment. I can only guess what gibberish the communication might have been when spoken by a frantic two-year-old. But, to her credit, Dot figured it out and helped save the day.

I had made friends with Dot and Fred but had spent more time with Dot. My memory of time spent with Fred was when he took me for a scary ride on the handlebars of his Whizzer motorbike. Those events are the only recollections I have of interaction with either of them.

Several weeks later, Dad returned home with Mom, who was encapsulated in a near-full-body plaster cast. She had been in Houston, where a spinal fusion had repaired a broken back. Then, about fifteen months later, in February 1944, Dad and Mom came home with a baby sister, Barbara Ann.

Barbara and I temporarily shared my room until Dad enclosed our garage to make a new bedroom for me, complete with a built-in bed.

From time to time, Dad and I would occasionally drive to Houston to spend the weekend with my grandparents, Wyatt and Lizzie, who had by then become "Pa" and "MeMama" at their chicken and egg farm on North Road on the outskirts of Houston.

Sometime after selling the store in Leggett and following the unsuccessful attempt at Beaumont-area land speculation, they had acquired the farm. Getting up in the dark with Pa to feed the livestock (a milk cow, chickens, and, occasionally, a pig) and gather the eggs from the previous day's laying hen production was the closest I ever came to becoming an East Texas farmer. Pa and I would then go in for breakfast—always a bowl of oatmeal and a cup of coffee. And, later, MeMama would make biscuits.

It was while visiting the North Road farm that the three closest cousins—David Brock, Glen Brock "Buddy" Roberts, and I—got to know each other at age three. MeMama's North Road kitchen sink included a hand pump for water; an adjacent antique gas stove turned out her soda biscuits, an East Texas farm country version of a scone. I still feel considerable affection for those biscuits with home-churned butter; I have never found any to match.

MeMama's butter churn was always good for a squabble among the cousins over who got to churn the cream into butter. The privilege lasted for a short couple of minutes before we were all bored and would argue over who had to finish the work.

The Leggett household Dad had grown up in may have been loving, certainly caring, but my recollection of my paternal grandparents was that neither openly demonstrated physical affection. Both were patient with all eleven of us cousins and showed the same rugged stoicism that was consistent among Thicket residents. It seems reasonable to assume that the same environment prevailed as Dad and his siblings were growing up.

Dad and I made several trips to North Road until, as if the Great Depression was not enough, another economic tragedy struck. In the dark of night, thieves had stolen every chicken. Pa mentioned having been awakened during the night by the smell of gas, but a search found no leaks in the house. What he smelled was the thieves' use of gas to quiet the chickens.

Apparently, the incident was enough to finish off their economic circumstances; they were broke.

MeMama and Pa moved to College Station and into our little backyard apartment while a small cinder block house was being built for them on Jane Street. Their house had one bedroom where MeMama slept; Pa's nights were spent on a sleeping porch off the living room and kitchen. When I slept over, I spent the night with Pa.

We would get up early to work the garden before coming in for the traditional bowl of oatmeal and cup of coffee. After that, we fed the chickens, then Pa and I would usually sit, and he would reminisce about life as it had been in the Thicket during his days as a young guy back in Moscow.

As a fourth-generation Thicket inhabitant, Pa had inherited the chiseled features common to those who lived in the Thicket. And that characteristic, along with sandy hair color, was passed along to Dad, his brother, Hermes, and his sister, Louise. Aunt Louise later had a surgical correction made to a nose that looked better on my uncle Hermes than it had on Louise. Dad and his brother, Carl, escaped that feature.

MeMama was prim and seemed an inch or two taller than Pa when she was dressed in the granny shoes she always wore. Neither ever had a weight problem, seeming instead to outwardly maintain an unchanging physical appearance. By the time I really came to know them, they each exhibited a determined seriousness, presumably a result of having encountered too much hardship for too long.

MeMama, in her early sixties, maintained a grandmotherly facial expression, defined by perpetually tight, thin lips and rimless spectacles that hid her eyes. Her wardrobe never changed including the same nightgown at bedtime; during the day, a guinea-hen-patterned dress was the consistent choice.

Pa wore the same pair of khaki pants and a nondescript workshirt every day regardless of the season. During the growing season a well-used fedora covered his head against the morning sun.

It was after MeMama and Pa's move to College Station that Dad responded to an itch to tap into some latent artistic skills. In support, a small studio building was constructed behind the apartment and wash house to provide space to delve into a new interest—pottery sculpting and ceramics artistry.

Making a pest of myself, I regularly joined Dad to watch him sculpt clay into pottery shapes and to try my own versions of what he was doing. At five years old, I never got the hang of using a pottery wheel. And, given sufficient time, I still may not have, but the prospect was definitively eliminated one day.

It was summer, and the long weeds had become very dry when the field caught fire. Watching Dad's attempts to save the pottery studio was probably as traumatic to me as it was to him. But there was just no way to save it; the studio had been built right on the lot line where the long weeds began. Something had to give; it was the weed fire's day to win out. So much for pottery sculpting.

World War II was progressing, requiring that almost everything was rationed; families were issued small books containing stamps good for food items and essential items like gasoline. Saving gum-wrapper foil and bacon grease in a Folgers coffee can on the stove gave everyone the opportunity to participate in supporting the war effort.

Support also included a victory garden, a rabbit hutch, and a chicken coop. One or the other of the latter two always contributed to Sunday dinner. Victory gardens were standard in most backyards during the war and continued as a holdover when the war ended.

To capitalize on opportunity, an older Black gentleman with a mule and a plow came around in the spring to offer his services. When he left the neighborhood, gardens were properly turned and ready to plant.

The chicken coop and rabbit hutch were removed at the war's end. Rabbit's popularity as a food staple also ended, probably a casualty of the Easter Bunny's image or possibly because chicken was cheaper. But whatever the reason, rabbit's disappearance from the dinner table was sudden, and timing of that event seemed to have been the same with everyone.

Sunday's chicken moved from the backyard to Luke's grocery store, which sold fresh chickens that were killed out behind the store on Fridays and Saturdays. The pungent smell of scalding feathers permeated our side of town for most of both days.

In the space of a few weeks, several family members returned from military service, including my uncles Carl Brock, Ansen Sewalt, and Harry Wood. Cousin-by-marriage Willie Williams, who was married to my cousin Ramona Pittman, had an impressive Samurai sword he had taken in combat from a Japanese officer on the island of Guadalcanal. And Uncle Carl's forearms displayed an impressively ornate set of dragon-themed tattoos he had acquired when his ship had been docked in the Far East.

During the war, a German POW camp had been located in Hearne, twenty miles from College Station.[3] The camp's presence prompted a playground rumor once that a couple of German internees had escaped and had not been captured. I never heard if the story was true, but, for our needs, truth was unimportant. The story was exciting and good enough to be kept alive for a while.

I've had a dog for most of my life. My first dog, Boots, was a black-and-white female mongrel. Boots and I were inseparable until one day, while playing in the long weeds, Boots trotted onto the highway and was struck by a fast-moving car. Losing Boots was my first experience with death.

Through example, I learned early about the value of thrift. My first recollection was a rusty old wagon that had passed its best-used-by date well before Dad brought it home. But I loved it.

A frequent playmate, Johnny Turner, lived a few blocks away. I would regularly go to see Johnny, one knee in the wagon, the other foot propelling me forward. If that wagon had ever had wheel bearings, they were long since rusted out. Now, they were replaced by more nearly the recognizable sounds of a sack full of cats on the way to the river. The noise was sufficient to agitate every dog in the neighborhood into chasing me on my trip to Johnny's and again on the return trip home.

Early 1940s Christmases were memorable. Among my earliest Christmas gifts was a vintage Lionel electric train that smelled of ozone when it ran, but it was neat looking, like the old-fashioned electric railyard switch engines that were seen in Eastern United States cities. That train was later replaced by a newer, more modern Lionel steam engine that emitted smoke when a white pill was dropped into the stack.

Sometime around my seventh Christmas, Santa brought an Erector Set. A lot could be done with an Erector Set, and, once complete, whatever was built was usually difficult to keep together.

Our neighborhood along Foster and adjacent streets was populated by a lot of younger-than-school-age kids. Mike and Jimmy Walton lived across the street, the Anderson sisters lived next door to us, Elaine Chalk lived a couple of blocks away, and Ronnie Berta, the neighborhood's very pampered little boy, lived just down the street.

Among the advantages of living on an unpaved street was that plenty of ammunition was available for occasional rock fights with the Walton brothers. But their two-against-one advantage in firepower was usually to my detriment. We called a truce when Mike and I began first grade.

Polio was the 1940s version of a pandemic. Several years later, when Doctor Jonas Salk announced on March 26, 1953, that he had successfully tested a Polio vaccine, relief sounded across America.

Polio often caused permanent muscle atrophy to affected parts of the body, resulting in permanently shriveled arms or legs. It was a nasty disease that mostly affected children, but adults were not immune. Our homeroom teacher freshman year in high school was crippled.

In our small town, several kids had been afflicted, some ending up for a time in an iron lung. I don't recall any deaths, or any kids being crippled by atrophied limbs as a result of paralysis, but polio was a frightening illness. Nearly everyone knew someone who had been affected by the disease. The problem was that no one had been able to determine how it was transmitted or how to treat it, once contracted.

Dad's nose for thrift meant that he was always happy to make a deal. I was five when one of my parents' favorite couples friends, the Spears, made Dad a good deal on Mildred Spears's bicycle. It came pre-faded and well-worn, but its condition made no difference to me. It was the best-looking machine I had ever seen. And it was mine.

It didn't take long for me to be riding my new bike all over the neighborhood and, immediately after, for every kid I knew to point out that I was riding a girl's bike. After registering a few complaints to Dad about the disadvantages of that feature to me, the problem was solved. Dad's solution? Convert it (in his mind) into a boy's bike by welding a beat-up steam pipe in place to provide a boy-like appearance. I had that bike for several years.

The *Bryan Daily Eagle* included *Puck*, a weekly comic for small-town newspaper Sunday insertion. I developed an affinity

for *Dick Tracy, Alley Oop, Smokey Stover, Gasoline Alley, Li'l Abner, Little Brother Hugo, Nancy, Blondie,* and *Prince Valiant.* Before I could read, I would pour over the comics every Sunday,
attempting to decipher what was being said. And when I was
lucky enough to find someone to read them to me, I became a
pest until they were convinced that the only way to relieve themselves of this nuisance was to read the comics to me.

When no one was available to read to me, I found entertainment in the Montgomery Ward catalog's farm implements
section, fantasizing for hours over one day becoming an East
Texas farmer. The fantasy was entertaining but short-lived.

A certain amount of College Station's life centered
around the town's ice plant. Weekdays at noon, the plant's whistle would sound, and everyone would break from what they were
doing to head home for a quick dinner, then return to work. At
5:00 p.m., the whistle's musical sounds would send dutiful
household heads home for a 5:30 p.m. supper.

The ice plant's primary function was to provide air conditioning for Texas A&M's administrative building, but, in addition to the whistle, it also served a couple of other useful
functions, such as supplying meat storage and block ice for home
iceboxes.

Neither Luke's nor May's markets were capable of carrying much of a meat selection, and their meat pricing was expensive for the average pocketbook. It was possible to acquire a
quarter section of beef directly from the rancher at an improved
price over grocery stores, but the luxury of large refrigerators or
home freezers was still to come. For bulk cold storage, it was

necessary to make other arrangements. I remember visiting our quarter section of beef many times at our meat locker at the ice plant when the mood struck for chicken-fried steak or pot roast.

The manufacture of block ice for some of the town's kitchens was supported by ice delivery in the same manner as dairy delivery by the milkman.

While I was busy experiencing my early childhood, Dad was working on his engineering degrees and writing a textbook: *The Art of Free Hand Drafting as a Reference Manual for Engineers, Technical Students and Draftsmen*. And when he wasn't teaching, he was Boy Scout Troop 102's Scoutmaster. Dad never seemed to tire of doing some kind of project.

The Texas A&M student population of 6,500 or so "Aggies" was more than twice the town's resident population. A&M was a land-grant college chartered to provide a source of future United States Army officers. The all-male student body was given a free education and, for that, was expected to graduate as Army Second Lieutenants.

College Station's housing within the town limits was mostly located in two concentrations—along the Hempstead highway and on the other side of the A&M campus.

A few retail businesses that mostly served the student population were located along the campus's fringes. Black's Pharmacy, the Magnolia service station, Cecil Culpepper's insurance and real estate office, a beer bar, the Blue Top Courts, and two mom-and-pop grocery stores served our part of town, fronting along the Hempstead highway like dominoes.

If we wanted air conditioning, other than Guion Hall, A&M's movie theater and concert hall, and A&M's Memorial Student Center, Black's Pharmacy had the only air-conditioned commercial space in College Station.

Groceries were provided by one or the other of two mom-and-pop stores located at opposite ends of that strip. Luke's Grocery Store served our part of town, and May's Market served their end of town. MeMama shopped at May's, which was conveniently located just around the corner from their house on Jane Street. I have recollections of the impressive number of flyspecks on the strings used to turn the hanging fans on and off at Luke's.

Neither offered much in the way of grocery selection.

When Safeway opened a store in Bryan, grocery selection took a great leap forward. Safeway's freezer case included products previously unknown in our parts. Among the more exciting culinary innovations, Mellorine, a highly touted ice milk substitute for real ice cream, was offered in half-gallon containers of vanilla or cherry-vanilla flavors. And an innovative new concept was introduced—Birds Eye frozen vegetables.

Until Safeway's opening, ice cream had only been made available to College Station residents at Black's Pharmacy. Ice cream cones or hand-packed pint containers were scooped from a metal cylinder by Mr. Black himself.

The new Safeway's effect on Luke's Grocery Store was probably more profound than on the folksier May's Grocery Store. May's didn't sell dressed chickens for Sunday dinner, but

a smokehouse around back turned out some interesting variations on cured meat.

The dark side to this was shopping amenities were restricted to a select group—the town's White population. I don't
remember the condition ever being discussed; that component
of College Station life had an eerily silent aspect to it. It never
occurred to me that there was something missing relating to the
Black population's low visibility or that Black households had
few rights.

The poorest of White sharecropper households lived on
a considerably grander scale than the best of Black households.
For Black individuals, housing was an unpainted shack located
on a pothole-infested dirt lane that was nearly impassable when
it rained.

For those taking the Southern Pacific train to Houston,
the station had three bathrooms—men's, women's, and coloreds'. The town's only two movie theaters, Guion Hall and the
Campus Theater, were off-limits to Black patronage. A separate, consolidated school located on the edge of town served
Black students.

Conditions were the same when we traveled to Houston.
If there was a drinking fountain in the grocery store for the pa-
trons, it was labeled "Whites only;" a second fountain would be
labeled for "Coloreds." When I took a bus with my Houston
cousins, Black passengers rode in the back or stood.

The openly restrictive conditions imposed on Brazos
County's Black population never occurred to me until the Civil
Rights Act was passed in 1964. But for my time in College

Station, we lived in two separate worlds: one privileged; and the other, grossly mistreated. Consideration was never given to whether the Black population's treatment was the right thing. No. It was "just the way things were."

Following the completion of his master's degree in mechanical engineering, Dad was promoted. Things were going well:

> *I finished both undergraduate and graduate degrees and, at the same time, made a modest living for the family. Then, in 1945, I was made an Assistant Dean of Engineering.*

The first movies I remember were *Bambi* and *The Jolson Story* starring Larry Parks playing the part of Al Jolson wearing blackface. There were other films after that, but none struck my memory in the same way.

There were occasional Saturday morning "kid's club" programs at the Campus Theater. The program involved singing, then somehow tying in with Smilin' Ed McConnell, Froggy ("hiya kids, hiya"), and Smilin' Ed's trusty dog, Tige.

Besides speech accents, food choices are often recognizable differentiations defining one geographic region from another. For me, my preference was—still is, for that matter—Southern cooking. My mother's Southern cooking was self-taught. Leaving nothing to chance, she cooked everything until it was well-done, at times leaving it more edible than others.

We also had food traditions. Fried chicken was reserved for Sundays, and pot roast was standard on Wednesdays.

Occasionally, Mom would slip in a couple of my other favorites—like chicken-fried steak or pinto beans. Chicken-fried steak was made with round steak, a notoriously tough piece of meat. Mallet in hand, Mom would, with energetic determination, pound that piece of meat until it begged for mercy before breading it and tossing it into a cast-iron skillet. Despite her hard work, short of needing a set of power tools to cut it, the steak still assumed a certain measure of determined chewing to get it down. But chicken-fried steak was one of my favorites. It still is.

Side dishes could include any of several forms of my favorite plant life: fried okra, black-eyed peas, speckled lima beans, crowder peas, and fried green tomatoes. Leaving the possibility open, I haven't seen any of these making top-five appearances on lists of food preferences for most people if they weren't part of their childhood supper table.

For the most part, I ate whatever food was placed on the table. And, like most kids, I ate whatever was on my plate one ingredient at a time. No bite of this followed by a bite of that. Nope. I ate the spinach, then the mashed potatoes, then the chicken. The concept worked just fine until vegetable soup was served.

I had quite a set-to with Mom over the vegetable soup she served for dinner one day. The gag reflex that came on full choke when she tried to coerce me into eating that soup was real. And so was her reaction.

I "could just sit there" until I ate it. The battle of wills ended in a standoff when the ice plant sounded the five o'clock whistle. It was several years before I managed to agree that vegetable soup was something good to eat.

As dinner and supper table preferences went, only a few other exceptions landed on the list of inedibles along with vegetable soup. I never could handle the bitter taste of most greens—turnip, collard, and mustard—or the mouthfeel of any form of squash.

Some additional vegetations that suited me best came straight from the Big Thicket—pinto beans served with cornbread (fried or baked) on the side. And MeMama's tart blackberry cobbler was unforgettable. Possibly both went the way of the Big Thicket's forests. But I haven't given up pinto beans and fried cornbread now and then or a hankering for a touch of cobbler.

Black's Pharmacy had a soda fountain that served a few sandwich types. I tried many times to talk Dad and Mom into eating there but had no luck. It was not a family inclination to dine out. The Southern Pacific *Sunbeam* was my first out-of-home eating experience.

Twice when I was five, Mom and I took the train to Houston to see Dr. Ramsey, who had been the family doctor through the years, including for my deceased sister, Shirley Jean, and brother, Eugene Harry. Our first appointment was to determine why I was so incredibly skinny. Dr. Ramsey felt that I needed to back off on outside play for a month to stay in bed, presumably to cut back on calorie usage. The experience provided a painful recollection of seeing my friends playing outside while I was stuck in bed.

When we returned to Houston for a follow-up appointment, traveling again on the *Sunbeam*, I once more had a chicken salad sandwich on white bread. Dr. Ramsey apparently decided I passed the test; I was able to go outside and act like a kid again. And the *Sunbeam*'s chicken salad between two slices of Wonder Bread remains as a most-memorable-food moment.

More moderate pleasures included miniature wax containers shaped like Coke bottles filled with some sort of green or red liquid. If we preferred, wax lips or wax teeth were also available. Any of those, when chewed, had a faintly sweetened flavor that was soon used up, leaving a mouthful of paraffin in need of a place to put it.

More substantive were Hershey bars, Baby Ruths, and Butterfingers. Lesser candy forms included root beer barrels, cinnamon balls, Necco Wafers, Tootsie Rolls, Walnettos, and a still larger array of other sugary forms disguised as candy.

Among soft drinks, Coca-Cola and Dr. Pepper were the most popular. Those favorites were occasionally followed by 7UP, RC Cola, and Pepsi. Then there was Delaware Punch, Grapette, and a full range of Nehi flavors made available at the Magnolia service station's horizontal soft drink cooler. RC had a big bottle and was part of a favorite combination—an RC topped off with a nickel bag of peanuts poured in.

I don't know exactly when things changed, but my awareness of 1940s tobacco advertising was that it insisted smoking was good for you. Camels advertised the "T-Zone," illustrating a diagram of the mouth and throat as being greatly benefited by a healthful bathing of cigarette smoke as it was inhaled.

L&M cigarettes even more assertively staked a claim that cigarettes were "Just what the doctor ordered!" Lucky Strike, while making fewer claims to health benefits, was satisfied with simply stating LSMFT— "Lucky Strike Means Fine Tobacco." I vaguely remember Dad smoking Camels, then later Pall Malls. Neither worked out well for what was a three-packs-a-day smoking habit.

Early 1940s radio music didn't require translation. My favorites were "Tumbling Tumbleweeds," "Ole Buttermilk Sky," and "Deep in the Heart of Texas." Mom played Tchaikovsky on a record player, apparently for my benefit, to expose me to a little culture. Tchaikovsky was supplemented by Prokofiev's *Peter and the Wolf*, which I listened to repeatedly.

Inspiration also stimulated one of Mom's more futile attempts at teaching me some musical skills. The idea might have worked but for one thing: Mom had a sometimes-fearsome temper. When I heard her speech switch to heavily clipped tones and saw her posture go super straight, I knew from the thunder-and-lightning look that the dreadful one was about to make a visitation.

Mom's plan to teach me to play the piano on our old upright was an attempt that turned out badly. I never really got beyond "Little Ducky Duddle" or "Postman I'll Be" before she became frustrated and her temper would flare, resulting in her expressing herself in terms not conducive to teaching small boys.

Admittedly, I was a less-than-stellar pupil. Things didn't work out for that particular aspect of either of our futures.

Other than an occasional trip to Galveston for a day at the beach and to visit my parent's friends, the Vardens, we weren't accustomed to holiday trips. But the summer between kindergarten and first grade included a trip to visit Dad's cousin Cecil Morrison in Colorado. The trip was likely a nostalgic revisitation of the honeymoon trip Mom and Dad had taken following Dad's graduation from Texas Technological College.

I was not prepared for my first trip to the Rockies from the Texas flatlands and was seriously unaccustomed to mountain driving. With little effort, the winding roads made me carsick. The sickness always passed once we stopped, but that nuance didn't work out once while we were driving from Durango to Silverton.

The Million Dollar Highway, as it was called, was reported to have received its name because it had cost a, then record, million dollars per mile to build. That was even though the roadway was dirt, winding, and relatively narrow. I was sitting between Dad, who was driving, and Cecil, who sat in the passenger seat. Mom, Cecil's wife, and Barbara were in the back seat. At five years old, sitting in the middle of the front seat did not allow me to see out. But motion on a winding road was readily discernible as we went around first one turn, then another.

When I felt the sickness coming on, I became insistent that Dad needed to stop to let me out, but there was no place convenient to do that. I was stuck. A "just a minute" response, spoken one time too many, left me unable to accommodate the request. I leaned over and filled cousin Cecil's conveniently available lap with that morning's pancakes. As I recall, Dad had no problem pulling over then; I don't remember ever going back to Cecil's house again or traveling on any more mountain roads for several years.

I was growing, and there was a lot to be learned. For teaching moments, Dad, being an enthusiastic outdoorsman, would occasionally take me fishing for catfish on the Navasota River. We would get up early to set trotlines along the riverbank, then later, eager to see what we had caught, pull in the lines we had set earlier. We usually had catfish for supper.

I learned early that there were a couple of variations of good-sized fish—bass were caught in the lakes, and catfish were mostly caught by trotline in the Navasota River. Catfish had several names, but mostly we caught "yellow cats," so named because of their skin's yellow shades.

Yellow cats grew to be big fish, tasted good, and had few bones to contend with. Before our garage was converted into my bedroom, Dad would hang a catfish catch from a rafter to skin. It never occurred to me, until many years later, that catfish came in any size smaller than thirty inches.

Brazos was a dry county; sale of "hard" liquor was prohibited. Of course, that created opportunity for liquor stores in Burleson County, the "wet" county, just on the other side of the Brazos River. And that meant that the first liquor store was available as soon as the river was crossed.

The Brazos River was spanned at that point by a hundred-foot-long county-built wooden bridge with no side rails and was composed of a collection of loose boards that made a horrific racket while crossing in an automobile. The experience, apparently designed to scare the pants off anyone crossing, resulted in a seriously dramatic adrenaline spike until the other side was safely reached.

The problem was that having reached the Burleson County side, it was necessary to turn around and return to the Brazos County side. The result was the same every time we crossed it. Hard liquor was not one of Dad's weaknesses—consequently, we hardly ever had reason to take a trip into Burleson County. But I do recall one purchase—a fifth of Hill and Hill bourbon that lasted for several years in our cupboard.

Saturday night was bath night. One of my memorable baths came after a more than usually productive week of play; the bathwater that drained from the tub that night was only slightly better than the Brazos River's water consistency.

Sunday mornings began with Sunday school, which was followed by church service. Then, we would come home for a dinner that was always fried chicken, the same Sunday afternoon dinner standard in just about every house in town.

Because Sunday dinner was generally fried chicken around mid-afternoon, Sunday night supper was often skipped. On those occasional times when Dad felt in the mood for a snack later, it was nearly always designed to appease someone with no appetite—milk toast, chipped beef on toast, or leaden pancakes covered with blue label Brer Rabbit syrup. None of these had the remotest affinity to kid food. I have, with little effort, avoided all of them since.

Like many 1940s small towns, College Station's telephone service was by a party line. When a call was made or received, it was expected that the neighbors would listen in to catch up on the latest gossip. If the call was long-distance, the connection was relatively primitive; conversations required raising the participant's voices, even to the point of yelling, to be heard by the other party. Mom did this during her out-of-town calls to any of her sisters.

The yelling to accommodate a long-distance call was not lost on Mom when we moved to Los Alamos a few years later. Phone service was considerably improved, but Mom held to the old habit when making a long-distance call.

Much began happening when I became eligible for kindergarten. Public schools began with the first grade but required pupils to be six years of age; kindergarten was private and accommodated five-year-olds. When I turned five, school began for me at Mrs. Lyle's kindergarten. Memories of kindergarten centered on one part of each day being a rest period, lying on pallets brought from home. And during another part of the day, Mrs. Lyle would read to us in grandmotherly fashion from her rocker, all of us in rapt attention seated on the floor around her.

One day, overcome by a desire to help her with the story she was reading, as I had heard the story before and knew the punchline about what the crocodile did, I leapt up to yell, "*Splash!*" It was my first experience occupying a chair facing into the corner. It was also in kindergarten that I met Richard Badgett, who became a lifetime friend.

A&M Consolidated was composed of grades one through twelve, segmented into five elementary school grades, while junior high school included grades six through eight, and four years of high school rounded out the rest.

First grade was taught by Mrs. Sloop, a kindly older lady. I remember little about that time other than when Mary Garcia locked herself in the bathroom and was unable to open the door to get out. The result caused quite a stir until the janitor took the door off its hinges, freeing a thoroughly shaken Mary.

Second grade was taught by Mrs. Buchanan, the sort of teacher one would hope would be assigned to teach one's own second-grade children. Between Mrs. Sloop and Mrs. Buchanan, it seemed that both ladies were almost perfectly selected by central casting's version of the ideal teachers of small children.

Pupils were a mixed bag, divided about equally between town kids, whose parents, for the most part, were associated with Texas A&M, and country kids, primarily from farm families and uniformly poor.

Notably absent from A&M Consolidated were a few kids who were from College Station's more affluent households, such as Cecil Culpepper's, Doctor Andre's, or college professor-types'. Those parents drove their kids to Bryan for "a more suitable education."

That left A&M Consolidated heavily populated by a lot of kids whose names started with something conventional, then added a second name—most often Ray or Joe, as in Bobby Joe, Billy Ray, James Ray, and Alton Ray. Town kids usually settled for just a single name, although Cecil Culpepper's son, John

Cecil, was an exception. And John Cecil was driven to Bryan for his education.

I learned early about summertime weather in College Station. Rivulets of sweat running down the back started around the beginning of May and remained a steady torrent until toward the end of September. The only air conditioning I was exposed to with any regularity was at Black's Pharmacy. It was a serious treat to walk into Black's and feel the dry air-conditioned air.

As grade school kids, the moment school was out for the summer, the shoes and shirt came off, and, within a short time, our feet became tough as leather.

But even when feet were at their toughened best, not watching for a particular kind of sticker called a "goat head" would be at our peril. The problem was that by the time realization struck that we had stepped into a goat head patch, it was too late. Any kid who lived in rural Southwestern areas can tell of the horrors a goat head visitation brought on bare feet.

### An End to Innocence

On August 6, 1945, Colonel Paul Tibbets, piloting the *Enola Gay* B-29 bomber, dropped the world's first atomic bomb on Hiroshima, Japan. World War II ended shortly thereafter with Japan's unconditional surrender. Within the following few months, the world was adjusting to what was to come next.

Circumstances required rethinking the future. What was to be done with Los Alamos? And who would participate? Recruiters were searching for replacements for the Manhattan

Project scientists who had moved on to academia. And Texas A&M was interested in the new field of nuclear physics:

> *The Dean of Engineering requested some of the staff to make an effort to become acquainted with the field of atomic energy, and I elected to take a one-year leave of absence from my work if I could find a suitable job.*

The opportunity for Dad to learn more about the recently disclosed, newest scientific field—discovery of the atom's power—had touched on a craving for new experiences too enticing to resist:

> *I applied and was accepted at the University of California, Los Alamos Scientific Labs in Los Alamos, New Mexico.*

Dad's acceptance of a position with the Los Alamos National Laboratory (LANL) was in March 1948. When school was out, we were on our way to Los Alamos.

> *So off we went to Los Alamos—the high city in the Jemez mountains. We were settled in by the latter part of July 1948.*

## CHAPTER FOUR

# Los Alamos

Except for the times we had visited Dad's older brother Hermes and our cousins in Lubbock, I was unfamiliar with West Texas. Now, our trip was taking us through the same sort of landscape Dad had experienced when he left the Big Thicket for Texas Technological College.

A tree-starved stretch of West Texas and New Mexico was a notably unpleasant change from the woodsy Central East Texas live oak forests that I knew. Those had surrendered to a scene of dirt and rocks punctuated by waves of sagebrush.

I wasn't uncertain about my feelings as we made our way through one small West Texas and New Mexico town after another; the new terrain had the undesirable appearance of a planet from a Flash Gordon serial. And the continuation of the culture shock when we arrived at Santa Fe was remarkable.

I developed an appreciation for Santa Fe's quaint charm several years later. But for that day? No. The view from the back seat of the Chrysler Windsor Dad had purchased new just before we left College Station for the trip to our new destination had left me unappreciative. I was used up, hungry, and, for the moment, too young to acknowledge Santa Fe's uniqueness.

"Quaint" had not yet moved the needle on my appreciation meter.

But the long day had a surprising bright spot; we were going to spend the night in a motel! I was fascinated by the Blue Top Courts in College Station but had never been in one. Now was the moment; the excitement was intense.

What I wasn't prepared for was that Dad's sensible dedication to thrift meant the night was to be spent in a room for two in Santa Fe's King's Rest's "Court Inn." Reality struck before the lights were out: stifling heat, no air-conditioning, and a room marginally larger than a broom closet. Mom and Dad's night was spent in a double bed as quaint as the rest of Santa Fe's surroundings; Barbara and I slept on a pallet on the floor. It would be a long time before I could work up excitement over spending another night in a motel—any motel.

The next morning, only thirty-five miles remained before we were to reach our destination. Even at the inexperienced age of eight, it was apparent that Dad, while not a particularly careful driver, could be a very fast driver. And, on that day, he was in a hurry.

A few miles after crossing the Rio Grande River, the thrill ride began. The roadway had only relatively recently been improved from an unpaved dirt-and-rocks, pothole-infested road during wartime when only authorized personnel could travel toward Los Alamos. Now we were on a paved, barely two-lane improvement.

The trip wound upward through a series of switchbacks bounded by a rugged cliff face on one side and frighteningly impressive views on the other, thanks to a mind-numbing, sheer drop into a canyon that seemed several thousand feet deeper than its few hundred feet. It's doubtful that the trip would have been any less terrifying if such niceties as safety barriers along the cliff edges had been thoughtfully installed to keep surprised drivers from unintentionally finding themselves at the canyon's bottom.

Then we arrived at our destination—Los Alamos's Main Gate.

A fifty-foot machine gun tower, a tank parked beside the road with its canon pointed threateningly toward incoming automobiles, barbed-wire-topped fencing, and armed security guards provided a menacing first impression. Dad had been to Los Alamos to line things up for his new job but had mentioned none of that! We were ordered by a guard with no-nonsense written all over his face to get out of the car and proceed into a guardhouse.

Apart from four-year-old Barbara, our introductory entry was processed by a steely-eyed type whose demeanor reeked of an opinion that he took himself and his work seriously: "And so should you."

Where were we? And why were we here? This was Los Alamos? Where were we going to live? I was not aware our new town's output was top secret or even what the term meant. But with the war ended and most presumably having knowledge of the bomb, the public still hadn't been made fully privy to Los Alamos's secrecy.

I learned soon enough that the town was surrounded by a seven-foot-tall barbed-wire-topped perimeter fence patrolled by security guards. And for anyone age seven and older, a security badge was required to enter the city.

We made the trip back down, and returned many times afterward, but none rivaled the first time. I wasn't alone in having had a similar first impression.

A few years earlier, Ruth Marshak, along with her husband, Robert, who was part of the initial wave of Manhattan Project scientific personnel arrivals, had her own impression of that first trip up The Hill from Santa Fe. She was not sure of her destination, but her first take on the trip up was that the experience had been an awe-inspiring endorphin rush:

> As we neared the top of the mesa, the view was breathtaking. Behind us lay the Sangre de Cristo Mountains, at sunset bathed in changing waves of color . . . Below was the desert with its flatness broken by majestic palisades that seemed like the ruined cathedrals and palaces of some old, great, vanished race. Ahead was Los Alamos, and beyond the flat plateau on which it sat was its backdrop, the Jemez Mountain Range.[1]

Ruth was more circumspect in a later recollection of that first trip:

> The site *began* with "the first guard house," the "seven-foot chain link affair with three strands of barbed wire"

that was the perimeter fence, the threatening signs phrased in the imperative, the guards with their "bulldog faces," the ritual of being inspected, of having one's credentials checked before being allowed to pass inside.

Eleanor Jette, metallurgist Eric Jette's wife, expressed a similar first impression:

> We stopped at the first guard house about half an hour after we crossed the Rio Grande. It stood just east of the fence which was a seven-foot chain link affair with three strands of barbed wire at the top of it. It was liberally festooned with signs which read: U.S. Government Property DANGER! *PELIGRO! Keep out* [2]

That's how our part of the story began.

But first: For any of this narrative to have been told required a coming together a few years earlier of the combined brilliance of a majority of the world's most eminent scientists and the peculiar circumstances that drew them together at the precise moment fission was discovered.

### Fission's Discovery

If the start of modern nuclear physics can be measured with any reasonable precision, the possibility of an atomic bomb was discovered in Nazi Germany in 1938, less than a year before the Second World War's beginning.

Radio chemists Lise Meitner and her nephew, Otto Frisch,[3] had mathematically proven the possibility that a nuclear chain reaction, if left unchecked, could create an explosion of huge force. They named the process "fission." Without intention, Lise Meitner had inadvertently discovered the source of what potentially could be a bomb ten thousand times more powerful than any other bomb then in existence. Only, she didn't want any part of that prospect.

Intrigued by her findings, in December 1938, physicists Otto Hahn and Fritz Strassmann, close associates of Ms. Meitner, performed an experiment that confirmed the Meitner-Frisch calculations.[4] Hahn and Strassmann communicated their findings to Niels Bohr, a Danish physicist who, along with Italian physicist Enrico Fermi, was preparing to depart for the United States.[5]

Bohr, having confirmed the Meitner-Frisch findings' validity with Otto Hahn, arrived in New York City on January 16, 1939. The developments were immediately made known to European scientists who had preceded them in coming to the United States.

A second watershed event occurred on January 26, 1939. At the opening session of a theoretical physics conference in Washington, DC, Bohr communicated the Meitner-Frisch calculations, supported by the Hahn-Strassmann experiment results, to members of the American scientific community.[6]

Theoretical physicists worldwide scrambled to act on Bohr's message, resulting in numerous projects initiated immediately. Two University of California, Berkeley scientists—

Glenn Seaborg, a research chemist, and J. Robert Oppenheimer, a theoretical physicist—took their own immediate actions.

And on June 27, 1940, the British government formed the British National Defense Research Committee to "organize scientific research on the atom, and the fission of uranium" under the code-name "Tube Alloys."[7] Tube Alloys physicists Otto Frisch and Rudolf Peierls were among the first to reach some startling conclusions subsequently memorialized in a famous report: the Frisch-Peierls memorandum.[8]

Published in March 1940, the Frisch-Peierls memorandum explained the feasibility of creating an atomic weapon:

> . . . a "super-bomb" which utilizes the energy stored in atomic nuclei as a source of energy . . . about the same as that produced by the explosion of 1,000 tons of dynamite . . . The blast from such an explosion would destroy life in a wide area. . . .
>
> In order to produce such a bomb it is necessary to treat a few hundred pounds of uranium by a process which will separate from the uranium its light isotope (uranium-235) of which it contains about 0.7 percent. . . .
>
> It is a property of these super-bombs that there exists the "critical size" of about one pound. A quantity of separated uranium isotope that exceeds the critical amount is explosive; yet a quantity less than the critical amount is absolutely safe. The bomb would therefore be manufactured in two (or more) parts, each being less than the

critical size, and in transport all danger of a premature explosion would be avoided if these parts were kept at a distance of a few inches from each other.

The bomb would be provided with a mechanism that brings the two parts together when the bomb is intended to go off. Once the parts are joined to form a block which exceeds the critical amount, the effect of the penetrating radiation always present in the atmosphere will initiate the explosion within a second or so.

The mechanism which brings the parts of the bomb together must be arranged to work fairly rapidly because of the possibility of the bomb exploding when the critical conditions have only just been reached. In this case the explosion will be far less powerful. . . .

. . . the following conclusions seem certain:

1.  As a weapon, the super-bomb would be practically irresistible. . . .

2.  Owing to the spreading of radioactive substances with the wind, the bomb could probably not be used without killing large numbers of civilians . . .

3.  We have no information that the same idea has also occurred to other scientists but since all the theoretical data bearing on this problem are published, it is quite conceivable that Germany is, in fact, developing this weapon. . . .

4.  If one works on the assumption that Germany is, or will be, in the possession of this weapon, it must be

realized that no shelters are available that would be effective and could be used on a large scale. . . . Therefore it seems to us important to start production as soon and as rapidly as possible, even if it is not intended to use the bomb as a means of attack. . . .

. . . The only uncertainty concerns the critical size for the bomb. We are fairly confident that the critical size is roughly a pound or so, but for this estimate we have to rely on certain theoretical ideas which have not been positively confirmed.

On July 14, 1941, the British National Defense Research Committee issued the codenamed "MAUD Report,"[9] restating the Frisch-Peierls memorandum, maintaining that "a sufficiently purified critical mass of uranium-235 could fission." Building on theoretical work performed by Peierls and Frisch in 1940 and 1941, the MAUD report estimated that "a critical mass of ten kilograms would be large enough to produce an enormous explosion. A bomb this size could be loaded onto existing aircraft and be ready in approximately two years."

The report went on to state that "uranium research could lead to the production of a bomb in time to affect the outcome of the war." It also served as a reminder that fission had been discovered in Nazi Germany almost three years earlier and that "since spring 1940 a large part of the Kaiser Wilhelm Institute in Berlin had been set aside for uranium research."

While the Tube Alloys group was making considerable headway toward understanding the fission process and its potential implications, US scientists had developed their own concerns.

### Einstein's Letter to President Roosevelt

Adolph Hitler's prohibition of uranium shipping from an important Hungarian source raised alarms among the United States scientific community. As a result, a letter was drafted by physicist Leo Szilard to be sent to President Franklin D. Roosevelt stating their concerns.

Because of his known personal relationship with President Roosevelt and his international reputation for scientific expertise, the letter was signed by Albert Einstein. Delivered to President Roosevelt on August 2, 1939, the Szilard-Einstein letter focused on the "potential of a chain reaction in a large mass of uranium resulting in a considerable release of energy, and the possibility that extremely powerful bombs of this type may thus be constructed."[11]

The letter went on to say, "I understand that Germany has actually stopped the sale of uranium from the Czechoslovakian mines which she has taken over. That she should have taken such early action might perhaps be understood on the ground that the son of the German Under-Secretary of State . . . is attached to the Kaiser-Wilhelm Institute in Berlin where some of the American work on uranium is now being repeated."[10]

The letter emphasized the urgency of the need for research dedicated to developing an atomic bomb. The thought that Hitler could not be allowed to be first with an atomic bomb was made clear, as a result prompting immediate action. Roosevelt's reply thanked Einstein and informed him that "I found this data of such import that I have convened a Board . . . to thoroughly investigate the possibilities of your suggestion regarding the element of uranium."[11]

The board Roosevelt referenced, the Advisory Committee on Uranium, chaired by Lyman James Briggs, director of the Bureau of Standards, convened on October 21, 1939. The board's first action authorized the purchase of uranium and graphite for Szilard and Fermi to conduct nuclear chain reaction experiments using uranium.

On December 2, 1942, at 3:25 p.m., Enrico Fermi's team produced the world's first sustained nuclear fission chain reaction at the University of Chicago.[12] In investigating the possibility of producing a nuclear chain reaction, the question extended to which of the three uranium isotopes fission was most likely to occur; U-235 was the isotope of U-238 that fissioned.

While this activity was evolving, plutonium, a radioactive metallic element with the atomic number 94, was discovered in December 1940 by Glenn Seaborg and his associates.[13] who were studying how to make an atomic bomb by bombarding uranium-238 with neutrons. Their experiment resulted in forming U-239. Then, through a two-stage process, PU-239, a new element, was formed. The discovery was followed by a March 28 experiment in which Dr. Seaborg, in association with physicist

Emilio Segrè and chemist Joseph W. Kennedy, demonstrated that the isotope of plutonium PU-239 underwent fission, making it potentially capable of providing fuel for an atomic bomb.

Einstein sent two more letters—one on March 7, 1940, and the other on April 25, 1940—calling for action on nuclear research. During that period, events were progressing rapidly. On July 14, 1941, the MAUD Report had concluded that "an atomic bomb is feasible." The announcement prompted an October 9, 1941, request to Vannevar Bush by President Roosevelt to "determine the cost of an atomic bomb, and explore construction needs with the Army."

Soon after, in January 1942, Roosevelt authorized full-scale development efforts.

### The Manhattan Project

Fission research was assigned to the United States Army Corps of Engineers' Manhattan Engineer District in June 1942 to direct an all-out bomb development program. Two months later, on August 13, 1942, the "Manhattan Project" was formed. Colonel Leslie R. Groves assumed command on September 17, 1942.[14]

While that activity was developing, J. Robert Oppenheimer, a theoretical physicist and professor of physics at the University of California, Berkeley, held two conferences in June and July 1942 in Chicago and Berkeley where engineers and physicists discussed a potential nuclear bomb design.[15]

On August 20, 1942, Glenn Seaborg stated, "Perhaps today was the most exciting and thrilling day I have experienced.

Our microchemists isolated pure element 94 (plutonium). . . . It is the first time that element 94 has been beheld by the eyes of man."[16]

In September, Robert Oppenheimer was selected to head the Manhattan Project's secret weapons laboratory.

Driving the Manhattan Project's implementation forward, Colonel, now Brigadier General, Groves determined three sites, codenamed "W," "X," and "Y," that were to be selected, each for different applications and each geographically independent of the others. Two selections were immediate:[17]

On September 19, 1942, Site X (the "Clinton Engineer Works"), the Project's uranium processing production site, was selected.[18] Sixty thousand acres in the Oak Ridge, Tennessee, area were acquired to accommodate three plants: K-25, S-50, and Y-12, each dedicated to yet-unproven processes for separating the U-235 isotope from "natural" uranium, U-238. A separate plant, X-10, was to be a pilot for plutonium production.

The architectural firm Skidmore, Owings and Merrill was contracted to provide a town layout and structural designs for improvements of a massive scale. Town facilities ultimately served what became a city of seventy-five thousand residents, with three hundred miles of roadway, fifty-five miles of railroad tracks, ten schools, seven theaters, seventeen eating facilities, thirteen supermarkets, a library with ninety-four hundred books, a

symphony orchestra, sporting facilities, and church services for seventeen denominations.

On January 16, 1943, Site W (the "Hanford Engineer Works"), a five-hundred-thousand-acre site recommended by General Groves's staff and DuPont, the
primary operating contractor, was officially endorsed by
General Groves[19] to be the Manhattan Project's primary
plutonium production site. Initial plans called for three
or four reactors and one or two chemical separation complexes. Nothing would be allowed within a four-mile
separation of complexes over concerns of potential for
radioactive accidents.

By the summer of 1944, Hanford's population had
reached fifty thousand.

**Site Y**

Site Y, the Scientific Research Laboratory, the development's third component, had more complex location demands.[20]

Unlike Sites W and X, whose location requirements
were reasonably straightforward—geographically large
and sparsely populated in the event of a nuclear accident—Site Y's needs were more refined. The Groves-
Military Policy Committee team had specified "must-
have" criteria for the highly specialized location to be
suitable. The project's top-secret status made secrecy
paramount and isolation a first requirement. "Isolated,
yet accessible," was the phrase.

Furthermore, the location needed to be:

Safe from enemy attack; climate moderate enough to continue work year-round; geographic location west of the Mississippi, and inland a minimum of two hundred miles from the Pacific Ocean; terrain providing hills close by to allow guarding the site from above; at least rudimentary in-place facilities to provide for offices and test facilities; and preliminary housing for scientific personnel to allow immediate start of research.

## Los Alamos Ranch Preparatory School

Site Y's location attention had focused on sparsely populated New Mexico with several alternatives meeting many of the required parameters; one, the Los Alamos Ranch School at Otowi, thirty-five miles northwest of Santa Fe, appeared to have an edge.[21]

The school's 7,300-foot Pajarito Plateau location was placed conveniently within the caldera of an ancient, once-monumental volcano that, around 1.61 million and, again, 1.22 million years ago, had thrown catastrophic volumes of debris into the atmosphere as far away as Kansas, burying the surrounding countryside under several hundred feet of ash that fused into a light-colored layer of soft rock called Bandelier Tuff.[22]

Sometime after the second eruption, the volcano collapsed on itself, forming the Valles Grandes caldera, which included the Pajarito Plateau. At 176 square miles, Valles Grandes was one of the largest volcanic craters on Earth.

A fifty-square-mile piece of the Pajarito Plateau is dedicated to Bandelier National Monument, which includes Frijoles

Canyon, its walls lined with cliffs composed of tuff. As with other Pajarito Plateau canyons, Frijoles Canyon is populated with caves excavated by early Native Americans for housing. Bandelier's occupancy was maintained until abandonment sometime during the sixteenth century when, coincidental in timing, the province of New Mexico was established by the Spanish government in 1598. Santa Fe was declared the province's capital in 1610.

Descendants of early Spanish occupiers began settling on Pajarito Plateau land grants in the nineteenth century. Among twentieth-century Plateau occupants, the Los Alamos Ranch School had been the brainstorm of a former Detroit entrepreneur with the Hollywood-inspired name of Ashley Pond II.[23]

The purportedly disappointing scion of a wealthy, driven father, Pond had grown up in boarding schools and, following graduation, had enlisted with Teddy Roosevelt's Rough Riders. Apparently not up to the endeavor, Pond collapsed before seeing action and was subsequently sent west to recover his health.

Finding his way to the Jemez Mountains, Pond discovered the Pajarito Plateau, which held desired characteristics he had defined for a contemplated new business venture—a "progressive school for boys." The area's attraction led him to Harold H. Brooke, a Plateau settler who, in the early 1910s, had developed an assemblage of crude cabins, sheds, and barns on 380 acres.

Following the acquisition of Brooke's homestead, Pond's Los Alamos Ranch School opened in 1917 with the auspicious mission "to help shape strong young men through a combination of rigorous outdoor living, and classical education." The school was patterned after the Boy Scouts of America's outdoor-oriented teachings.

All students, "mostly problem children from the East," were required to belong to Boy Scout Troop 22, which was formed for school purposes. Boy Scout uniforms—neckerchiefs, shorts, and long socks—were the school's year-round, all-weather uniform. To graduate, students were required to have achieved at least the Boy Scout First Class rank.

Maintaining exclusivity, the student body never exceeded forty-six boys. Between 1920 and 1940, attendance averaged about forty students between the ages of twelve and eighteen. [24] Matriculation costs kept all but the most upper of upper-class families out of a highly exclusive clique. During the depths of the 1930s' Great Depression, tuition and housing ran $2,400 annually ($44,000 in 2022 dollars), and students were required to buy a $380 ($7,000 in 2022) riding outfit.

During its time, the school educated an array of seriously impressive attendees: writers William S. Burroughs and Gore Vidal (who attended for a short time); Arthur Wood, who became president of Sears & Roebuck and Company; famed anthropologist Edward T. Hall; John Crosby, founder of the Santa Fe Opera; artist Wilson Hurley; Roy Chapin, president of American Motors; John Reed of the Santa Fe Railway; Professor Edward Hall of Northwestern University; Bill Veeck, who became the owner of the Chicago White Sox; and Sterling Colgate. An heir to the Colgate toothpaste family fortune, Sterling Colgate later earned a doctorate in nuclear physics and returned to Los Alamos, where he worked with Edward Teller on Teller's hydrogen bomb project.

Narrowing in on concluding a final Site Y selection, representatives from the Manhattan Engineer District, Albuquerque District, and the Southwestern Division Real Estate Branch met at the Los Alamos Ranch School in November 1942 to critically consider the location's suitability.

At a difficult-to-access altitude of 7,300 feet, the school's Pajarito Plateau location occupied a region of erosion-caused 800-foot-deep canyons; it was impossibly rugged terrain provided by sheer cliffs dropping off on three sides to the east combined with the Jemez Mountains forming a semi-circular ridge overlooking the plateau on the west.

Of the nearly 59,000 surrounding acres, most were government owned. Eighty-nine hundred acres of privately held property were distributed among a couple of dozen small homesteaders and two larger properties—the 380-acre Los Alamos Ranch School and the nearby 320-acre Anchor Ranch.[25]

Beyond the school's location advantage, in-place infrastructure totaling 29,560 square feet included fifty-four buildings: twenty-seven houses, dormitories, and living quarters, totaling 46,626 square feet, and twenty-seven miscellaneous buildings—a school, an arts and crafts building, a carpentry shop, a small sawmill, barns, garages, sheds, and an icehouse. Anchor Ranch facilities added four houses with twenty rooms and a small barn. The school's recreational facilities included tennis courts, football and baseball fields, a ski run, and an ice-skating pond.[26]

Sparse population, existing infrastructure sufficient to fit the "immediate move-in" criteria, self-sufficiency provided by the school's in-place water and power systems, and the security of easily controlled access provided by steep canyons and a high mountain ridge were deciding factors. Cumulatively, the Los Alamos Ranch School site was a near-perfect fit.

General Groves discussed the school site with J. Robert Oppenheimer (who, on October 19, 1942, had been selected as the Manhattan Project director) for further confirmation of the school's desirability. Oppenheimer was fully in favor. After consideration of the cumulative reports and recommendations, General Groves made the decision: Project Y would be centered at the site of the Los Alamos Ranch School in Otowi, New Mexico.[27]

A contract with the W.C. Kruger Company, Architects and Engineers, was immediately negotiated. Kruger had an office in Santa Fe and was in a good position to cooperate with a construction contractor. Kruger's contract called for providing plans for adapting 31 existing buildings, drawing plans for 111 new buildings, and planning utilities and streets.

In December 1942, the Army Corps of Engineers awarded a contract to M. M. Sundt Construction Company of Las Vegas, New Mexico, to make necessary modifications to existing structures, construct initial buildings required for housing scientists, and support personnel, the Main Tech Area buildings, and military-style barracks.[28]

Until that could be done, "what was available at the moment would have to do." Construction needs were so urgent, buildings were often reportedly in process before the completion of superstructure drawings.

Before awarding its final diplomas in January 1943, the school had graduated over two hundred students.[29]

## The Hill

On February 1, 1943, the United States Army took control of the school. In official Manhattan Project correspondence, the school became "The Project" or "Site Y." To Santa Fe and surrounding area, residents, and project scientific personnel, Los Alamos was more simply referred to as "The Hill."[30]

Secrecy was an obsession. All project personnel shared a single mailing address—P.O. Box 1663, Santa Fe, New Mexico—and to anyone not associated in some capacity with Site Y, the location remained occupied by an exclusive preparatory school. Only this preparatory school's perimeter was secured by a seven-foot chain-link security fence, topped by three strands of barbed wire.[31] Nine-foot security fences of similar construction surrounded the Main Tech Area and test sites. Test sites were located across several mesas north and south of the main tech area, where central research facilities were to be located.

What was now a military camp and soon-to-be scientific laboratory was accessed only by NM 4 from the south and NM 502 from the east. Manned security gates controlled entry access, with vehicles and their passengers subjected to ID checks. And anyone operating a vehicle anywhere near the town or lab was expected to produce proper identification when requested by military police.

The *Daily Bulletin*, an informational newsletter distributed to Los Alamos employees and residents, advised, "It cannot
be overemphasized in the interest of preservation of life, limb
and property that all individuals—either on foot, mounted or in
vehicles—STOP whenever it appears that a guard indicates such
a desire, either by actions, or by order."[32]

During Manhattan Project times, central facilities, and
later the town of Los Alamos, occupied two primary mesas,
bounded on the north by Pueblo Canyon and on the south by
Los Alamos Canyon and DB Canyon.[33] Other canyons, key to
scattered Site Y facilities, included Sandia Canyon and Pajarito
Canyon to the south and Bayo Canyon to the north.

Experimental work was conducted at twenty-five "sites"
composed mostly of crude houses and other support spaces principally located south and north of town, each identified by name
or numerically with a prefix of "TA": [34]

- **The Main Technical Area**: TA-1, an imposing set of
  buildings, housed the "Tech Area" on both sides of what
  would later become known as Trinity Drive.

  The north side was adjacent to Ashley Pond; south
  of Trinity was bounded by Los Alamos Canyon's north
  rim. Facilities within the Tech Area in which general laboratory or process chemistry and radiochemistry wastes
  were produced (TA-3) were served by "acid sewers," industrial waste lines extending north to a discharge point
  (TA-45) at the edge of Pueblo Canyon.

Tech Area security was extreme: security guards oversaw nine-foot fences topped with three strands of barbed wire; during nighttime, over 150 fifteen-hundred-watt floodlights illuminated the fence's perimeter and area vicinity.

- **V-Site:** V-Site buildings included TA-16-515, 516, 517, 518, 519, and 520. TA-16-516 housed plutonium implosion device development activities. When it was determined that implosion was going to work, "Fat Man" Trinity test bomb assembly and, subsequently, the bomb used on Nagasaki were assembled in building 516 on a floor padded with wrestling mats.

- **S-Site:** V-Site's neighbor. High explosives were melted, mixed, and poured into molds at S-Site to produce the explosive lenses that were to surround Fat Man's plutonium core.

- **Gun Site:** TA-8-1, TA-8-2, and TA-8-3 supported "Little Boy" uranium bomb concept testing, where project scientists and engineers developed and tested the gun-type trigger design.

- **Delta Prime Site:** TA-21, located on DP Mesa, was bordered by two canyons—DP Canyon on the south and Los Alamos Canyon on the north. Research to determine the chemical and metallurgical properties of nuclear materials was conducted during wartime. Following the war's end, work transitioned into plutonium production, extending from 1945 until 1978.

DP Site was composed of two primary research areas: DP West facilities were constructed in the mid-1940s to process plutonium and uranium; DP East consisted of two tritium facilities that later provided energy, environmental, and weapons defense research.

- **Bayo Canyon:** TA-10, located two miles north of the Main Tech area (later, Los Alamos Town Center), was used between 1944 and 1961 for radioactive lanthanum (RaLa) experiments.

  The original 350-acre TA-10 Site contained a radiochemistry laboratory, solid waste disposal facilities, two assembly buildings, an inspection building, a personnel building, control buildings, two RaLa detonation complexes with adjacent firing pads, and contaminated leach pits from the radiochemistry laboratory.

- **Radioactive Waste Treatment Plant:** TA-45 was located within TA-10 on the south rim of Pueblo Canyon and above the acid sewer waste outfall. Untreated liquid waste discharges from the acid sewer lines extending from TA-3 began in late 1943 or early 1944 and continued through April 1951. Radioactive isotopes from research and processing operations associated with nuclear weapons development were the primary waste ingredients. Barium-140 shipped to the site for RaLa tests

contained quantities of strontium-90, which also ended
up in Acid Canyon during the radioactive lanthanum-
barium-140 separation process.

- **Pajarito Site:** TA-18-1, TA-18-2, and TA-18-29 were
  used during the war for plutonium chemistry research.
  After the war, the site became the main location for critical assembly.

These sites were required for initial research, making it
expedient that use be made of existing structures. But, with that
urgency satisfied, the need for housing personnel became considerably more critical. For project activities to proceed, there
had to be living space for scientific personnel and their wives, a
need so urgent that little time was made available for planning.

Simultaneous with addressing apartment construction,
Sundt was erecting the Main Tech Area and making Kruger-
recommended improvements needed on existing site structures
to render them usable.

Preliminary planning profoundly understated estimates
of the project's need. An ambitious assumption was that 300 of
the best scientists, engineers, and technicians would be seques-
tered and build a bomb.[35] Instead, initial Site Y's population of
1,500 added another 4,200 residents from early 1943 through
1944 year-end, increasing the resident population to 5,700.

Demand for housing outstripped the capacity to maintain an adequate housing supply. Sundt-built apartment buildings were filled as soon as they could be completed. Even so,

infrastructure sufficient to accommodate scientific and support personnel needs remained chronically inadequate for several years.

The overwhelming immediacy for necessities couldn't wait for new construction to solve the problem. Temporary housing brought in included privately owned trailers and "Wingfoots," or government-owned expandable trailers. All shared common-area laundry and bath facilities that were functionally dismal. Their "temporary" status remained for several years.[36]

## The Scientists

With the exception of Albert Einstein, who had been assessed as a security risk, a more extreme collection of the world's top physicists working together in a single isolated location was beyond any reasonable imagination.

Among the first to arrive was a group of Nobel Prize winners and future prizewinners referred to by Oppenheimer as his "luminaries." This first assemblage included Enrico Fermi, Leo Szilard, Hans Bethe, John Van Vleck, Edward Teller, Robert Serber, Emilio Segre, Edwin McMillan, Robert Bacher, Isidor Rabi, J. M. B. Kellogg, Edward Condon, L. D. P. King, Richard Tolman, Donald Kerst, and mathematicians J. Carson Mark and Stanislaw Ulam.[37] And more were to come.

Many had fled Europe's totalitarian regimes or Germany's progressing war. To satisfy several of these individuals' concerns over "anything military," program management control, initially planned to be under US Army supervision, was revised to purportedly be under the supervision of the University of California and Dr. Glenn Seaborg. Actual oversight remained under General Groves and the Department of the Army.

All were brilliant scientists, but not all were theoretical physicists. For most, physics related to nuclear fission was new. Addressing the issue, a series of introductory lectures was initiated by Robert Serber, a Theoretical Physics Division group leader. Dr. Serber's lectures were subsequently published in a book called *The Los Alamos Primer* and provided to incoming staff.

**The Gadget**

Prior to the completion of secure Main Tech Area facilities, conceptual development brainstorming sessions were often inconveniently required to be held while construction was in process.[38] To avoid raising worker concerns that a project of mega-proportions was in the offing, "Gadget" was euphemistically substituted during discussions for "bomb." The term remained through the Trinity test detonation

Conclusions summarized in the MAUD report and agreed as workable in the Oppenheimer conferences had settled on a gun-type trigger design—firing one piece of fissile material into another to result in achieving the critical mass required for detonation.

Planning focused on two bomb formats—the Mark 1 bomb was to make use of U-235 as the fissile material; the Mark 2 was to use PU-239:

Note: Materials capable of sustaining a chain reaction are called "fissile;" the two fissile materials used in atomic weapons are U-235 and PU-239.39 Uranium's most common isotope, Uranium-238, composes 99.3% of natural, or unenriched, uranium. U-238 is fissionable but not fissile, meaning it cannot sustain a chain reaction by itself. The uranium isotope U-235 is the only naturally occurring substance which can break apart. It can split because the U-235 nucleus is unstable. When it breaks apart, the atom's neutrons are released, hitting other U-235 atoms and causing them to also split. With enough intensity, such as in a bomb, the effect is an impressive explosion. The potential for that condition had been determined mathematically by Lise Meitner before being confirmed by Hahn and Strassmann.

The Mark 1 bomb, code-named "Little Boy," was not particularly problematic by Manhattan Project standards. Enrico Fermi's experiments had proven U-235's potential, and Britain's MAUD Report had concluded that one pound of uranium achieving full fission was capable of yielding an explosive force of eight kilotons—sixteen million pounds—of TNT. A proper mechanism needed to be developed, but, as applied to a uranium bomb's probable success, concerns were limited.

The Mark 2 bomb, codenamed "Thin Man," proved unworkable. Test results supported an already open skepticism raised by the Tube Alloys group in England. The MAUD Report had raised doubts over plutonium's suitability for making a nuclear bomb at all; plutonium's physical properties were too inconsistent. Now Manhattan Project scientists had cause for their own concerns.

In one of the Oppenheimer-sponsored, pre-Manhattan Project discussions, a conference participant, physicist Richard Tolman, had suggested the concept of an implosion-type device but had raised no support among conference participants.

But taking a cautious view, Oppenheimer had anticipated a need to mitigate risks associated with plutonium as a bomb component. While maintaining priority on the gun-type trigger format during Thin Man bomb testing, a separate group under physicist Seth Neddermeyer had been investigating implosion as a plutonium bomb trigger.

Neddermeyer's belief was that Tolman's idea had merit; implosion could be practical by making use of a hollow cylinder of plutonium surrounded by an explosive shell. The conceptual use of shaped charges in three-dimensional explosive "lenses" was reported to have earlier been broached by British physicist James L. Tuck. And Robert Christie was credited with calculations that concluded plutonium sphere compression could result in critical density. But complications in dealing with both considerations were profoundly complex and currently unsolved.

In September 1943, Oppenheimer made one of his more astute managerial conclusions when he requested mathematician John von Neumann to provide his thoughts on implosion.[40] Von Neumann, regarded as the world's most brilliant mathematician at the time, had developed an expertise in mathematically difficult-to-model explosions and was the leading authority on the mathematics of "shaped-charges." A Princeton mathematics professor and member of Princeton's Institute for Advanced Study, von Neumann had joined the institute, along with Albert Einstein, in 1935, following both of their escapes from Germany's threat.

A review of Dr. Neddermeyers's study results prompted von Neumann to discuss his observations with Edward Teller. Teller's input concerning the potential for compressing PU-239 to a fissionable core density was convincing. Von Neumann concluded that the use of high-explosive shaped charges to implode a plutonium sphere could result in sufficient fission to create a bomb.

Further, his mathematical conclusions were that the implosion design, which later would be used on the Trinity and Nagasaki bombs, was likely to be more efficient than the Mark 1 bomb gun-type trigger design.

The following month, in October 1943, George Kistiakowsky, a Ukrainian-born explosives expert and Harvard professor, was persuaded to join the Manhattan Project, replacing Dr. Neddermeyer as head of the Explosives Division. Kistiakowsky's work focused on the shape and composition of the high-explosive lenses calculated by von Neumann to be the most promising design for implosion bomb success.

In December 1943, the Brits joined the effort when a Tube Alloys contingent, led by Sir Rudolf Ernst Peierls and including Niels Bohr, Otto Frisch, Klaus Fuchs, and Ernest Titterton, arrived to add their expertise to Manhattan Project activities.[41] At that point, there was expressed concern by

Manhattan Project participants that their activity was proceeding satisfactorily without the Tube Alloys group's assistance. The reaction would likely have been even more strident if it had been known Klaus Fuchs would one day become one of the Manhattan Project's most notorious participants.

Several months later, on July 17, 1944, a final decision was made to abandon prospects for a plutonium bomb to use the gun-type trigger. The hypothetical plutonium fission-by-implosion problem's status remained unchanged, but it was no longer simply an option; it had to be solved. Manhattan Project research was reorganized to focus efforts entirely on a third bomb format: The Mark 3 bomb, codenamed "Fat Man," was to trigger plutonium detonation by implosion.[42] That much was certain.

Two requirements still had to be addressed: unsolved difficulties associated with how to enable casting a spherical plutonium core and the need to overcome significant plutonium inconsistencies. Both were concerns, as had been stated in the MAUD Report. The ultimate tasks of the metallurgists were first, to cast plutonium into the shape of a perfect sphere, and second, to eliminate the corrosive effects of exposure to air.

Assuming plutonium inconsistencies could be overcome, the plutonium sphere's compression had to be precise, meaning the explosive lenses had to be perfectly configured for uniformity of the compression wave required to condense the plutonium into a critical mass. The implosion process would squeeze a softball-sized solid plutonium sphere into a tennis ball size as dimensionally precise as the softball had been.

Assuming both a way could be found to cast plutonium into a perfect sphere and an answer to plutonium's susceptibility to atmospheric degradation could be discovered, existing technology was still incapable of meeting the explosive lens detonation timing required. To be successful, the lenses had to detonate precisely within a fraction of a millionth of a second. If the implosion was even the slightest asymmetric, the plutonium core might be caused to shoot out one side, producing a fizzle—a considerably reduced result.

Intense testing of lens shapes, explosives compositions, and manners of detonation would be required to study the behavior of the shockwave needed to uniformly compress the plutonium sphere. The question for testing was how. Robert Serber, who had earlier been instrumental in his lectures defining a nuclear bomb's physics, had the answer: radioactive lanthanum as a plutonium surrogate.[43]

Lanthanum-140, a lanthanum isotope, was chosen because of its short half-life and ready availability. Barium-140, a fission product produced in uranium slugs at Oak Ridge's X-10 graphite reactor, was separated from the uranium, then shipped in lead-lined containers to Los Alamos where the lanthanum-140 and barium-140 were separated at the TA-10 Site for use in Bayo Canyon RaLa shots.

The first RaLa test was conducted on September 22, 1944, by a team led by Italian experimental physicist Bruno Rossi. Several generations of RaLa program testing solved detonation circuit timing difficulties, explosive lens composition, and lens configuration. Meanwhile, plutonium inconsistency problems had also been separately resolved. To overcome decomposition resulting from atmospheric exposure, the plutonium core was cast in two nickel-plated hemispheres.

Combined, the results led to a February 1945 conclusion: test participants were satisfied that an atomic explosion using PU-239 could be produced. Robert Oppenheimer, General Groves, James Conan, George Kistiakowsky, and three others met in Robert Oppenheimer's office on February 28, 1945, to approve the implosion bomb's design.[44]

Mark 3 was now referred to as Fat Man. Fat Man's structure was to combine five concentric spheres:[45]

- **A high-explosive lens system:** an 18.5-inch-thick assembly of thirty-two explosive lenses cut into shapes of five- or six-sided pyramids with their tips cut off, giving the appearance of a soccer ball. Each lens was attached to its own dedicated detonator.

- **The "pusher":** A 4.5-inch-thick, 264.6-pound aluminum absorber shell. The pusher's purpose was to maintain the implosion's effect through mitigation of a drop in pressure directly behind the lens' explosives' shockwave.

- **The "tamper":** a uranium reflector shell of nine-inch diameter, 2.75-inch thick, 265-pound natural uranium (U-238) layer surrounding the "pit." (The core of an implosion weapon—the combined fissile material and initiator—was referred to as a "pit"). The tamper's function was to redirect neutrons back into the plutonium core to allow fission to become more fully involved before the mass erupted in an explosion of monstrous proportions. Placing the fission process in context, the entire process, start to finish, occurred within a few billionths of one second.

- **The core:** a 4.44-inch diameter, 13.67-pound sphere of plutonium that was solid except for an approximate one inch in diameter cavity in the center where a "neutron initiator" was to be placed.

- **The "initiator":** the initiator's job was to start the chain reactions in both bombs. But the plutonium bomb, in particular, would require the "neutron initiator's" neutron boost as a "kickstart" to raise the core's explosive capacity to a higher level. The initiator's construction combined radioactive polonium and beryllium into a sphere weighing about seven grams called the "Urchin."

The entire apparatus was enclosed by a three-eighths-inch thick steel outer casing, accounting for almost half of the Fat Man bomb's 10,800-pound weight.

With the approval of Fat Man, two legitimate atomic bomb prototypes had been developed: Little Boy (the Mark 1), a 9,700-pound bomb using U-235 as the fissile core, and Fat

Man (the Mark 3), a 10,800-pound implosion-type bomb using PU-239.

Little Boy's U-235 was separated into two pieces: the "bullet" and the "target." The bullet was a cylindrical stack of six uranium rings just under four inches in width and 6.3 inches in length.[46] The target, nine U-235 rings, was contained in a 6.3-inch-long hollow cylinder.

Detonation was to be initiated by firing the bullet into the target by a six-foot, 992-pound high-powered antiaircraft gun. Cordite, a conventional artillery smokeless powder, was the propellant that was to drive the bullet into the target.

Little Boy was 126 inches long, 28 inches in diameter, and, like Fat Man, was also encased by a three-eighths-inch-thick steel casing to complete the bomb package.

If results were as anticipated, the bombs would be one million times more powerful than the then most powerful bombs in any arsenal.

### Trinity and Tinian

Decision-makers had agreed that Fat Man's format should work, but the plutonium bomb's reliability remained a concern. To address the issue, a Fat Man prototype test was scheduled for "Trinity Site" at the Alamogordo Bombing and Gunnery Range, two hundred miles south of Los Alamos in Central New Mexico's Jornada del Muerto desert.[47]

Preparing Trinity Site for the test, miles of roads were paved to support the transport of materials to the test site, and thousands of miles of electrical wiring and cables were laid to provide communications and the power that would detonate the Gadget. On July 15, 1945, all was ready.

The Gadget could be placed into position at the top of the one-hundred-foot tower built for the test. The collected assemblage's feelings were running high with unbridled enthusiasm. Then, during a painstaking inch-by-inch winching the Gadget up the tower, the sort of frightening event really scary movie drama thrives on occurred. In one mind-numbing moment, the Gadget became partially unhinged.

And 10,800 pounds of shockingly malevolent fury began to sway.

The prospect of Fat Man falling from the tower, and the very real potential for it detonating while everyone was at the scene, was the sort of scenario where the collective lives of all involved may have flashed before their eyes.

Such a spectacular occurrence would surely have resulted in making world news. Intended secrecy, along with a significant assemblage of among the world's most brilliant scientists, would have been instantly vaporized. But on that day, such a disaster was not to be. The Gadget was eventually secured at its planned top-of-the-tower position.

But reason for anxiety remained.

Other than the mathematical models created in proof of the Gadget's concept, there was no precise answer as to what to expect from the moment of detonation. Concerns regarding potential Trinity test outcomes were sufficiently extreme that General Groves contacted New Mexico's governor, John Dempsey, to inform him that, tentatively, martial law might have to be implemented. General Groves was even said to have expressed concerns regarding the City of Amarillo's population of seventy thousand, three hundred miles away.

The next morning, July 16, 1945, an assembled gathering of a majority of the universe's eminent scientists waited with an indescribable intensity of anticipation. Was what they had been working on with no letup for three years going to work? The theory was right; the testing had been satisfactory; the design seemed reasonable.

But were they right?

The answer came at 5:30 a.m. [48]

In a thunderous moment of triumph, the Gadget detonated with an explosive equivalent of twenty-one kilotons, forty-two million pounds, of TNT.[49] The temperature at the detonation's center was four times that of the sun's core. Men standing 10,000 yards away were knocked flat as the shockwave's massive force swept over them. The detonation's flash was visible more than two hundred miles away and was heard at least forty miles.

The Gadget was a success!

The steel test tower vaporized instantly, and a six-foot-in-depth depression that was four hundred yards across was left where the sand had melted and solidified into a carpet of a greenish glass-like substance. "Trinitite," the newly created glass, was to be a feature of all future atomic explosions.

Brigadier General Thomas F. Farrell described his impression of the Trinity detonation:

The whole country was lighted by a searing light with the intensity many times that of the midday sun. It was golden, purple, violet, gray and blue. It lighted every peak, crevasse and ridge of the nearby mountain range with a clarity and beauty that cannot be described but must be seen to be imagined. It was that beauty the great poets dream about but describe most poorly and inadequately.

The bomb development was over. Consideration now turned to "how quickly can we turn bomb test results into action?" The answer was already underway.

## Japan's Bombing

Immediately following the Gadget's detonation, the Navy destroyer USS *Indianapolis*, which had been standing by pending notification, was ordered to "proceed without delay."[50] Its cargo, a partially assembled Little Boy, was secured to the *Indianapolis'* deck in a wooden crate.

Little Boy's bullet was stored in a lead-lined steel container locked to brackets welded to the deck of the *Indianapolis'* Captain Charles B. McVay III's quarters. The nine U-235 target rings were flown to Tinian on three separate aircraft, arriving July 28 and 29.

Tinian, one of three main islands included in the Marianas chain of mostly uninhabited islands, was a convenient 1,500 miles, six-hour-flight time from Japan's key cities.[51] The XXI Bomber Command consisted of 269 B-29 bombers; two, specially modified, had been selected to deliver Little Boy and Fat Man to their Japan destinations.

Upon arrival at Tinian, both bomb's components were delivered to an air-conditioned assembly building to be completed prior to being loaded onto their delivery B-29s. Little Boy was unsafe once the gun was loaded with the Cordite propellant; anything that ignited it would cause a full-yield explosion. For that reason, the propellant was to be loaded into the gun only after takeoff, eliminating concerns related to the B-29's take-off reliability to be no more than usual.

But Fat Man didn't come with the same comfort. Fat Man's format had to be made fully live and ready to detonate before the delivery B-29's wheels left the ground. The ability to leave the island without incident was of utmost importance; a crash almost assuredly would have resulted in wiping out most of the island and the entire US arsenal of B-29 bombers.

Japan's destiny began at 2:45 a.m. on August 6, 1945, when *Enola Gay*, the B-29 Superfortress powered by four 2,200-horsepower Wright turbocharged radial engines, cleared the Tinian runway. The six-hour flight to Hiroshima was piloted by Col. Paul W. Tibbets, carrying Little Boy and a twelve-man crew. *Enola Gay* was accompanied by *The Great Artiste*, a B-29 carrying instrumentation, and *Necessary Evil*, a second B-29, commanded by Captain George Marquardt, who was to take photographs.

Mission commander Captain William S. Parsons armed Little Boy during the flight; Captain Parson's assistant, Second Lieutenant Morris R. Jeppson, then removed bomb safety devices thirty minutes prior to reaching the target area. At 8:15 a.m., 1,980 feet over the city, Little Boy, the world's first atomic bomb used in war, detonated with a calculated yield of fifteen kilotons of TNT.

President Harry S. Truman's announcement was brief:

> Sixteen hours ago, an American airplane dropped one bomb on Hiroshima, an important Japanese Army base. That bomb had more power than 20,000 tons of TNT. It had more than two thousand times the blast power of the British 'Grand Slam' which is the largest bomb ever yet used in the history of warfare." The announcement went on to state, "It is an atomic bomb. It is a harnessing of the basic power of the universe. The force from which the sun draws its power has been loosed against those who brought war to the Far East. . . ."

> The Secretary of War, who has kept in personal touch with all phases of the project, will immediately make a public statement giving further details.

> His statement will give facts concerning the sites at Oak Ridge near Knoxville, Tennessee, and at Richland near Pasco, Washington, and an installation near Santa Fe, New Mexico. Although the workers at the sites have been making materials to be used in producing the greatest destructive force in history they have not themselves been in danger beyond that of many other occupations, for the utmost care has been taken for their safety.[52]

Henry L Stimson's statement, released that same day, described the new weapon as perhaps "the greatest achievement of the combined efforts of science, industry, labor, and the military in all history." Improvements would be made "increasing effectiveness, and possibly the scale of magnitude."[53]

Three days later, on August 9, 1945, Major C. W. Sweeney, piloting the B-29 *Bockscar*, cleared Tinian's runway uneventfully to deliver Fat Man to Nagasaki. Detonation, at 11:02 a.m., was 1,650 feet over the city with the effect of twenty-one kilotons of TNT. Fat Man's cloud rose 60,000 feet over Nagasaki.

On August 15, 1945, in a reversal of a prior stated position of "fighting until the last man standing," Imperial Japanese forces surrendered. World War II was over; Project Y's purpose was complete.

## Post Manhattan Project

With the war ended and the Manhattan Project's purpose a success, The Hill's future was uncertain.

Had the Japanese not surrendered, a third plutonium core was ready for another bomb. When it was determined that the additional bomb was not necessary, the core was sent to Los Alamos to be used in Omega Site critical mass experiments. The extreme danger of plutonium was quickly proven. Two separate experiments on the core resulted in the death of scientists.

On August 21, 1945, Harry Daghlian accidentally dropped a tungsten carbide brick onto one of the core's hemispheres, resulting in it showering him with fatal radiation.[54] His death followed twenty-five days later.

Nine months later, on May 21, 1946, Louis Slotin was engaged in an experiment on the core, "tickling the dragon's tail," when a screwdriver separating the plutonium hemispheres slipped, accidentally allowing them to come together.[55]

One of the individuals present described "a blinding flash of blue light, accompanied by heat." Dr. Slotin personally separated the two suddenly highly radioactive hemispheres by hand, incurring a fatal radiation dosage and saving the lives of several others present. His reportedly agonizing death occurred nine days later.

The "demon core," as it had become known, was subsequently melted down for use in other applications.

On July 1, 1946, ten months after the Hiroshima and Nagasaki bombings, the US conducted the first of two Operation Crossroads tests.[56] Captured Japanese and German ships and a few ready-to-be-scrapped US Navy vessels were targeted to test nuclear weapons' effects on military hardware. Two Mark 3 bombs, identical to the Trinity and Nagasaki bombs, were detonated on Bikini Atoll with the same approximate explosive yield of around twenty-one kilotons.

"Able," the first Crossroads test, was dropped from an airplane, detonating at a 520-foot altitude. "Baker," the second test, was detonated on July 25, ninety feet under the lagoon. The resulting radioactive contamination was so dangerous, a planned third test was canceled.

Site Y Lab employment had declined as most of the pioneering team of Manhattan Project physicists had resigned to move on to academia or prestigious research positions, with only a few remaining. For the moment, all things bomb related ended. But plans for Site Y weren't over.

On August 1, 1946, President Truman signed the Atomic Energy Act.[57] The act outlined the development and regulation of military and civilian use of nuclear matters and provided for government control of fissionable material. The act also assumed control over the Manhattan Engineer District on January 1, 1947, by the newly formed Atomic Energy Commission.

## Los Alamos Scientific Laboratory

Site Y was officially rededicated as "Los Alamos Scientific Laboratory" and the town as "Los Alamos" on January 1, 1947. Robert Oppenheimer had moved on to Caltech as a professor but soon realized he was no longer interested in teaching and accepted a position as director of Princeton's Institute for Advanced Study. Norris Bradbury had been elevated to Los Alamos Laboratory director.

Los Alamos's new mission required a mostly new cadre of engineers and technicians, resulting in renewed spectacular town population growth. When we arrived in June 1948, Los Alamos's population was already 8,200, and by January 1, 1950, the decennial census counted 10,476 Los Alamos residents.

The lab's new mission: improve on what the now-legendary Manhattan Project scientists had accomplished.

Engineering and scientific personnel demands resulted in an international search for scientists, engineers, and technicians to carry on expanded activities; pay scales were made sufficiently attractive to acquire the needed talent.[58]

Los Alamos's $3,371 average annual household income at the time was high compared to the $1,500 national average. Top lab scientific personnel earned $10,000 annually; Lab Director Norris Bradbury's annual salary was reported to have been $12,500.

With the surge in demand for lab employees, site support personnel needs were also growing. Bus operations had become necessary as housing facilities were so limited. The sixty or so Native American ladies who worked as housemaids on the project used the buses each day to commute to their place of employment from their pueblos.[59]

In March 1946, thirty daily buses were collecting passengers from locations within a fifty-mile radius of the project; by December 1946, the number had increased to forty-three buses in service. Three buses were for schoolchildren, seven operated on the project, and the balance continued to make their round trips to nearby towns and pueblos.

In November 1943, Sundt completed their contract, resulting in the Robert E. McKee Company from El Paso, Texas, being engaged in January 1944. Construction had been authorized for housing fifty-six families in a combination of one-, two-, and three-bedroom duplexes. Need for expediency directed the contract to the Ready-Cut House Company in Dallas; Morgan and Sons Contractors was selected to erect the buildings.

The lab's rededication required temporary housing, a Manhattan Project carryover, to remain important, now including fifty-one winterized hutments, forty-seven government-owned standard trailers, twenty-five Wingfoots, fifty-six Pacific Apartments, thirty National Hut apartments, and something near 250 privately owned trailers. This group primarily provided housing for service personnel and temporary laboratory workers.

On June 27, 1947, six months after the LANL dedication, President Truman authorized Operation Sandstone. Another bomb test, Operation Sandstone, was conducted this time under LANL supervision on Enewetak Atoll in the Pacific.[60] Three tests on new bomb design options were detonated from 200-foot towers: on April 14, 1948, "X-Ray" yielded thirty-seven kilotons; on April 30, "Yoke" yielded forty-nine kilotons; "Zebra," yielding eighteen kilotons, concluded testing on May 14.

The key to increasing a fission explosion's yield was sustaining a chain reaction long enough from initiation to produce the optimum explosive energy released before the core's internal pressure caused it to rip itself apart. Operation Sandstone's tests were the beginning of rethinking atomic bomb formatting.

Results from the two bombs used to end the war with Japan had clarified that a fission weapon's best trigger design was implosion. With that conclusion, the Sandstone tests focused on three pit-type variations: a composite core of PU-239 and U-235 in the "X-Ray" test, "Yoke" made use of an all-U-235 core, and "Zebra," in addition to an all-U-235 core, tested a new initiator format that reduced the amount of polonium required.

Also departing from the Mark 3 bombs' solid plutonium cores, the three Sandstone test pits were hollow, and each made use of pit "levitation." Pit levitation had been understood in Los Alamos before the war ended but required more testing. Consequently, use of a hollow core and pit levitation were set aside for Fat Man's solid core.

Hans Bethe, after the war, used a hammer and nail analogy when talking about the Mark 3: "Do you put the hammer on the nail and push, or does it work better to swing the hammer and get some momentum going before you hit the nail?"[61] The Mark 3 design's hammer had pushed—pit components were in physical contact, leaving no room for the implosion's force to build momentum before hitting the pit.

The first levitated pit design suspended the pit on wires. An air gap between the U-238 tamper and the pit provided the tamper room to build momentum before compressing the pit. Beyond supporting more energy to be delivered to the pit, levitation also served to smooth out explosive shockwave irregularities.

Test results revealed the Zebra format was most effective, leading to Zebra's format becoming the Mark 4, the first mass-produced atomic bomb. The Mark 4's physical configuration was essentially the same as the Mark 3, only slightly larger in length and diameter. Aside from pit levitation, a revised initiator, and a hollow U-235 pit, the Mark 4's mechanism included one other significant difference—a sensible improvement to safety referred to as "in-flight insertion."

For this refinement an open pathway inside the bomb allowed the pit to be carried inside the aircraft. Just before the scheduled drop, a "weaponeer" manually inserted the pit through a doorway in front of the bomb casing, added the final explosive layer, and closed the bomb to arm it.

A set of wires physically connected to the airplane were pulled from the bomb as it fell away, enabling the firing circuit.

As the world's first atomic bomb detonations, Trinity, Hiroshima, and Nagasaki had made some serious impressions. But concerns regarding future bombs were considerable.

Little Boy had used up Site Y's entire wartime U-235 production in one magnificent, if inefficient, explosion. A sixteen-kiloton yield had been achieved with only two pounds of U-235 undergoing fission. The remaining 139 pounds, 98.5 percent of the 141-pound pit, contributed nothing to the event.[62]

The problem was "pre-detonation."

Pre-detonation was a condition when fission occurred in only a portion of the fissionable material before the whole mass blew itself apart. Further, the gun-type trigger made the bomb's instability infinitely dangerous.

Fat Man had been the more powerful of the two bombs; the fourteen-pound PU-239 pit had achieved a twenty-one-kiloton yield. Implosion's greater efficiency was attributed to the massive U-238 tamper's effect, holding Fat Man's plutonium core together for a few hundred nanoseconds longer. The extra time allowed the urchin to do its job, boosting yield efficiency as more of the core had time to become involved in fission before predetonation blew it apart.[63]

John von Neumann's calculations had concluded mathematically that implosion would be the more productive of the two trigger formats, and the wartime bombs had proved von Neumann's calculations correct beyond any doubt. But the problem remained that the Mark 4 bomb was still too big and unwieldy. And it had to be solved.

At 10,800 pounds, 60 inches in diameter, and 128 inches long, the Mark 4 was only barely accommodated by the Air Force's biggest bombers. And while improvements in safety for in-flight arming had been made, the bomb remained unacceptably cumbersome.

The Air Force needed a smaller, lighter bomb. Los Alamos's mission had shifted from Site Y's conceptual development—how to build an atomic bomb in the first place—to how to make it a lot easier to use. When decisions were being made about who to hire to solve the problem, dad was among those on the way.

Dad's position with LANL was as life-altering to his future as had been the Depression and the war, each in its own way. And we were all going to participate in the new adventure.

## Life in Los Alamos

The day of our arrival in Los Alamos, Dad became immediately immersed, sometimes working six days a week, with Saturdays being at least half a day. His work was to participate in what was to bedone to reduce a 10,000-pound instrument of destruction to a more congenial size, capable of being loaded onto smaller aircraft while retaining the same frenzied capability to wreak pandemonium on a large expanse of unfriendly territory.

Also, on the day we arrived, we moved into a three-bedroom, one-bath apartment in a new "Morgan" apartment community, conveniently located off Canyon Road, near the town center. Our apartment was also adjacent to Pueblo Canyon, one of the several canyons creating the mesas on which the town of Los Alamos and the lab were located.

Los Alamos had some eccentricities. Over time, most became just another part of the landscape, but others, for this story, became apparent only after I was able to take a more adult view in retrospect when I began researching conditions as they had been at the time.

The Atomic Energy Commission had replaced the Army as Los Alamos's town manager in March 1947, in the process assuming oversight of security from the military. The Zia Corporation, a Robert E. McKee Company subsidiary, assumed Los Alamos's town operations management; at the same time, the University of California retained lab operations oversight.

Our arrival to the town now known as Los Alamos had been a year and a half after Site Y's rededication to the Los Alamos National Lab. Most of the Manhattan Project scientists had moved on to other activities in academia and research.

Getting over the initial greeting, our introduction to Los Alamos was that the town appeared mostly as it had been under the Manhattan Project's Project Y. But a furious rate of redevelopment was about to change that and was already in process. New construction implemented during the next few years physically changed the appearance of both the town and the lab. But other Manhattan Project attributes remained unchanged during the four years we spent in Los Alamos:

- **The town was exclusive:** It was a place whose near sole function was to support the development of new generations of spectacularly destructive weapons.

- **Security was extreme:** Access remained restricted. The city was surrounded by seven-foot chain-link perimeter fencing; a nine-foot chain-link fence surrounded the Main Tech area and each test site. Three strands of barbed wire topped each.

   The Main Tech area and test sites were further access restricted. Only individuals authorized to be there were allowed entry and, to prove it, were in possession of a badge specific to the area.

   Los Alamos's airspace was restricted; no private airplane overflights were allowed. Once, a private plane was said to have strayed too near and, to the pilot's undoubtedly considerable surprise, was intercepted by Air Force fighters dispatched from Sandia Air Force Base to escort the pilot back to Albuquerque for a question-and-answer about what his thinking may have been.

   Street lighting was minimal. It's doubtful that there were many American towns of Los Alamos's size having such an exaggerated absence of nighttime light pollution. As a result, aside from always-spectacular starlit night skies, an occasionally really cold winter night produced an eerie flickering of emerald-green lights illuminating the northern sky.

Some cocoon-like conditions kept anyone who didn't belong there out; individuals within the fenced perimeter had been investigated and were presumably authorized to be there. It isn't clear when Los Alamos first became recognized by mapmakers, but it remained a blank spot on published maps prior to the 1950s.

Sometime in the late 1940s and early 1950s, Los Alamos was reported to have included over eight hundred security guards among a population of ten thousand. Residents were not bothered by door-to-door salesmen, and there was little need for concern over the prospect of encounters with unwanted strangers or for locking front doors. With the town protected by fences and guards, Los Alamos was safe from criminal activity.

- **Lab scientists and engineers were bound to strict secrecy:** Families knew little about what was done at their household head's work. I knew only that Dad worked in the Tech Area, was somehow involved in other test site activities, and often worked at least a part of Saturdays. I wasn't alone among kids whose fathers were lab employees, and I don't recall their fathers' work being mentioned in playground conversation.

That didn't keep us from speculating about the bomb's size. We concluded that an atomic bomb was probably the size of a thumbnail. Knowledge of the 10,000-pound soccer ball-sized reality would have to wait. What I now know of what Dad was doing when he went to work every day came several years after we left and the need for security had loosened. He was blowing things up as he tested new trigger designs.

- **Los Alamos's environment held potential for exposure to radioactive contamination:** Beginning in late 1943, when Manhattan Project scientists were fully engaged in a day-and-night schedule to develop a workable Gadget, expediency compromised prudence. The TA-3 Site generated highly toxic radioactive waste from uranium and plutonium testing and, later, plutonium production, and RaLa program-generated strontium-90 waste was dumped untreated into Pueblo Canyon. The highly toxic contaminated area, later known as "Acid Canyon," was sixteen hundred feet from Central Grade School and directly below the town center.

Los Alamos's first impressions had been a culture shock. My small-town manners and Southern-accented speech stood out, providing an excellent opportunity for other kids to make fun of me. A few playground skirmishes settled things, generally ending amicably. One in particular, Jess Siglow, became my closest friend, and we had a lasting friendship.

In coping with adjustments to the peculiarities of the Los Alamos environment, I wasn't alone. Peggy Pond, having spent her early childhood in Los Alamos, wrote of her sadness at seeing Los Alamos's transformation from an open wilderness camp to a closed bomb-producing city, "with its fears, and guarded laboratories . . . and the forbidding metal fences bearing, in enormous red letters, the warning: DANGER! PELIGRO!"

For adults, adjustments were more extreme. Los Alamos had the trappings of a socialized society; other than personal belongings, there was no private property. Everyone rented from and was beholden to the federal government. Government ownership applied to everything—housing, schools, commercial development, and recreational facilities.

## Life in Los Alamos Begins

I began third grade in September at Central Elementary Grade School, a former Sundt-constructed building from Manhattan Project times. Two months later, we moved to a Western Housing Area duplex at 1374A 40th Street, immediately adjacent to the more recently completed Mesa Elementary Grade School.

Our new address was as basic as the College Station home we had left. Government housing was never better represented by a more triumphant attempt to offer niceties beyond bare necessities. Finishing details included black asphalt tile flooring, a sensible kitchen minimally equipped with a stove and refrigerator, and a gravel pad for one car to park. A narrow stoop accessed through a back door off the kitchen provided space for a clothes washer. Clothes were hung out to dry on a backyard line during all kinds of weather.

A single-floor furnace was a notably inefficient heating source, made more apparent because it was the home's only heating source. It was no problem during the summer, but winter nights were different. My parent's frugality continued in Los Alamos; the floor furnace was all but turned off at night, not to be turned on again until the following morning. Even when it was on, the floor furnace never actually heated much of the house beyond the living room.

During the winter months, our home's interior became an Arctic-hut equivalent. Getting into bed was shockingly cold for the first few minutes until, gradually, my body heat warmed the sheets. That worked fine until changing positions, in which case the warming process began again.

In the mornings, it was usual to wake up to ice accumulated inside my window. A near-daily first-thing-in-the-morning argument erupted between Barbara and me over the amount of floor furnace space to be allocated to each of us when the thermostat was turned up for the day.

Mesa Elementary School's third-grade classroom was a Quonset hut—a Manhattan Project leftover moved in to support an outsized western area grade-school population. Having next-door proximity to Mesa Elementary School provided a considerable convenience; I could hear the bell ring and mosey over to class, arriving perfectly on time.

Mesa Elementary also had a distinct peculiarity: like Garrison Keillor's Lake Wobegon, Los Alamos's children tended to be "above average." A fair sampling of Mesa Elementary students had super-smart fathers; inherited genes meant that some precocious kids sprang from a few of those parents.

The condition was showcased in 1949 when an article in the *Denver Post* reported, "intelligence tests have rated a number of Los Alamos's pupils in the near-genius class, a situation that challenges the professional competence of their teachers."[64] The observation was reiterated in author Jon Hunner's book *Inventing Los Alamos*. Our Mesa Elementary principal, Sam Miles, was quoted as having stated, "Genius is common, and the circumstances fitted to develop it, very rare."[65]

But a father's employment played no part in the kids' social interactions. Some kids may have been at a classroom disadvantage, but if so, no one gave attention except maybe the teachers. In hindsight, I can see how there could have been at least some teacher prejudice.

Third grade was taught by a pleasant young woman, Miss Caldwell, and, for the most part, my third-grade experience was not particularly memorable except for one event. An overnight Arctic temperature had made the air so cold that grabbing the metal door handle to enter our Quonset hut classroom required a seriously painful disengagement from the handle, leaving copious amounts of DNA in the form of near-perfect replicas of fingerprints. Conditions were perfect for making dares only small boys could reasonably be expected to take up. And one classmate did. He licked the playground flagpole.

In retrospect, it doesn't seem particularly surprising that the effort to loosen a tongue under such circumstances, without leaving at least a few taste buds with the flagpole, involved a certain amount of pandemonium.

While the rest of the class was being appreciatively entertained, Miss Caldwell and one of the school's administrative staff busily engaged in administering to a screaming basket case while mounting a diligent effort to correct the problem with the least amount of damage. I don't recall anyone ever having accepted that particular dare again or whether that kid returned to class that day after a visit to the school nurse. In fact, I don't recall whether he came back at all.

Fourth grade was taught by a diminutive young woman, who, with great consistency, exuded the unmistakable impression of a shrew that derived pleasure from humiliating small children. I observed this trait during several instances throughout the year, but one particularly notable event related to a classmate named Bobby. Bobby had a more advanced playground mouth than the rest of us, it seemed—at least as applied to word selection—but none of us had the nerve to express ourselves as openly and loudly as Bobby.

During one of Bobby's more impressive recesses, the shrew caught wind of Bobby's enthusiastically expressed speech indelicacies. Not to miss an opportunity, when recess was over, the shrew made a request for volunteers—anyone who had heard Bobby say "naughties"—to line up and whisper the salacious words into her eagerly cupped ear. The spectacle required the rest of us, Bobby included, to observe as some classmates, mostly little girls, paraded by to whisper their collective tattled delights.

That event made me fantasize unseemly mayhem on an adult. But the shrew didn't satisfy her bitchy little self with Bobby; there were other incidents. One, more personal, had to do with her making recommendations for safety patrol positions when we moved on to the fifth grade. She made a point to the class that she "couldn't recommend Ronnie" because she was "afraid Ronnie would beat up kids if they didn't do what he told them." That got quite a laugh out of the class and further enhanced my already enthusiastic dislike for her.

Following another recess, the shrew discovered her teacher's closet had been violated. Someone had pilfered a couple of crackers out of a stash she had apparently planned for a later snack. As usual, quite an issue was made of the outrage to the entire class, apparently prompting someone to snitch. This time, the culprit, a female classmate, was once again subjected to the shrew's requisite public humiliation. A conference with the girl and her parents was held before school started one morning, the rest of the class observing the goings-on through the glass classroom door after the bell had rung.

At the end of the year, three classmates failed to pass fourth grade. They would not be progressing on to the fifth grade for what was understood to be "reasons of immaturity." Bobby and the unlucky cracker thief were among the threesome; no apparent reason was given for the other girl's inclusion.

On reflection, if immaturity was, in fact, the real reason for the shrew's actions, as opposed to a venomous dislike toward those kids, most of the boys in our class would have been hard put to move on to the next grade. To be fair, the shrew provided a valuable lesson: sometimes we learn best from those who provide the worst examples of human behavior.

Not to be outdone for a useful learning experience, the fifth grade had its own "aha" moment. Apparently, to supplement the student experience, Mr. Miles had our teacher, Mr. Payne, set up a retail "store" where members of our class took turns selling school supplies at a small table each day prior to the start of class and during recess. That little store provided what had to be my earliest awakening—I *liked* selling; I *really liked* selling. The realization resulted from a particular circumstance.

One of our little store's offerings was an eight-and-a-half-by-eleven-inch pad of lined paper like the ones on which my generation practiced alphabetic figures. Only, in this pad, minute wood chips were embedded in the paper. In an apparent attempt to compensate for such an obscenely crappy product, the manufacturer had included photos of old-time movie stars on each pad's coversheet. The problem was that even grade school kids weren't fooled by such a blatant sham. The pads didn't sell. Our store was hung with an inventory of unsalable product. Then came inspiration: I would move the junk inventory!

My aggressive "sales" tactics worked. I found of-the-moment results can be considerably satisfying. But I soon discovered what snake-oil salesmen had always known: without the ability to be on the next stage out of town, there are nearly always consequences. One of the little girls in a lower grade had, as a result of my enthusiastically, apparently overbearing, persistence, purchased one of the offensive notepads, then immediately burst into tears. Word got around fast. I was chastised by every other little girl on the playground, including my own class-mates. "Wait! I got rid of the bad merchandise, didn't I?" At least that's what I would like to have said, but no one was going to cut me any such slack.

Okay, the little girl's money was returned, and I recovered from the group reprisal and sold the remaining unsatisfactory pads to less vulnerable individuals. With the experience, I had discovered what was to become a lifetime passion for selling—the "real way," not the aluminum-siding way. And I would soon get the new challenge I needed.

With secrecy and security as tight as they were, one might think Los Alamos's environment would be smothering. And to some adults, it may have been. Historical accounts of Los Alamos life have acknowledged adult residents' challenges in adapting to the many inconveniences of living within a restrictive environment. But for kids, it was no problem.

My and my friends' lack of concern for security impositions was likely attributed to our having been allowed to move around reasonably unfettered. No doubt our freedom was under the watchful awareness of unobtrusive security guard surveillance, likely more dedicated to seeing that we didn't get ourselves into too much trouble than concerns over secrecy violations. This was made apparent a couple of times when our activities stretched the limit beyond what security guard tolerance could ignore.

Once, on a north-of-town Boy Scout hike, our group's encroachment on the Bayo Canyon Test Site was too much for the security guards' comfort. The ride back to our campsite loaded with five Boy Scouts and two security guards about did the Jeep in. But everyone enjoyed the experience—even the guards.

Among adults, Los Alamos's social stratifications were similar to a university town's pecking order hierarchy was accomplished in a sly manner—by housing type. Housing was dependent on the household head's stature within the lab's hierarchy. A McKee single-family home indicated a reasonably well-placed position in the lab pecking order. Rent paid was then assessed according to a household head's salary.

Apart from Director Bradbury's home, even the Western Housing Area's best were unimpressive. By Los Alamos standards, the Bradbury family's housing had a cachet more appropriate to "El Jefe."

Kids, at least those in grade school, were influenced by none of this. No apparent distinction resulted from where we lived or what our fathers did. Most of us didn't know with any certainty about our father's occupation. In contrast, College Station's distinction between town kids and farm kids had been more apparent.

When we arrived in June 1948, Los Alamos housing, support buildings, and the Main Tech Area were still predominantly Manhattan Project-era vintage. The 1953 film *Stalag 17*, starring William Holden, could have been shot in Los Alamos before Manhattan Project removals and replacements. During the 1948 through 1950 period, the town's appearance transformed from a military outpost to a more modern city.

Six aptly named "Bathtub Row" homes, originally occupied by school administrators, then senior Manhattan Project
scientists during the war, had included the town's only luxury—
bathtubs.[66] Supplementing Bathtub Row were two-bedroom,
one-bath, and three-bedroom, one-bath Sundt-built apartments. Each unit included a shower and was notably finished to
a less-than-fashionable level, best described as "good enough."

Also, apparently "good enough" was over three hundred
service and construction families continuing to occupy temporary housing types in an assortment of privately-owned trailers;
expandable, government-owned Wingfoots; and "hutments,"
square 260-square-foot structures brought in from Fort Leonard
Wood immediately after the war.[67] As before, this housing group
shared central bath and laundry facilities.

Two buildings, Theaters #1 and #2 during Manhattan
Project times, had served a variety of Project Y needs, including
social events. After the war, Theater #1, renamed the "Hill"
Theater, served as the town's movie theater when we arrived.

On Saturday afternoons, Mom would take Barbara and
me to the Hill Theater for whatever Hopalong Cassidy Western
was playing. The feature film was always preceded by that week's
serial starring various heroes: Superman fighting for truth, justice, and the American way; the Lone Ranger, disrupting bad
guys and their sordid ways, along with his trusty sidekick, Tonto;
and Flash Gordon, exploring distant galaxies in a rocket ship,
which almost always showed a faint line of the string that held
it up while filming was taking place.

An impressive three-story log structure, Fuller Lodge had served as the school's main building before becoming the Manhattan Project's community dining and meeting hall until 1945, when it became the town's only restaurant. Our family had little dining-out experience, but our first Thanksgiving dinner in Los Alamos was at Fuller Lodge. Apparently, the experience had been enough to satisfy; we never went back.

Across from the Main Tech Area and adjacent to the infirmary, Ashley Pond, named after the school's founder, had been a school amenity until a student drowned. My recollection of Ashley Pond was a murky waterhole, made aggressively unattractive by the thoughtful enclosure of a surrounding chain-link fence.

Dr. Bradbury's mission to remake Los Alamos to accommodate the lab's expanded mission and the population required to support it had begun soon after the war's end.

A new high school, opened in the fall of 1949, was proclaimed by a magazine as "one of the most modern and beautiful school buildings in the country." The high school included a community auditorium and an indoor swimming pool that, to our delight, was occasionally made available for elementary school student use. About the same time, a new town center accommodating a movie theater, bowling alley, bakery, sporting goods store, the Santa Fe New Mexican newspaper circulation office, and bank was also completed.

With the new came the removal of the old. In 1950, the iconic Manhattan Project's Main Tech Area was demolished following the completion of a bridge spanning Los Alamos

Canyon. Main Tech Area functions were moved to South Mesa, becoming Technical Area-53, "the Mesa." The new bridge, spanning Los Alamos Canyon to accommodate South Mesa access, was touted as the "third highest arch bridge in the world." Its spans also became one of Jess's and my frequent recreational facilities.

TA-53's completion was celebrated with an open house event, giving employee families a tour. Two features were memorable: at eleven stories in height, the world's largest Van de Graaff generator was on display, and a remote-controlled manipulator demonstrated the handling of radioactive materials behind thick, lead-glass windows in the "hot cell" area of the lab's chemical and metallurgical building. The whole thing, in sum, was a seriously impressive event.

Continuing Los Alamos's transformation, many Central Los Alamos Manhattan Project facilities were razed during that period. A few remaining Manhattan Project facilities were later saved from the wrecking ball when declared National Historic Landmarks.

The town's first new single-family homes had been constructed in the Western Housing Area during 1946 and 1947. One mile west of the town center, the new development was composed of a mixture of 150 two-bedroom and three-bedroom housing units, including duplexes constructed by Morgan and Sons Contracting and single-family homes constructed by the Robert E. McKee Company.

Whether single-family or duplex, Western Housing Area units were one-bath floor plans and were equipped with such up-to-date conveniences as bathtubs and clothes-washer hookups on back porches; single-family units included more upscale details such as carports, living room carpeting, and fireplaces.

Likely in recognition of the urgency of the need to speed the availability of housing, Western Housing Area homes included eleven curiously unique "Lustron" houses.[68] Lustrons, a postwar anomaly composed of prefabricated porcelain-enameled steel walls and roofs on steel frames, had been mass-produced in Columbus, Ohio, each in thirty-three hundred or so components. Parts for each house were placed on a specially designed truck and delivered to the site for assembly.

Lustron Corporation made several models of these life-size Erector Sets available. Los Alamos's only Lustron model was a 713-square-foot two-bedroom, one-bath unit with a living room, pocket kitchen, and bath. And the Lustrons included one ultramodern feature—a living room picture window, not included in McKee homes.

Only 2,498 Lustron homes are reported to have been completed and installed in thirty-six states and Venezuela between 1948 and 1950. Today, with fewer than a confirmed two thousand remaining, the Lustron has been elevated into something of a collector's item. Two of the original sixty remaining Lustrons at the Marine Base Quantico in Virginia have been placed on the National Register of Historic Places.

At 7,300 feet, Los Alamos was subject to an all-seasons climate. Contrasting with the Central East Texas woods I had been accustomed to, Los Alamos's forests of pine trees and junipers were just as enjoyable to spend time in. During warmer months, climbing, hiking, and camping were the activities of choice; in winter, outdoor activities included ice skating on an outdoor rink in Los Alamos Canyon or sledding on a favorite hillside.

Whatever the activity, after school and weekend time was often spent with Jess Siglow, bumming around in Los Alamos Canyon or playing an intense game of Monopoly at his house. A Monopoly game could last for days after school.

And when an occasional night was spent at Jess's house, his oversized tomcat, Tippy, provided excellent entertainment of the sort appreciated mostly by small boys. One such event related to Tippy's genetic affinity for catnip, which made him the equivalent of a scary drunk. If he had been human, Tippy's reputation would have been as an openly hostile Saturday night brawler, best to avoid.

The discovery resulted in a game: the three of us, a dark room, a closed door, and a catnip mouse on the floor. Having acquired his full cataleptic dose and becoming a pharmaceutically-enhanced cat version of Dr. Jekyll's Mr. Hyde, Tippy enthusiastically began attempting to dislodge us from beneath the bed covers protectively pulled over our heads. His undisguised mission was likely vengeance for perceived prior indignities resulting from Jess's and my tricks imposed on him.

Jess's mother would eventually become aware of the commotion and come to our rescue, letting Tippy out for the evening to relieve his frustrations on any small mammal sufficiently unfortunate to land in a crazed tomcat's crosshairs.

Times in Los Alamos provided other spontaneous opportunities for the chronically inquisitive. One such event was a Saturday discovery of a tractor that had been in use that week doing work around the high school football field track. Now idle for the weekend, the tractor was available for other uses.

I had no experience with having driven tractors, and neither did Jess, but we didn't see that as necessarily being a problem. Investigation disclosed that starting a 1940s Ford tractor was as simple as pressing a button. The discovery was at first startling. When we recovered—no one had seen what happened—realization overcame initial fright; here was an opportunity too enticing to pass. We would drive it, each having a turn at the steering wheel. And it seemed there was no reason we couldn't be involved together: one steering, the other responsible for operating the throttle, an adjustable lever discovered to be conveniently located adjacent to the steering wheel.

A quick scissors-paper-rock negotiation settled the order of activity. I would take the first driver's seat turn; Jess, while standing on an adjacent step, would manage the throttle. Then, of course, we would exchange places.

I had no previous driving experience but understood that it was necessary to depress the clutch before engaging a gear. Having done that, I removed my foot—too suddenly, as it turned out. The tractor's startling forward lurch violently ejected Jess from his perch, and in the process of attempting to save himself, he yanked the throttle lever down into a near-full-on position.

With Jess now flat on his back, the tractor and I left the scene at the machine's best possible pace, my hands gripping the steering wheel as a petrified, nonfunctioning passenger. The sprint ended conclusively in a collision with a chain-link fence, ordinarily functioning to separate spectators from the field during athletic events but proving even more helpful at the moment.

My leap from that tractor left my feet hardly touching the ground before I caught up with Jess, who, having recovered, was already furiously on his way. The two of us flew out of there like it was a jailbreak. On Monday, when explanations to the real operator were required, the tractor was left to fend for itself.

For less spontaneous entertainment, Jess and I became avid Hardy Boys mystery books fans. To better enable our reading habit, we would each acquire a different new Hardy Boys book, read it, then trade with the other. It worked great; we always had a new book to read.

### The Manhattan Project's Secret Spies

While Los Alamos's bomb improvement development was progressing, two other disclosures added urgency to the United States' atomic weapon improvements pace.[69] Most vexing, on August 29, 1949, the Soviet Union detonated its own atomic bomb. Then insult was added when, on January 27, 1950, it was confirmed that the Russians had been notoriously stealing Manhattan Project secrets during World War II, and after.

The news about spies had come to the playground one day at recess; the excitement was that two German spies had been captured in the lab. What they had been doing and how they had been caught triggered a range of speculation.

It was years later that I learned that bit of elementary school playground gossip had some substance; there really had been spies. And one of those spies was German, but this spy hadn't been spying for the Germans or was only recently arrested. These spies were more subtle and were of the Soviet variety. And their clandestine thievery of atomic secrets wasn't even discovered until four years after the Manhattan Project had ended.

The late 1949 disclosure resulted from the United States Army's Signal Intelligence Service's decrypted cables revealing that Klaus Fuchs, a Tube Alloys contingent member, had been more than just a physicist;[70] he had also been an important Soviet spy. Like a Tom Clancy spy-novel character, Fuchs was apparently as seemingly unlikely to acquaintances to be a spy as could have been cast to play such a role. It was reported he was struck by most as "a very shy young man," fitting in well with key project scientists. In a few instances, he had served as a babysitter for some.

Fuchs's January 27, 1950, arrest led to a January 30 statement in which he admitted that in June 1945, shortly before the Trinity test, he had provided the Soviets a report fully describing the plutonium bomb, including a sketch of the bomb's components and important dimensions. Fuchs's subsequent testimony led to Harry Gold, a KGB agent codenamed "Raymond."

As it turned out, Gold had served as a courier for several Manhattan Project Soviet spies. One, David Greenglass, a machinist on a team making molds for Fat Man's high-explosive lenses, had, with his wife, Ruth, been a member of the Young Communist League prior to joining the Army in April 1943.

As a member of the Army's Special Engineer Detachment, Greenglass had been stationed at the Manhattan Project's Oak Ridge, Tennessee, facility before being transferred to Los Alamos in August 1944. In November 1944, Greenglass's brother-in-law, Julius Rosenberg, recruited him to spy for the Soviet Union, assigning him and his wife the codenames KALIBER and OSA. Responding to Julius Rosenberg's request, a sketch and detailed notes on the implosion-type bomb Greenglass sent to Rosenberg turned out badly for both Rosenbergs.[71]

Greenglass's arrest led to his February 1951 testimony disclosing his sister and brother-in-law's participation in passing information to the Soviet Union. The Rosenbergs' subsequent arrests and convictions resulted in their being sentenced to death and executed for their part in Soviet atomic bomb espionage.

The Rosenbergs' death penalty likely resulted from the relationship between the two countries having deteriorated to a state of extreme animosity by the time their and others' betrayals were discovered. Someone was going to pay; the Rosenbergs drew the unlucky straw.

The discovery that there had been Manhattan Project spy activity at all only came about as a result of a secret US Army counterintelligence program, codenamed VENONA.[72] VENONA had been initiated in February 1943 to examine coded Soviet diplomatic communications. But the effort was not successful until much later when the code was broken and Klaus Fuchs's role became known. But two others, discovered later, were equally destructive:

- **George Koval**, a Soviet citizen codenamed "Delmar," had enlisted in the United States Army and was also assigned to the Special Engineer Detachment. Given top-secret security clearance, Koval, while stationed at Oak Ridge, was made "Health Physics Officer," providing full access to all Oak Ridge facilities.[73]

  In June 1945, Koval was transferred to the top-secret Dayton, Ohio, Manhattan Project laboratory, where he did his most serious damage. Once again, as Health Physics Officer, Koval was provided free access to all Dayton facilities.

  From 1945 into early 1946, Koval met regularly with "Clyde," his Soviet contact, to pass along detailed information about the "Urchin," the implosion bomb's initiator; the initiator played a key role in the Mark 3's performance.

  Koval's activities had been so covert that his espionage was undiscovered until November 2007, when Russian Prime Minister Vladimir Putin posthumously awarded him the Hero of Russia medal, acknowledging Koval's contribution to the Soviet Union's development of the atomic bomb.

• **Ted Hall,** code-named "MLAD" after recently completing coursework at Harvard at age 19, had been invited by Oppenheimer to join what Oppenheimer called "this somewhat Buck Rogers project."[74] On October 15, 1944, Hall left Los Alamos for a two weeks annual leave, ostensibly to celebrate his nineteenth birthday with his parents in New York. He instead decided to inform the Soviets of the secret bomb project's existence. In cooperation with his Harvard roommate, Saville Sax, contact was made with Sergei Kurnakov, who became his Soviet contact.

Through Sax, Hall provided full information key to the plutonium bomb's invention. He continued to spy for the Soviets after the war was over, passing secrets about the hydrogen bomb. When the VENONA papers were declassified in 1995, Hall's role was made public.

How the Soviets were able to pull off such a notorious theft of top-secret information was reflective of an apparently diverted American security apparatus focused on the Germans, leaving the Soviets an open field to gather just about any kind of information they wanted.

The Special Engineer Detachment, formed to ensure that there were enough Manhattan Project high-grade technicians, had been an open entry for the Soviet spy apparatus.[75] Apparently, communist connections were unimportant to membership; at least George Koval and David Greenglass were members of that elite group.

Nearly a dozen Manhattan Project individuals were reported to have been identified as having served as Soviet spies. And most were Americans sympathetic to the communist cause and the Soviet Union.

While life in Los Alamos had its restrictions—more so for adults—there was a lot to do nearby.

When Dad wasn't working Saturdays, family activities were often spent somewhere outside the city—trout fishing along the Rio Grande between Santa Fe and Taos, picnicking in Bandelier Monument, or spending time in Santa Fe art galleries, San Ildefonso, or Santa Clara Pueblo. Lunch, on rare occasions, was at Santa Fe's newly opened Pink Adobe restaurant, where the poor boy sandwich was a menu item staple.

Mom and Dad had a considerable interest in Native American history, even having collected Native American artifacts on their honeymoon trip during the summer of 1933. The interest extended to contemporary Southwestern art, resulting in the tribes and their pueblos often being sources of weekend entertainment. The timing was near-perfect; contemporary Native American art as important collector pieces had its serious beginnings during the 1940s.

San Ildefonso Pueblo's Maria Martinez was already developing notoriety for her contemporary black pottery.[76] Another San Ildefonso potter, Crucita Calabaza, later became famous under her Native American name Blue Corn. But during the Manhattan Project, Crucita had been employed as the Oppenheimers' housekeeper. Tony Da, Maria's son, had also been employed as a Manhattan Project Laboratory technician before later taking his turn as a talented potter.

It was on one of those weekends in 1950 that a Hollywood film crew was making use of a dressed-up San Ildefonso Pueblo as a cinematic frontier fort. I had not previously seen a movie production, so when I heard from a grade school friend that a film was being made at San Ildefonso, I convinced my parents to take a Saturday trip to see what was happening.

We arrived at San Ildefonso during a break in the action that had everyone waiting around for the next scene to be filmed. Taking advantage of the break, I approached a group of three people engaged in conversation and dressed in appropriate frontier style. "Excuse me, sir, can you tell me where I can find Joseph Cotten?"

Mr. Cotten got quite a laugh from the people he was speaking with and everyone else within earshot when he volunteered, "That would be me," or some response to that effect. He then graciously turned to the two people he was speaking with and who I had interrupted to introduce Cornel Wilde and Linda Darnell. A wave of disbelief washed over me. *What?! These aren't people! They're MOVIE STARS!*

It doesn't take much from actual Hollywood film stars and the considerably lofty pedestals they occupy to mortify a star-struck ten-year-old. As it turned out, I was able to recover and, after a while, came to the reality that movie stars were actually rather like real people.

I had learned of the filming from Eric Peterson, a friend who had snagged a bit part in a film crowd scene, and had hoped to see him in action. While I was impressed by his participation, I was never able to actually pick Eric from the crowd scenes when I saw the movie. Maybe I'll try again sometime. But I never forgot the film's name, *Two Flags West*, or the stars' gracious manners.

Thirty-four years later, I would spend some time with Dale Robertson, who had been cast in a supporting role in *Two Flags West*, when we were discussing a television show featuring Dale, tentatively to be sponsored by a company I was briefly associated with in one of my 1970s career moves.

## Meanwhile, Bomb Improvement Was Progressing

The work Dad had come for and was now actively engaged in was being hotly pursued.

Operation Sandstone tests had verified a few bomb improvements over the original Mark 3 bomb: levitation had suspended a much lighter hollow pit a few inches from the tamper, replacing a solid 14-pound plutonium core, and a smaller initiator had replaced the Urchin initiator—a pellet composed of polonium-210 and beryllium.[77]

Sandstone test yield efficiency had further disclosed that whatever the fissile material, the shockwave would result in a hollow pit compressing into a solid sphere, requiring a smaller U-238 tamper and eliminating the need for the aluminum pusher.

Eliminating the need for the 4.5-inch thick, 264.6-pound aluminum pusher and reducing the 2.75-inch thick, 265-pound U-238 tamper was a good start. But the Mark 4 remained a five-ton soccer ball of mega-proportions. Bomb efficiency left several immediate components to be addressed:[78]

- **Explosives:** Explosives accounted for 4,000 pounds of bomb weight, and the 15-inch explosives depth accounted for 30 inches of the Mark 4 bomb's 48-inch diameter.

- **Inefficient in-flight insertion:** The Mark 4 pit required storage in a separate space within the plane and needed a dedicated weaponeer to manually insert the pit into the bomb at the time of arming.

- **Initiator efficiency:** The modified initiator tested in the Sandstone test's Zebra format resulted in the Mark 4 weapon incorporating a "B" initiator, using less polonium but still needing to address some significant drawbacks: polonium was extremely toxic, making it consequently dangerous; and polonium's half-life of 138 days required bombs to be disassembled and initiators to be replaced regularly.

- **Pit composition:** Sandstone tests had proven that hollow pit core composition options beyond purely U-235 or PU-235 could be effective and demonstrably reduce pre-detonation concerns. But more testing was required to further increase efficiency.

- **Bomb casings:** Mark 1 and Mark 3 bombs were armored, encased in 3/8-inch steel casings, to survive flack and machine-gun bullet impacts during delivery to the target. Weighing over two tons, casings accounted for half of the bomb's total weight.

Apart from the casing, extensive testing of alternatives was required. Manhattan Project participants had already recommended increasing the number of explosive lenses in the bomb's trigger and changing from a solid to a hollow core. Next, the best lens configuration had to be determined.

Post-war RaLa testing resumed with raucous results; thunderous shockwaves from impressively large explosions rattled our classroom most school days, becoming so routine that, other than when a test was even more robust than usual, no particular notice was given. It seems strange thinking back to how such formidable detonations nearby could result in little notice from a room full of otherwise curious grade-school kids.

Like during Manhattan Project times, RaLa tests were conducted on two test pads in Bayo Canyon, two miles north of town. Because a certain amount of nuclear fallout resulted from the activity, tests were restricted to times when the weatherman predicted that the wind direction was north. But a surprise shift in Mother Nature's wind direction plans occurred twice—once in 1949 and once again in 1950. Radioactive fallout over Canyon Road, one of Los Alamos's main roadways, resulted in the road's closure, with men in respirators and white suits engaged in cleanup for several days.[79]

As radiation exposure was concerned, those events were probably relatively minor. The more notorious radiation contamination resulted from the highly toxic radioactive wastes generated by Pajarito Site plutonium testing being dumped into Pueblo Canyon along with strontium-90, a by-product of separating lanthanum for Bayo Canyon's RaLa testing.[80]

The Pueblo Canyon location was expedient during Manhattan Project times, but the acid sewer's outlet was now inconveniently located just north of the town center and 1,500 feet from Central Elementary School. But that didn't necessarily result in a sensible conclusion. Dumping radioactive materials into Pueblo Canyon continued after the war, resulting in the contaminated area becoming known as "Acid Canyon." To mitigate the problem, the contaminated area was fenced, with warning signs stating "Danger—Contaminated—Do Not Enter," only after pressure from town residents.

What appeared as casual handling of nuclear waste materials likely resulted initially from jaded views of the possible effects of radiation among the scientists involved in testing programs. The Post-Manhattan Project era provided clarification: "playing around" with radioactive materials was dangerous to the extreme. Fatal accidents involving overexposure to radioactivity occurred in 1945 and again in 1946.

And Dad's work in the design and testing of a trigger compatible with the objective of reducing the bomb's size had its own extreme danger. Dad spoke of one incident a few years after we left Los Alamos. He had overheard my conversation with a friend regarding a newspaper article describing an individual's adrenaline-fueled superhuman act of lifting a car off someone pinned underneath.

Dad mentioned, in an offhanded manner, having had such an experience of real danger of his own, one which had inspired a similar impulsive act to save himself. He said, "Preparation for a RaLa test went wrong, resulting in the group of us who had been preparing the test to react, simultaneously clearing the site's security fence and tearing out for cover.

*It was a few minutes before things settled down. No one involved had any recollection of how they had cleared a barbed-wire-topped, nine-foot-in-height chain-link fence or how they had torn out of there so fast. And it all happened with no one seriously injured. But it was several days before any of us got over the experience.*

I never heard any more about the incident but assumed that a pre-detonation of the radioactive lanthanum, used in RaLa tests as a plutonium surrogate, was about to result in a miniature, inconveniently timed, premature atomic explosion.

One other Bayo Canyon incident is worth mentioning. Extending back to the post-graduation honeymoon, one of Dad's enthusiasms had been exploring Native American ruins and areas previously occupied by Native Americans. In the process, he recovered artifacts.

The Pajarito Plateau and canyons contained hundreds of pre-Columbian ruins encompassed by Bandelier National Monument, and many more were also located on Los Alamos

Laboratory property. Three major ruins—Tsirege, Cave Kiva, and Otowi—stood out. The Otowi ruins, composed of two large unexcavated pueblos, were located in lower Pueblo Canyon at a point where the canyon wall between Pueblo Canyon and Bayo Canyon was partially collapsed.[81] The area was inaccessible to the public but clearly was attractive to someone with legal access who found such a prospect impossible not to explore.

When downtimes in Bayo Canyon testing allowed, Dad's curiosity led him to look into a small cave he had noticed in the canyon wall. He was rewarded with a discovery of a partially buried fragment of conquistador chain mail armor. It was several years before governmental impositions relating to artifacts found on public lands prohibited collecting. But, at the moment, no such restriction existed.

For most, a find of such historic value would be extraordinary, but for Dad, the fragment was just another bit of history to add to his souvenir collection.

## Computers in Los Alamos

Anyone assuming the Manhattan Project to have had cutting-edge computation capabilities would be correct, although the high-speed systems we know today were still futuristic. The most advanced "computer" at the time applied simply to an individual using a Marchant or Friden desktop adding machine to complete the overwhelming number of calculations required for atomic fission's theoretical equations.[82]

Manhattan Project computers were principally scientists' wives spending long days at their adding machines. Wear and tear from the intense usage resulted in frequent equipment breakdowns, which were exacerbated by wartime shortages restricting replacements' availability. As a result, critical computational needs were disrupted with inconvenient frequency.

To solve the problem, two young physicists—Nicholas Metropolis and Richard Feynman—assumed the task of learning how to repair the non-functioning machines, in the process becoming indispensable.[83] Then, nearing the war's end, it was discovered that newly developed IBM punch card machines could perform needed computation tasks at a rate faster than even the highly-accomplished ladies could muster.

Manhattan Project's dependence on human computers ended, freeing Metropolis and Feynman to return to their Manhattan Project activities. The punch card machine was the beginning of another scientific revolution—a mechanical means of increasing the speed of calculating complex problems.

John von Neumann, the genius who had played such an integral role in calculating the viability of the implosion bomb, had, postwar, made his brainpower available to another scientific breakthrough—electronic computing. Von Neumann had returned to his position with Princeton's Institute for Advanced Study and had begun serving as a consultant to the University of Pennsylvania's Moore School of Electrical Engineering, where he was exposed to another breakthrough in technology—the EDVAC (Electronic Discrete Variable Automatic Computer) and ENIAC (Electronic Numerical Integrator and Computer). Both were advanced electronic computing projects being developed for the Army by Moore faculty members John Mauchly and J. Presper Eckert.

ENIAC, the first electronic general-purpose computer, had come online in February 1946 for calculating artillery firing tables.[84] Capable of handling a then-unheard-of fifty thousand instructions per second (an ordinary cellular telephone processor today can handle over five billion instructions per second), ENIAC was clunky: weighing more than sixty thousand pounds, covering eighteen hundred square feet of area, and costing $500,000 to build (about $6 million in today's dollars). But, for the time, the machine was impressive, and von Neumann was becoming as thoroughly engaged with computing technology as he had with enabling the plutonium implosion bomb.

His collaboration with Mauchly and Eckert resulted in von Neumann's *First Draft of a Report on the EDVAC*, in which he proposed the use of a "stored-program" concept. "Von Neumann architecture," storing the system's operating program in the same memory address as the data, remains in use today.

In 1948, Nicholas Metropolis returned to Los Alamos from the University of Chicago to lead a team in constructing a still more advanced computer, the "Mathematical Analyzer, Numerical Integrator, and Computer" (MANIAC). Introduced in 1951, MANIAC made advanced use of von Neumann architecture and von Neumann himself. Physically, MANIAC was substantially more efficient, reduced in size to six feet high, eight feet wide, and one thousand pounds.

Von Neumann's considerable Manhattan Project value had been in his ability to complete calculations confirming the plutonium bomb's implosion viability. That work, in part, re-sulted from consulting with Edward Teller's verification con-cerning increased plutonium density's effect on detonation efficiency.

Working once again with Teller and fellow mathemati-cian Stanislaw Ulam, von Neumann wrote programs for MA-NIAC in which he and Ulam developed simulations for working out the steps necessary to understand atomic particle behavior in thermal nuclear reactions, verifying the Teller-Ulam design's feasibility.[85]

It's worth noting the peculiarity of the anonymity that seems to have followed John von Neumann. Books written on von Neumann since, attempting to disclose what was behind von Neumann's brilliance, provide superlatives not matched by any known scientists other than Albert Einstein, his peer at the Princeton Institute for Advanced Study. Von Neumann was the premier mathematician of his time and has been acknowledged to be among the most brilliant mathematicians of all time.

Dad had been exposed to MANIAC and the new scien-tific field of high-powered electronic computing. The experience triggered an infatuation, leading to him one day becoming an internationally acknowledged computer applications expert and chief of NASA's Computation and Analysis Division at Johnson Space Center in Houston.

But for the 1948 to 1952 period, Dad remained engaged in developing a more usable atomic bomb, first through Los Ala-mos's RaLa testing, then as the new Mark 5 plutonium bomb's chief test engineer at Nevada's Yucca Flats.

Along with being engaged in the US's next-generation nuclear bomb, Dad found time to draw and paint, in the process becoming an accomplished artist.

Dad's natural artistic talent had led him to be drawn to spending time with local artists. Most notable, Georgia O'Keeffe, well known in Eastern art circles, had recently taken up residence north of Santa Fe at a Ghost Ranch home in the village of Abiquiu. And Dad was *on it*. It was Dad's considerable luck in timing that Ms. O'Keeffe was willing to teach her passion for illustrating intricate flowers and New Mexico landscapes.

That Dad was an attentive student was reflected in a series of pueblo and New Mexico countryside oil paintings and watercolors we inherited, along with a pencil drawing he did of an O'Keeffe-style flower. Prior to the O'Keeffe period, I had been aware of Dad's interests in just about every artistic media.

In College Station, he had constructed the pottery studio, complete with pottery wheel and kiln, behind our house and had created several other artistic works in a spectrum of media— pen and ink, pencil, and wood and copper engravings. He never seemed to run out of inspirational ideas to consider, then act on.

Brilliant engineering minds were expected to have well-developed analytical qualities. But coupling such skills with exceptional creative characteristics expected of types dedicated to the arts was not frequently seen; Dad was gifted in both. He possessed a curiosity that led him to know a lot about a lot of things, making him a perfect representation of a polymath.

Adding mystery to his generously endowed brainpower was a unique physical ambidexterity. He could bowl right-handed or left-handed and could also play golf with either one. There are undoubtedly others just as unusual in that sense, but they are sufficiently rare that I haven't been aware of having met anyone else with that ability.

His boyhood spent among the shadowed peculiarities of East Texas's Big Thicket had included hunting and fishing as both recreation and a way of supplementing food for the family dining table. And he remained an avid outdoorsman. As a fisherman, he would catch his limit for the day, then relax while others with him were hoping for a bite. He took up fly-fishing while we were living in Los Alamos, extending what became fly-fishing expertise to tying his own flies.

He was a frequent hunter of wild game—deer, elk, and antelope. Once, he brought home a bear roast, the product of a hunt with a friend. Presumably, the friend took the rest of the bear. We had the roast for a few meals, but I never did develop a hankering for haunches of bear. Venison chili was shared frequently with Mom's sister Kathleen's family, the McWilliams. My uncle, Bill McWilliams, Los Alamos High School's football coach, an avid outdoorsman, and a former Texas farm boy, kept the McWilliams' freezer well stocked with wild game as well.

Dad took me along on fishing trips to what were often difficult-to-reach, always out-of-the-way locations. One such place was New Mexico's Rio Grande Box Canyon. A steep path along the canyon wall led down to the river and accessed some deep fishing holes, requiring considerably more fishing expertise than I had. Dad was game to go where the fishing was more likely to be good, and I was grateful to be able to tag along. My recollection was that the trip up the path to return to our car seemed considerably steeper than it had been going down.

The New Mexico summer sun almost always shined. In combination with Los Alamos's clear mountain air, summer days were nearly always pleasant. But when the sun went down, summer nights were cool, at times bone-chilling. In the highest elevations, the possibility of a hailstorm pelting the daylights out of everything in sight with near golf ball-sized ice balls was not unusual.

We discovered that while on another trip to a hard-to-get-to kind of place for the possibility of good fishing. This time, the trip required horses. Dad and I and another father and son packed in to Lake Katherine, a deep volcanic lake at a 12,622-foot elevation in the Pecos Wilderness outside Santa Fe. Trailhead signage had warned of "sometimes dangerous weather."

When we reached Lake Katherine, several vantage points around the volcano's rim provided excellent views into the lake's crystal clear waters. An array of trout could be seen swimming tantalizingly below, none of which had been willing to give a carefully selected assortment of bait the slightest notice. The day at the fishing hole had begun badly.

Then, without warning, the trailhead sign's meaning was clarified. A parade of seriously ominous dark clouds, like the ones seen in scary movies, rolled in like the devil's caravan. As if on cue, the parade was followed by a howling windstorm, rain, and a Fourth of July lightning show. And the hail that accompanied the event was more of what the trailhead sign had promised. Our group dived for cover under a tarp set up earlier as a lean-to in anticipation of such a surprise.

While foolishly leaning my head up against the tarp, I caught a hailstone's direct hit, leading me to black out for a few moments. When the storm ended, the quest to have another go at bringing home dinner resumed. And, this time, like a bad comedian's telling of a joke, sometimes it's only a matter of timing. The unsatisfactory fishing had turned into a trout feeding frenzy; we had fish for dinner.

The next morning while saddling up for the return trip down the mountain, Rusty, Dad's mega-sized sorrel quarter horse, took advantage of an early morning opportunity to stand on my toes, which I had carelessly placed adjacent to a front hoof while adjusting his halter. A horse standing on one's foot is never acceptable, but the event's importance is exaggerated when one's toes are cold, one's shoes are Keds canvas high-tops, and the horse is a very big horse.

At such moments, the need to remove a half ton of horse from one's toes overshadows any other distractions. Horses can wake up grumpy; for them, finding a misplaced foot is made more pleasurable on chilly mornings. The event was a good reminder of the need to pay attention to what one is doing anytime one is around a horse.

## A Different Perspective

I owe quite a debt to a few, what seemed at the moment, inconsequential experiences.

The bicycle I took to Los Alamos from College Station was well-worn and was an undisguised girl's bike in spite of Dad's creative solution—a crossbar welded on where a boy's bike bar was expected to be.

The bar still had the appearance of having served as a former steam pipe before being salvaged from a junkyard. It was apparent that, until something more positive could be arranged, whatever was to be done to improve circumstances was up to me. Three years was long enough.

First thing—paint! Two small touch-up-size bottles of maroon 1947 Mercury automobile paint acquired at the Santa Fe Western Auto store covered the offending bar, then the rest of the bike. When complete, the effect was that I was still riding a no-less-unattractive girl's bike.

The bicycle had been an understandable nod to Dad's thrift. Our Scotch lineage may have had some influence, but likely it came just as much from a mindset acquired by those who had spent time in the poverty of early 1900s East Texas farm country then survived the Great Depression's devastation. For that, Dad had endured a stint of homelessness during his college days and had a well-earned right to be financially sensible.

My first ice skates, a pair of somebody's cast-off, too-small women's skates, confirmed by their all-white appearance, were just as sensibly acquired. Even so, the notice I attracted with those skates wasn't enough to keep me away from the outdoor rink in Los Alamos Canyon. Fortunately, by the next season, I had outgrown the already too-small-for-my-feet skates by a couple of sizes. The skates from Santa were black and in the right size.

The bedroom Dad converted for me from our College Station garage included a built-in bed, requiring the bed to remain when we left College Station. When we arrived in Los Alamos, my sleeping arrangements temporarily became an air mattress and sleeping bag on the floor.

Then, in an "aha!" moment of inspiration, Dad discovered that an abundance of war surplus furniture from Manhattan Project times was available. Military barracks standard-issue sleeping-room furnishings had included a metal cot with a two-inch felt mattress, thirty-six-inch wide four-drawer chest, and twenty-four-inch by thirty-inch footlocker, and all was now available for the taking. I moved off the floor and into a bedroom furnished like the big boys had once used.

Thrift's effect also carried a motivational lesson: I wanted to be able to get my own stuff—a new bicycle, neat Boy Scout and Army and Navy surplus equipment, comic books as they came out on the first of each month, and more—all I needed was a job.

I hadn't heard an explanation describing when the entrepreneurial bug bites, but my personal curtain opened when a schoolmate made me aware I could make $0.90 a day ($9.40 today) after school peddling *Santa Fe New Mexican* newspapers in Los Alamos's town center. I was quick to bite. Most days, as soon as school was out, I trotted down Canyon Road to the *Santa Fe New Mexican* newspaper's office in the town center for my paper allocation. Now I could put my fifth-grade bookstore-selling experience to work on something of substance—yesterday's news.

A first stop at the Bank of Santa Fe solicited captive teller-line customers. But the most productive location was a Trinity Drive stop sign in front of the Turquoise Post, a PX during wartime that had become a gift shop and now occupied one of the school's original buildings across from Fuller Lodge. The location conveniently allowed approaching stopped vehicles on Trinity Drive to corner drivers regarding my wares. A loudly proclaimed "*Santa Fe New Mexican!*" would attract two or three more sales before I completed selling out my papers most afternoons.

After a few months, Mr. Jernigan, Los Alamos's *Santa Fe New Mexican* circulation manager, agreed to trust me with a Western Housing Area paper route of 115 homes, our house included. I was thrilled but naive. The thirty-two dollars per month I was to earn was a serious motivator. I was able to make a six-dollar monthly payment on a new Montgomery Ward bicycle and still have plenty left to indulge in a lot of neat stuff I didn't need but wanted—Army surplus canteens, Boy Scout gear, an Army knapsack, ammunition boxes, sailor hats, some boots I particularly liked, and more.

One of my enthusiasms was getting Dell Comics when new issues hit the stands at the beginning of the month. I would run over to Dragon Drugs to make sure I didn't miss out on any of my favorites. Before we left College Station for Los Alamos, my source of comics was Black's Pharmacy, where, due to Mr. Black's studious oversight, he made it impossible to look at the comics without him suddenly materializing to invite us to, in effect, buy or leave.

My newfound solvency made it possible to do as I pleased as one of Dragon's paying customers. In addition to the relatively harmless Dell Comics, there were also scary comic books, such as *Tales from the Crypt*, and some more educational comics featuring literary classics. I never found *Archie, Jughead, Little Lulu,* or *Casper the Friendly Ghost* to have any attention-getting value.

The money from the paper route provided exactly what I had been looking for. But I soon discovered I had taken on an obligation as a seven-day-a-week serf. Worse, when I calculated what I was making, my daily take was little more than I had made selling papers on the corner opposite the Turquoise Post. Now I was making a couple of cents over a dollar a day in comparison with the ninety cents I had made selling the papers. And now there was no time off.

Job demands required twice-monthly subscriber collections; most of every other Saturday was devoted to the activity. And when I wasn't collecting, I was delivering papers Monday through Saturday afternoons. On Sundays around 4:00 a.m., two newspaper bundles—one for the front section and the other for the Sunday section—were delivered to our driveway. I would "stuff" the two sections together before heading out to make certain that subscribers received their Sunday comics by 7:00 a.m.

Getting up at such an hour was well below my threshold of like, but once out of bed, Sunday deliveries were not overly challenging during warm months. Winter weather made Sunday deliveries more interesting. Snow and ice, frequently enhanced by a jaw-rattling northern wind, often required hauling papers on a sled and returning home several times before completing the deliveries.

## A Memorable Experience

Before I had taken on the responsibilities of a paper route, I had been a Boy Scout. Thanks to a few dedicated adults, the focus on Boy Scouts established during preparatory school times continued in earnest after the school was taken over. My third and part of fourth grades were spent in Cub Scouts before becoming eligible to move up to Boy Scouts.

Troop 22, Los Alamos Ranch School's Scout troop since the school's 1917 founding, easily had the most illustrious alumni roster of any Scout troop in history. Every matriculated Los Alamos Ranch School student had been required to participate.

Now I was part of Troop 22, teamed up with Jess and several classmates, participating in hikes and campouts, including a week at Philmont Scout Ranch, the Boy Scouts of America's largest National High Adventure Base. Troop 22 had excellent leaders who motivated Scouts to participate in Scouting events and progress through the ranks quickly. I was enthusiastic about all of it, earning my Tenderfoot, Second Class, and First Class ranks in just over one year. The following year, I achieved the rank of Star and completed most of the Life rank requirements.

Two outlying campsites—Camps Hamilton and May—had been used by the Army for training and later became available for Troop 22's use for weekend camporees.

During a particularly memorable campout, one of our troop members discovered that Army troops had bivouacked in the area during Manhattan Project times, as unopened C-rations were found buried in several locations. Like a pack of wild dogs, the C-rations were quickly dug up, opened, and sampled. This was around 1949, probably six years after they had been so carefully stowed. They were not blatantly stale, but they were tasteless, a quality that didn't seem to bother anyone. We ate them anyway, just because of what they were.

I found the time spent in Boy Scouts to be valuable. But one experience was the most memorable:

Boy Scout troops are composed of patrols, each led by an elected patrol leader. Midway through my second year as a Troop 22 member, our patrol leader moved, necessitating an election that would be supervised with the results confirmed by an adult. Mrs. Siglow, Jess's mother, volunteered to supervise the election.

The secret ballot was counted and certified by Mrs. Siglow; I was elected Kiowa Patrol's leader. Only, the outcome was to the immense dissatisfaction of Richard, a patrol member who, being a year older, had apparently assumed the patrol leader position was to be his. But he had come up short in the voting.

I was unaware of Richard's displeasure with the election's outcome, so it was a surprise when Richard showed up at the next troop meeting with his hatchet-faced father in tow. After a few minutes' delay in starting the meeting, our Scoutmaster informed me that Richard's father had stated concerns over our patrol leader election.

Richard had alleged—tearfully, I assumed—that I had paid patrol members for votes on my behalf, costing him the election. Now his father was demanding that a new election be held then and there "to confirm election results." This time, the election was to be done by a show of hands.

Under Richard's father's buzzard-like, watchful eye and firmly set jaw, what was expected was clear—he wanted what Richard wanted. And his expectations were met; Richard was elected patrol leader. I was stunned. But we were a group of eleven- and twelve-year-old kids, and intimidation had done its work. Rosemary's baby had won.

My protests to our Scoutmasters regarding Richard's claim being fabricated had no effect; the result was final. Richard and his father provided my first experience with an adult playing such destructive win-at-all-cost chicanery of the sort parents have been accused of using to bribe their kids' way into elite universities today.

When Mrs. Siglow learned of what had happened, she hit the roof. And the roof she hit landed squarely on Troop 22's Scout leaders. I appreciated Mrs. Siglow's support and was told our Scoutmaster made a public statement of apology to the troop at the next meeting for the way events had been handled. But I found the experience to be too much; I wanted nothing more to do with Troop 22. I moved on to the recently formed Troop

450, where I remained until we left Los Alamos to return to College Station.

Richard and his father provided a useful, if painful at the time, object lesson. It's probable that the experience had more value to me than for Richard; I wonder how many other times his father stepped in for him when things didn't go his way. I don't think my dad ever knew what had happened.

## My Next Dog

We had not had a dog since Boots, my black-and-white female pup who died on the Hempstead Highway in College Station. While in the Fortieth Street duplex, we had acquired a dog of really interesting genealogy. Freckles was a curious mix of cocker spaniel and chow. As a puppy, he was cuddly and cute; as an adult, he was disarming.

As Freckles matured, he took on the appearance of a taller-than-usual cocker spaniel who had spent regular two-a-days at the gym and taken daily shots of testosterone. The dog had a seriously developed set of shoulders that tapered to athletic hindquarters and an attitude consistent with a gym rat on steroids. Not a dog one wanted to meet in a dark alley.

Freckles spent most of his time in our fenced backyard— never in the house, regardless of the weather. And, at 7,300 feet, winter nights spent outside could make even a golden retriever develop an attitude. But Freckles was my buddy, and we often found something to do together—a boy-and-his-dog sort of thing.

Once, when Freckles was following Jess and me in exploring the construction site of Los Alamos's three-story, forty-seven-bed acute-care medical facility, which was to replace the former Army infirmary adjacent to Ashley Pond, his naturally adrenaline-filled personality got the best of him.

We had reached the building's roof when Freckles, in a fit of enthusiasm, took a jubilant leap from a low wall protecting the roof's edge and sailed off into a startling three stories of air. Fearing the worst, Jess and I raced to the bottom floor to find Freckles limping but otherwise functioning surprisingly well. It turned out Freckles had incurred a bruised leg when he bounced off a second-level workmen's scaffold on his way down.

The dog was tough.

## The Mark 5 Bomb

Los Alamos had been an excellent experience, but more particularly for Dad. Our move to Los Alamos was for Dad to participate in the kind of project of which most scientific types can only dream. He was an essential part of a team whose mandate was to improve the bomb that had caused such a stir in facilitating the end of World War II.

Now, four years of design, redesign, and testing later, the smaller, lighter bomb the Air Force requested was a reality and had been given a name—the Mark 5.[86] The Mark 5 atomic bomb had been reduced in diameter from the Mark 4's 60 inches to 43.75 inches, and a 10,000-pound Mark 4 weight had been reduced to a range of 3,025 to 3,175 pounds. A trade-off was that bomb length had extended from 90 inches to 129–132 inches, but the Air Force had the bomb they had requested. The Mark 5 was suitable for delivery by a range of aircraft and had lost nothing in its lethal capacity to invoke massive damage when required.

To arrive at such a dramatic modification, the Mark 5 included several sweeping changes:[87]

- **Trigger design:** The Manhattan Project scientists had recommended a reconfiguration of the 125-pound explosive lenses, thirty-two of which originally composed the bomb's trigger. Dad's objective was to reduce lens weight and thickness without compromising the pit compression required to maintain yield efficiency.

  Through several generations of testing, the number of explosive lenses increased from the original thirty-two to sixty, then, finally, to ninety-two. A resulting thinner explosives layer provided an improved shockwave and a bomb that produced about the same yield in a smaller size.

- **Explosives:** More efficient next-generation high explosives, capable of generating greater compression with less weight and bulk, made use of Composition H6, rated 1.35 times more powerful than pure TNT.

  The explosives layer could now be reduced to only one to two inches thick and weigh closer to tens of pounds rather than tons. Reduction in the amount of explosives needed allowed bomb diameter to be further reduced. An added advantage was that "insensitive high explosives" (IHE) were less likely to detonate accidentally, making for safer bombs in the event of an aircraft crash.

- **Initiator construction:** Further initiator improvement was proposed in 1948 and placed into production in January 1950. The revised design provided two more advantages: a further reduction in the amount of polonium required allowed the initiator's outer diameter to reduce to two-fifths of one inch, and the period between initiator replacements increased from 120 days to one year.

  Still later, polonium/beryllium initiators were superseded by "pulsed neutron emitters," eliminating polonium entirely. Without the need for the inclusion of radioactive materials, decomposition requiring frequent replacement was eliminated. The "non-polonium" initiators were more controllable, and weapon reliability was further improved.

- **Pit composition:** Sandstone tests had determined that pit options beyond purely U-235 or PU-239 could prove effective.

  Composite cores containing highly enriched U-235 and plutonium-239 (in the late 1940s) had already eliminated the prospect of pre-detonation in which the pit blew itself apart before the fissile material had become more fully involved. Now a relatively small amount of

PU-239 combined with a mostly U-235 core were typical pit components.

The change had been enabled by a more efficient post-war process for separating U-235 from U-238 having become available. With several Mark 5 pit variants now available, a reported yield range extended from six kilotons to 120 kilotons.

- **Automated in-flight insertion:** The weaponeer, a second individual required to be on board a delivery aircraft to arm the bomb, was no longer needed. Now the aircraft pilot controlled arming the bomb from the cockpit; an automated mechanism inserted the pit into the explosives layer from an outside storage position.

- **Casing weight:** Postwar casing designs dispensed with the three-eighths-inch armored steel casing in the previous Mark bombs, opting for lightweight aluminum or steel casings optimized for aerodynamic efficiency. Casing weight was reduced from 5,300 pounds to under 1,500 pounds.

Mark 5 manufacture extended from July 1951 to early 1955. In addition to bombs to be dropped from aircraft, the Mark 5 was also configured for missile warheads as W5 bombs.

### Yucca Flats - Area 7

Dad's lab status qualified him for a housing upgrade. We moved from the duplex to a single-family home at 1336 Forty-First Street, the next street over. A few upgrades included a fireplace, living room carpet, and a carport. And the new home's backyard remained conveniently adjacent to Mesa Elementary School, still allowing me to hear the school bell ring and stroll over to class, arriving mostly on time.

But, while the Forty-First Street home was an attractive housing improvement, the upgrade also came at a price. Beginning in late 1950, Dad had completed his part on Mark 5 designing and testing bomb trigger formats to arrive at the optimal number of ninety-two lenses.

But now, he had a new job and had begun spending lengthy periods in Nevada; the effect placed stress on all of us, most particularly Mom.

Dad's Mark 5 bomb development experience had led to a position with the Atomic Energy Commission's "Atmospheric Atomic Testing" program conducted at Area 7 of Nevada's Yucca Flats, an isolated stretch of sand sixty-five miles northeast of Las Vegas.[81] On January 27, 1951, the first Mark 5 atomic bomb test was detonated at Yucca Flats from a five-hundred-foot tower.

It was sometime during that period that Dad made a trip to Washington, DC, to discuss bomb test results. A locked briefcase containing supporting documents was handcuffed to his wrist. Mom undoubtedly knew something of what Dad had been up to, but his absences had been a mystery to Barbara and me.

Then, in late 1951, Mom, Barbara, and I were invited to join him on one of his Las Vegas trips. Las Vegas was in its infancy as a serious adult entertainment venue, but the Flamingo and New Frontier hotels and casinos served up glitz every bit as stimulating to me as if they had been Disneyland. On that trip, Barbara and I were informed that the next morning, we were to see an atomic bomb detonation that Dad was conducting.

It was early morning; Mom, Barbara, and I parked beside a lonesome stretch of desert road. We were waiting for an event somewhere "that way." Then, with no warning, it happened. An atomic bomb detonation has been described similarly by close observers: "after a few seconds the rising flames lost their brightness, reverting to an impressive column of smoke with an expanded head like a gigantic mushroom that rose rapidly to a height of several thousand feet."

From our distance and lack of warning for the moment of detonation, our experience was less dramatic but still impressive—a distant thunderous roar was accompanied by a mushroom cloud rising the several thousand feet others had observed.

So that was it. Dad had been Yucca Flats' chief test engineer for the past year but now accepted Texas A&M's offer to return to academic life. A&M's offer to Dad's return to the faculty as a full professor of engineering was timely. He could have remained in his position with the Atomic Energy Commission as the chief test engineer on atomic bomb testing at Yucca Flats.

But there had been good reason for Dad to end the commute between Los Alamos and Yucca Flats.

Weeks-at-a-time periods in Nevada away from the family had resulted in considerable stress. Dad had found his time working on the bomb's reconfiguration and testing the new format immensely satisfying. But he had to decide which was more important—job or family.

Selfishly, the decision provided me with a guilt-free opportunity to resign from the newspaper delivery business for reasons other than laziness. I had enjoyed the financial freedom the newspaper route had provided, and newspaper delivery was acknowledged to have been an excellent character-builder, but I'd had enough of character building; I could find another way to acquire things.

## In Retrospect

Los Alamos provided some of my more memorable experiences. Los Alamos's culture and setting were unique—a moment in time.

In January 1952, I gave no thought to Los Alamos having been particularly unique, even though conditions had some significant inconsistencies with how people lived in other places. Any town resident from age seven had been cataloged for security, given a pass, and required to show the pass before being allowed to reenter the city when returning. It was always an event to stop at the guard gate to show our pass, a small gesture making life seem a little more important than was justified.

Before we arrived at Los Alamos, the Atomic Energy Commission (AEC) had assumed responsibility for security from the Army on January 1, 1947. Security guards were reported to number over eight hundred, but, after a short while, their presence was just another aspect of the community's fabric—no different than the intrusiveness of the powerful detonations heard on most days.

Life in Los Alamos was close to a fictional utopia for kid-oriented activities: plenty of places to hike, Boy Scout campouts, ice-skating, sledding, no abject poverty, no unemployment, people doing work they found interesting, no social hierarchy among kids, and no "bad" part of town. It wasn't apparent that the circumstances were not normal; most people didn't live behind locked gates in a socialized environment.

Crime was limited most probably to shoplifting by such hardened-criminal types as Billy, a Fortieth Street neighbor and grade-school schoolmate. One day, in suitably conspiratorial tones, Billy described how conveniently candy bars could be liberated from the IGA market where our mothers shopped. His story was convincing; it was easy.

Tagging along with Billy for a first-time "how-to" demonstration, the alert store manager, possibly previously onto Billy, suddenly materialized behind us as we stood, admiring the attractively tempting display. His helpful query of "is there anything I can do for you boys?" was given the weak response that we were "just looking." And, given our being there had no productive reason, we were invited to leave, apparently busted by an onto-the-caper store manager. The encounter was all the lesson

I needed. My life of crime was over. I didn't care that much for candy anyway.

We returned to College Station in early February 1952.

## CHAPTER FIVE

# Return to College Station

I was glad to be back in Texas. In hindsight, I'm not entirely certain Dad shared that enthusiasm:

*When, in 1948, I received a one-year leave of absence to work for the Los Alamos Research Laboratory, my work had begun in the role as a planning engineer. The position led through a series of promotions within the Los Alamos National Lab until I had the good fortune to become chief test engineer on the Yucca Flats Nevada Atomic Bomb Test Site with the Atomic Energy Commission.*

*The University of California had been persistent regarding the need for me to remain in my position, and, on a year-to-year basis, convinced Texas A&M administration to let me remain there until 1951, when they balked at further leave. So back to Texas A&M and a new home.*

To Dad's extreme credit, he returned to teaching without any openly stated regret. But teaching was clearly incapable of providing the same personal satisfaction attached to the excitement he had felt in his role in developing the Mark 5 atomic bomb and its subsequent testing. This was what he had to say in hindsight when he was drafting a version of his own memoirs many years later:

> *We bought a new home, and I went back to work as a full professor of engineering—a very good assignment. I was also doing a lot of consulting work on the side in the engineering field. We were happy.*

But Dad never adjusted to teaching again; he needed more. When we left College Station for Los Alamos, it was home with all of a home's familiarities. Our move to Los Alamos had required adjustment to a lot of strangeness, but once we had settled in, Los Alamos had assumed as much of the "old-shoe" comfort I had known when we left College Station. Now, there we were, home again.

The four years we had been away were equivalent to one-third of my life. Things hadn't changed much in College Station; it was still a time when no one felt the need to lock their house or to even know where the house key was located. Lock our car? Why?

The new home we moved into, in a wooded area, was quite an improvement over the little house on unpaved Foster Street and the government-owned housing we left behind in Los Alamos. Those were basic houses intended to provide basic shelter. They were nothing fancy. For that matter, neither was the new house, but it was a nice change. And, as College Station's environment presented itself, the town remained as unpretentious as it had been when we left.

Most College Station homes ranged from notably basic to only slightly better. And Chevrolets and Fords were the primary vehicles. But three households sported transportation that stood out from the rest—Doctor Andre's (the town doctor's) wife drove a "four-holer" Buick Roadmaster, and Cecil Culpepper (the local real estate and insurance entrepreneur) and Doctor Redmond (a medical doctor who practiced in Bryan) drove the town's only Cadillacs.

Together, the Andres, Culpeppers, and Redmonds comprised College Station's upper crust. Socially, they didn't have much of a high profile. That was except for Mrs. Andre. Her notoriety was unintentional, but we could hear her from anywhere in town as her straight-eight engine supported by a Dynaflow transmission struggled to haul her land barge of an automobile around. The three families also, as befitted society's elite, occupied the town's most important appearing houses. The Andre residence added a defining touch by sporting the town's (and, to my knowledge, the county's) only private swimming pool.

Our neighborhood included several large oak trees, one of which was immediately adjacent to my bedroom window. The front of our house was level with the street, but the lot sloped down to a wash, providing an open space finished in sand underneath the house. It was an excellent place to use the road grader I had received at Christmas.

Fortunately, some continuities that only seemed right remained: Black's Pharmacy was still the same, the town's only beer joint was still apparently well attended, the Blue Top

Courts were still standing, and the Magnolia service station still had a cooler where one could get a Pepsi, RC Cola, or a full range of Nehi beverages for a dime. All still fronted on the Hempstead Highway that led in one way to Houston and the other way to Dallas.

Luke's Grocery Store had sold. Manning Smith, the new owner, soon found after we returned that trying to make a success of a mom-and-pop grocery store in competition with Safeway in Bryan was a losing proposition. Mr. Smith changed to insurance sales and found success. May's Grocery, with its more specialized smoked meats and convenience-store size, managed to continue as a worthy Safeway alternative for a few more years.

Physically, College Station was little different from the town we had left four years before. A&M Consolidated was still three schools in one—grade school, junior high school, and high school—all on the same grounds. And all made use of the same cafeteria. School lunches before we left for Los Alamos were mostly sandwiches from home, carried in a lunch pail.

With the jump from second grade to sixth grade, I began having lunch in the cafeteria. A daily meal ticket was twenty-five cents for an entirely basic, sometimes inspired, lunch. One more memorable example was a scoop of mashed potatoes on a piece of fried bologna with a few sprinklings of cheese on top. That offering was not indicative of all our lunch selections, but even the best seldom raised a request for seconds.

With a little more lunch money, forty cents at Holick's across the street from the school would buy a hamburger and a Moon Pie. Most of the time, I settled for the cafeteria.

My second-grade schoolmates when I left for Los Alamos were seven- and eight-year-olds. Four years later had made quite a difference. Playground pals I had known were still friends, but the mix of kids had evolved in physical development. Beginning in kindergarten and extending into first and second grades, kids had been similar in size. Some had temperaments that made them tougher than others, but by sixth grade, hard physical work had added real toughness to the farm kids. Regardless of temperament, the farm-raised kids were generally just too tough to mess with.

In hindsight, an even more apparent observation was that many of those kids had probably bypassed a few of Maslow's steps and reached their full potential early. For some, there may have been an insidious factor: what seemed to have been exhibited by a few rural kids was the probable legacy of first cousins marrying first cousins.

A frequent giveaway was arresting physical features in the form of facial deformities. More importantly, the kids showed limited mental capacity in the ability to apply themselves to schoolwork. Possibly for some, their problem may have resulted from a home environment that didn't support finishing school. But for whatever reason, by the end of the eighth grade, most were gone.

Setting aside physical deformities, compromised mental capacity likely wouldn't be noticed in most low-performing schools today; kids with substantial learning disabilities in many schools are more likely to be simply passed on from one grade to the next until they drop out of school or are given a high school diploma. In many school circumstances, the reputation of a diploma is that it represents having done little more than show up for the required number of days in spite of having gained nothing in the way of knowledge for the time spent. But in Texas at that time, it was different.

Texas law at the time required kids to attend school through the eighth grade or until age sixteen, whichever came first. And that explained why some of our sixth graders were fifteen, just waiting for their next birthday when they could quit and disappear like most of those did who only stayed through the eighth grade.

My return to A&M Consolidated was a shock. When I began junior high classes midyear, I discovered my Los Alamos learning curriculum wasn't up to the same standard as College Station's. I was so far behind in English that, by the time sixth grade ended, I had flunked English, making me ineligible to be passed on to seventh grade. Fortunately, a conference between my junior high school principal, Mr. Riedle, and my mother solved the problem. I was able to move on to seventh grade with the assumption that I would catch up on my deficiency.

My collective Texas and New Mexico childhood academic experience was spent as a notably ordinary kid who ranged in status, at times being a reasonably good student, at others more average. Dad's extraordinary work ethic, as it related to studying, did not pass down to me until college when I was forced to bear down on the books. Until then, what I had preferred was spending time with friends after school and on weekends, doing whatever came to mind.

In returning to College Station, I reconnected with Me-Mama, Pa, and my cousins. David and John Brock had moved to College Station while we were in Los Alamos and were living next door to MeMama and Pa on Jane Street. My Houston cousins, Buddy and Penny Roberts, visited College Station often, and my cousins from Lubbock, Bill and Marsha Brock, came to town occasionally.

Whenever we got together, it was always about family time. Sometimes we would lie on our backs in the grass, looking for clouds shaped like animals or admiring a buttermilk sky. But mostly, we enjoyed just hanging out together.

Once, Buddy and I, making use of MeMama and Pa's living room rocking chairs, actively engaged in contesting who could rock the fastest and furthest. In his enthusiasm, Buddy neglected to pay attention to MeMama's cat's tail's location while amidst one of his more energetic backward rocks. The kitty's jungle-like scream as the carelessly placed tail received the full benefit of Buddy's enthusiasm sent a surprised Buddy over backward in the chair while the cat, now rocket-propelled, streaked for the back door.

In spite of the kitty's badly bruised tail, all seemed to have been forgiven. Buddy and the kitty seemed to have developed a mutual affinity. A few months later, Buddy and I sat in the same rocking chairs, this time with the kitty stretched out contentedly on Buddy's bare thigh. It was summer, we were both wearing shorts, and Buddy's legs had received an impressive sunburn the day prior.

He was stroking the placidly purring cat when a neighborhood dog came to the screen door and barked. The startled kitty, in a statement of defiance, arched her back to hiss at the dog while thoroughly anchoring her claws into Buddy's already offended leg. Buddy's shrieks were sufficient to have been heard as far away as downtown Bryan; an inspired cat, once again, streaked for the backdoor like having been shot out of a cannon.

I don't recall seeing the cat near Buddy again. I think the feeling was mutual.

While in Los Alamos, the East Texas summer, with air that was rich and sticky, had become a forgotten memory. But atmospheric effects that weighed heavily on the lungs were quick to restore what was now easy to recollect. College Station's summer weather was typical of East Texas—mostly steamy and hot. It wasn't usual, but it also wasn't unusual that daytime temperatures would approach a hundred degrees with humidity near the same number. Unlike West Texas, where dry air can support a swamp cooler, making indoor temperature passable, Central East Texas's humidity made no such option available. Sweat flowed freely beginning sometime in May and extended through sometime in September.

Summer nights were often made more pleasant by the punctuated sight of lots of fireflies glowing their tails off. Bedtime was another matter, made more interesting by the mosquitoes that attacked with wild abandon. Sleep without some sort of cover was not an option, even though the sheet stuck to me as I tossed restlessly through a hot night.

Nights were spent supported only by an attic fan for air circulation, relying on sleeping with a window open and hoping that the night air would give some relief.

On occasion, a thunderstorm would bring the sound of raindrops on the leaves of the oak tree outside my bedroom window. On those nights, relief would come to the oppressive atmospheric heaviness, making the air breathable. The result was as effective as any tranquilizer. A good rainstorm, accompanied by thunderous flashes of lightning and rolling thunder, still makes me want to find a place to hibernate.

But on most nights, sounds—the attic fan, barking dogs, birds, tree frogs, and crickets—were essential to getting to sleep. Nostalgia inspires me to say a few words in tribute to the tree frogs that sang me to sleep on those hot summer nights and the roosters who urged me awake on summer mornings with their early dawn acknowledgments of the approaching day. Recorded sounds of sleep inducements—rainstorms accompanied by rolling thunder or crashing waves on Galveston's seashore—were not yet available.

When the weather finally broke, summer was over. Winter days could also get chilly; on occasion, a day was cold enough to be attention-getting.

Our junior high school building was supported on pilings, leaving a crawlspace underneath. During some of the colder mornings, floors were cold, and classrooms were hard to heat. To solve the problem, oil stoves heated classrooms, the boy's bathroom, and (presumably) the girl's bathroom.

Actually, it seemed during colder months, classrooms never really got warm, prompting some kids to trade their jeans for more practical corduroy pants, which proved useful most of the time. But there was one notable inconvenience: for the most part, even in junior high school, most kids remained physically immature. Once, when entering the boy's restroom on a cold day, I found a friend standing at the urinal trough; it was an opportunity too obvious.

A slight bump resulted in his reaching out to the wall with both hands to recover his balance, his corduroys being dampened in the process. His get-even reaction missed when I jumped from my position in front of the stove. The stench dissipated after a few days, but before that could happen, the boy's bathroom remained mostly unused.

Sometimes, very small things result in memorable moments. I felt considerable pride when, in 1953, the *Bryan Daily Eagle* printed an article disclosing Brazos County's per capita murder rate to be the highest in the United States. The honor that we had made the national news was particularly special!

In recalling younger times, I occasionally am reminded of the two smells that were my particular favorites: new rubber tires and gasoline. Both attracted me in the way a dog finds pleasure in sniffing a fire hydrant. On occasion, when I was in Bryan, I dropped by the Western Auto store to linger a few minutes among the bicycles, which were fully equipped with brand-new rubber tires. It wasn't necessary to stop and sniff the tire itself. The aroma created by lots of tires in one space at the same time was sufficient.

Gasoline, like new rubber tires, had to be smelled to be enjoyed. I found, in the process of siphoning a gas tank a time or two, the flavor of gasoline to be immensely less attractive than its aroma implied.

Not long after we returned to College Station, doo-wop began to dominate popular music. Favorite 1950s singers included Pat Boone, Elvis Presley, Bill Haley and His Comets, Hank Williams, Lefty Frizzell, and Ray Charles "I Got a Woman". Later, when we moved to Arizona, I discovered that Hank Williams, Lefty Frizzell, and other performers of their type were "country-Western" singers. In Texas, their music was just music, along with the rest of what we listened to.

The 1950s included a few terms that were perfectly good for use at the time but unlikely to be understood by most of the population today: mimeograph, Cinerama, beatnik, hopscotch, marbles, 45 RPM records, dime store, icebox, Philco, Studebaker, Moose Lodge, mucilage glue, Radarange, Thermofax, bobby socks, stenographer, elevator operator, clothesline, beauty operator, painted turtles, diaper pins, garter belt, nylons, padded bra, Dixie Cup holder, jelly jar glassware, transistor radio, Hokey Pokey, sock hop, coke date, telephone party line, and more. We moved on.

Sundays meant Sunday school and church. Sunday dinner (called lunch in most parts of the country) was almost always fried chicken served up midafternoon. Later, I would occasionally return to Methodist Youth Fellowship (MYF) with the same kids who had been at Sunday school that morning.

An occasional Sunday evening potluck church supper would rally the Methodists to bring their favorite versions of fried chicken, deviled eggs, buttery mashed potatoes, beans with bacon, versions of creamed vegetables, Jell-O molds, and every sort of pie and cake. Several friends were also Methodist church-goers, so potlucks were social events as well as a shot at an abundant array of excellent home cooking.

Talk of down-home type cooking prompts my recall of the plant life that had the most cultural relevance to me. My favorites included black-eyed peas, fried okra, fried green tomatoes, speckled lima beans, crowder peas, and potatoes—that is, potatoes prepared in almost any form.

When we left College Station for Tempe, Arizona, I discovered the diet I was accustomed to was "soul food." And I liked most of it, with a couple of exceptions. In spite of a childhood in which greens were almost always an integral part of the family garden, I never did develop an appreciation for turnips, mustard greens, or any kind of squash. Moreover, I never became a fan of "soppin' syrup" poured over whatever was left on the dinner or supper plate to serve as dessert.

But I remain entirely partial to the rest.

## College Station Weekends

We had an array of options for things to do on weekends. During football season, almost every kid I knew took in a Texas A&M Southwest Conference football game when the game was in town on Saturdays. End zone seats were one dollar, and every team in the Southwest Conference was good during that period.

But, for undisguised malice, Texas A&M's rivalry with the University of Texas was the most intense. It was a good time for the Southwest Conference, not just for teams but for a lot of memorable players. One player, in particular, stood out. King Hill was a doctoral student in mathematics at Rice University while starring in football as an All-American, playing basketball, and playing golf. He was the NFL's number one draft pick his senior year.

Texas A&M students had several traditions. My favorite was the massive bonfire and rally held before the University of Texas football game. Of course, University of Texas students would try to set the fire earlier, so Texas A&M students guarded the woodpile 'round-the-clock until the actual scheduled night.

During football games, any football game, the A&M student body stood throughout the entire game. During the University of Texas game, the Aggie Corp would sway in unison, singing their favorite song, "Goodbye to Texas University. So long to the orange and the white . . ."

Texas A&M was a land-grant college, so it was consequently military. An all-male student body was dedicated to becoming second lieutenants in the Army upon graduation. But it was more than just a school. A tradition had been established that meant freshman students were indoctrinated, that is, inducted, into a fraternity of sorts. What that meant was a Texas A&M freshman's first year was one to be happily completed. Hazing from upperclassmen was a nonstop nightmare of unending harassment. The consequence was that the next year's freshman class was going to get it from the new sophomores.

College Station's only traffic circle had an adjacent drive-in theater, creatively named the Circle Drive-In. A frequent Friday or Saturday night activity involved gathering Dr. Pepper soft drink bottles on the Texas A&M campus to turn in for the two-cent deposit. The exercise was typically performed at night to avoid unnecessary attention and was usually done only after jumping the Circle Drive-In's chain-link perimeter fence for a viewing of that evening's silver screen offerings.

The drive-in had thoughtfully made air-conditioned seating available in the projector building for paying customers when sitting in a sweaty car or swatting mosquitoes became too uncomfortable. The indoor seats also served as a comfortable place to enjoy the movie for those who entered the facility over the perimeter fence.

Our reason for the unconventional entry wasn't that we were delinquents. Rather, successfully jumping the fence and watching whatever film was on simply seemed more attractive than actually driving in. I don't remember the thought that this was actually theft of some sort ever having occurred to any of us.

Supplementing the Circle Drive-In, two indoor theaters were available in College Station: Campus Theater, which wasn't located on the Texas A&M campus, and Guion Hall, which was. Saturday afternoon Guion Hall moviegoing was an excellent social event and always a double feature. The price of admission was ten cents, as was the price of a box of popcorn. Distributing circulars describing the coming month's film schedule earned a free pass that was good for the month. It never seemed to matter what the movies were; it was just an important Saturday afternoon something to do.

Fifties films were unabashedly wholesome. We watched them all: splashy musicals, excellent dramatic films, amusing comedies, sentimental romantic films, science fiction, some acclaimed, and lots of Westerns starring John Wayne.

But then word came that there was a new movie that had been "banned in Boston," tantalizingly precluding those of us too young for that sort of thing from seeing it. This, of course, required that the film, starring William Holden and Maggie McNamara, absolutely be seen. *The Moon is Blue*, having been singled out in Boston, required adapting our Circle Drive-In expertise in alternative ways to enter. Since it was apparent that the theater's front entry was not going to be available, we would adapt to the circumstances. Entering through Guion Hall's back door, we sat back in anxious anticipation of the implied magic moments envisioned. And then it happened.

Maggie said to William, "Are you going to seduce me?" What! That was it? That caused the film to be banned in Boston? It was going to take a lot more to satisfy a thirteen-year-old's licentious expectations. Not until *The Immoral Mr. Teas* came out several years later did we get sucked in like that again.

## Television's Arrival

Texas's first television station, WBAP-TV in Fort Worth, began operating on September 27, 1948. In 1950, three more stations were in operation in the Dallas-Fort Worth area;

two were broadcasting from San Antonio, and Houston had one station.

Television came to College Station in the mid-1950s. A special antenna capable of being rotated to catch the signal was needed for our first television set to function. One of my favorite uncles and aunts, Raymond and Edna Pittman, were owners of Denton's North Texas Electric and always were among the first to have the latest in cutting-edge electric gadgetry. Our first television set was one of their hand-me-downs.

Television programming was local to wherever the television station happened to be located and was always viewed through the appearance of a force 10 snowstorm. The television day ended promptly at 11:00 p.m. with the national anthem, leaving viewers breathlessly anticipating 6:00 a.m. when the test pattern would be once again replaced by the national anthem, followed by a cheery voice announcing that the station was now "on the air."

The seventeen hours between 6:00 a.m. and 11:00 p.m. might just as well have featured a bored piano player absently playing random show tunes from the 1930s and '40s while carrying on an animated conversation with someone off-camera. But we watched it anyway in case something interesting were to happen, such as what occurred in one of my most memorable early-television moments.

A live demonstration showcasing the talented capabilities of a man and his bullwhip, the sort of act we might see on *America's Got Talent* today, was to be staged. The demonstration included a shapely young female assistant who was to bend over while extending a cigarette between her legs, well behind her, of course. He was then to delicately remove the cigarette from her hands while leaving her remarkably shaped behind untouched.

Adding drama leading up to the event, he cracked the bullwhip around the stage several times, all the while steadily building the level of observer tension to a crescendo. Then came the moment of great anticipation. As he sized up the circumstances for just exactly how he would complete his amazing feat, I was mesmerized. Possibly it was the warm-up that resulted in a momentary loss of focus, but his genius failed him.

With a startling crack of the whip, the cigarette was removed from her delicate grasp, but the feat was accompanied by the assistant bounding energetically to a height roughly equivalent to the roof of a Ford F-150's cab following the whip's tip caressing her attractively flexed buttocks.

For me, it was television's first truly comedic moment, leaving me momentarily incapacitated by the fit of laughter elicited by the assistant's impressive response. No instant replay was available to recapture the event, but the memory still suffices. I smile when I think of that moment and wonder whether the rest of the assistant's television career was as stimulating or if men with bullwhips continued to be part of her act.

By 1953, TV was beginning to assume its first glimmer of sophistication. Four major networks were serving Texas— ABC, CBS, NBC, and DuMont—and television network programming had begun. Such shows and performers as *Your Hit Parade*, Sid Caesar and *Your Show of Shows*, Steve Allen, Perry

Como, Liberace, Burns and Allen, and a few others were all mostly shown on Saturday and Sunday nights.

*Your Hit Parade*, a show featuring each week's most popular seven songs, starred Gisele MacKenzie, Russell Arms, Dorothy Collins, and Snooky Lanson, a wholesome bunch putting on an always wholesome, fabulously popular family show. Then Bill Haley and His Comets stormed onto the scene. Wholesome was not sufficient for the show to survive when Snooky Lanson belting out "Rock Around the Clock" simply didn't register sufficiently on a scale of hipness.

Early TV shows had commercials often built right into the programs. What made it fun was when an announcer, through the breathless excitement he was experiencing while proclaiming the many benefits of Skippy peanut butter, would flub his lines. The attempt to recover his wits without letting on to the viewing audience he had been bothered at all by his figurative tumble down the stairs was an always entertaining part of the show.

*The George Burns and Gracie Allen Show* was sponsored by Carnation Evaporated Milk. During the show, Harry von Zell would wander onto the set to do a quick commercial, leaving George and Gracie to stand aside while he metaphorically explained how contented the lives of the cows were from which Carnation Milk came. Those were primitive, but also endearing, times. And the shows often included the sponsor's name: *The Colgate Comedy Hour, The Dinah Shore Chevy Show, General Electric Theater, Gillette Cavalcade of Sports,* and more.

Television during that early period, while it was rapidly improving beyond piano players or experts with bullwhips, was little more than radio with pictures. The really successful programs to make their way onto television were all radio-related: *The Adventures of Ozzie and Harriet*, *The George Burns and Gracie Allen Show*, *The Jack Benny Program*, *The Milton Berle Show*, and a few others.

Radio shows I discovered while in Los Alamos included *The Green Hornet*, *Sky King*, *King of the Royal Mounted*, *The Shadow* ("Who knows what goes on in the minds of men"), *Mr. and Mrs. North*, *Amos 'n' Andy*, *The Jack Benny Program*, and *Buster Brown* (and his dog "Tige"). They still made me want to sit by the radio Sunday and Thursday nights.

*The $64,000 Question*, television's first seriously watched quiz show for quite a while, featured a bright, unusually well-informed psychologist. I was infatuated with Dr. Joyce Brothers, who became one of television's major attractions as a boxing expert until she won the top prize of $64,000. I never missed an episode of *The $64,000 Question* until, one day, a crushing revelation disclosed the awful truth. Dr. Brothers was reported to have been given the answers to the questions ahead of time. It was the end of the show, but not for Dr. Brothers.

She made headlines once again by hitting someone over the head with a barf bag during an argument on an airplane. Then she went on to have fame as a talk show psychologist while still remaining well known for her former association with *The $64,000 Question*.

An array of new shows—situation comedies, mysteries, drama, Westerns, and others—included *The Many Loves of Dobie Gillis, Sea Hunt, Sugarfoot, Dragnet, Father Knows Best, Gunsmoke, What's My Line?, I've Got a Secret, Topper, 77 Sunset Strip*, and more—I watched them all.

Not to miss out on an opportunity, in 1954, Bryan's Safeway got into the act with C.A. Swanson and Sons, who introduced the perfect food for enhancing the enjoyment of the TV experience. Swanson's TV dinners were served on compartmentalized aluminum trays and featured soggy fried chicken, watery mashed potatoes, and strikingly tasteless frozen vegetables. Trying them once was more than enough; the end of home cooking would have to wait.

Still adding to the frozen foods magic, Birds Eye gave us frozen vegetables. In a geographic area in which most homes had a vegetable garden somewhere on the premises, or a neighbor who did, Birds Eye frozen vegetables were only marginally less attractive than TV dinners.

But, as innovations go, the inspirations behind both the TV set and TV dinners gave rise to another innovation—TV trays. Whatever TV dinner we chose could now be made readily available from the comfort of our couch while watching our favorite show.

For a kid in a small town, there was almost always something interesting to do. There may never have been a more easygoing time than the 1950s, or, more particularly, small-town Texas in the 1950s, provided one was born White. I have more to say on that topic later.

Fun was a different kind of thing in a 1950s small town. We learned to search out our pleasures. What I liked most was spending time with friends after school and on weekends, doing whatever was in season—softball, touch football, or shooting.

Weekends were sort of Huckleberry Finn enjoyable. Several friends and I had guns (we had all passed the National Rifle Association Gun Safety course), so snapping turtles, water moccasins, and any other sort of snake available along Carter Creek were fair game.

The Carter Farm and Carter Creek were among our favorite venues for weekend things to do. Grapevines had overrun most of the trees, so we took advantage of the convenience to cut pieces to smoke. On one occasion, while at the creek with a couple of pals, we had purchased a plug of Red Man chewing tobacco and were attempting to chew and spit like the big boys. It worked okay until I stepped on a slippery rock while crossing the creek. The resulting loss of balance caused me to swallow the plug of tobacco; regurgitation was instantaneous and complete, involving the plug of Red Man and lunch. The event curbed my enthusiasm for the taste of chewing tobacco again, ever.

As indicated by the family's gravestones, providing birth and death dates for several Carter family members, the Carters had apparently homesteaded the farm sometime during the 1800s. In addition to the small graveyard, an unmarked hole in the ground lined by a corrugated pipe had been a water well, probably adjacent to a house that was long disintegrated. It was always a little spooky to think about the possibility of falling into that hole and not being discovered.

Warm weather called for swimming. But we didn't have swimming pools, and Carter Creek was too shallow, too murky, and too full of snapping turtles. The problem was solved as a result of the hurricane that had devastated Galveston in 1900 when up to twenty feet of floodwater resulted in the city subsequently building seawalls to protect housing areas in the event such a storm was ever to occur again. Brazos County had excellent granite for that sort of thing, so a lot of Brazos County stone was quarried and shipped to Galveston by rail during the rebuilding period.

One of those quarries had filled with water and was conveniently located about four miles from College Station. In an apparent attempt to discourage trespassing, the quarry was posted for typhus. But the quarry was a favorite summertime spot, and I guess spending a hot afternoon cooling off negated concerns of acquiring a deadly disease. I doubt we ever believed the signs anyway.

Several attempts to touch the quarry's bottom were abandoned as too spooky. A few feet down, the water temperature dropped measurably, as did the resolve required to continue.

It was Dad's expressed opinion that "no one should grow up without having been frog gigging at night." By holding a lantern high while standing in the boat, the reflection in a bullfrog's eyes would light up like a neon sign. Identifying where they were located was no problem. I can't say how many times I went frog gigging with Dad, but one more memorable time, a water moccasin, apparently attracted to our lantern, attempted to join us.

Any snake trying to crawl into one's boat is a powerful diversion of attention from a search for frogs. Our immediate attempt to beat the snake back into the water was successful, and we remained in the boat rather than falling overboard during the pandemonium.

We always took home enough legs to be fried up for dinner, but I never developed a craving for frog legs any more than some of the other wild game we had on the table from time to time. Dad, the country boy, never really stopped enjoying the hunting skills he had developed during his boyhood in the Big Thicket or the considerable pleasure he derived from whatever he managed to bag ending up on the supper table.

My attempts at squirrel hunting with friends seldom— actually never—resulted in any positive result. Squirrels, being considerably craftier than small boys with guns, sensibly moved to the other side of a tree whenever we made an appearance. Although my father was very good at the process and we occasionally had fried squirrel for dinner, the genius required to outsmart a squirrel was another of the many skills that were not passed on to me. Just as well. I never really acquired the taste for squirrel, wild duck, antelope, venison, or dove, no matter how many times they had been cooked up.

The exception was elk meat, which was reasonably agreeable when made into chili or chicken fried. To just about anyone who has spent any of their early life in Texas, certain cuts of meat are better when chicken fried, but even venison was only moderately passable when prepared in any way but chili.

To add to the availability of bass fishing and duck hunting, Dad acquired a building lot on Camp Creek Lake, where he arranged to construct a fishing cabin. A slab for the cabin was poured on one weekend, then the next weekend, the cabin was framed, the exterior cladded, and the roof installed.

In one day, the cabin was complete. Work on that second weekend was done entirely by a crew of Cajuns who had driven in from Louisiana the day before. I thought I would be working on the cabin with them but was wrong. Not a word of English was spoken the entire day, and I didn't speak two-hundred-year-old French or, for that matter, French of any kind. It was clear those guys knew what they were doing and went about their work with an enthusiasm that never let up until the last board was nailed into place that night.

When the Cajuns left, the finished product was composed of two large rooms and a bathroom. The main room was heated by a potbellied stove that either had the place hot enough to run everyone out of there or too cold. A good fishing cabin should be a little rough around the edges; ours qualified.

Preparation for bass fishing usually called for stopping at a cattle watering hole to seine for bait—minnows and crawfish. With that out of the way, the next requirement was to locate where the bass were biting. To a professional bass fisherman, several qualifications are required to take advantage of the best probabilities, and Dad had a nose for the process. We almost always came home with a good catch.

The bass fishing was good, but the cabin's best use seemed to have been for duck hunting. We spent frequent early mornings on weekends in a duck blind, waiting for the sun to come up. With the temperature during duck season in the forties, one had to really love duck hunting to sit in an aluminum boat, waiting for sunup and the ducks to show up. I never learned to love those early mornings or developed an appetite for the ducks we took home.

During the early-to-mid-1950s, foreign carmakers hadn't made their mark in the US yet. But American car companies introduced new models, or at least some appearance of newness, every year. And every kid who was even remotely inclined toward cars knew every model in every year of the "Big Three" American car manufacturers.

Nearly every kid I knew was just as caught up in the excitement. Every year, changes in appearance and the frequent addition of such niceties as air-conditioning and automatic transmissions kept the adrenaline surging. Suddenly, Strato-Flight Hydra-Matic transmissions powered General Motors' Cadillacs, Oldsmobiles, and Pontiacs. Strangely, Buicks decided to go their own way with Dynaflow, and Chevrolet did the same with "Triple Turbine" Turboglide. Chrysler had their Power-Flite Range Selector, and Ford had its own automatic transmission version.

But mostly, what they had was glitz. They all, but more particularly Ford and Chrysler, were susceptible to the cars essentially falling apart at fifty-thousand miles, a term they referred to as "planned obsolescence." And that made them vulnerable, as foreign competition soon discovered.

Foreign carmakers found that improved quality gave them an edge; constant change in styling wasn't necessary if they built a better car. The change wasn't immediate, but it was lasting. Today's foreign cars seem to generically look a lot alike. I'm as likely to attempt to get into just about any black European-model sedan parked in the lot if I'm not paying attention to where my own car is parked.

As soon as we had arrived back in Texas from Los Alamos, I began to develop a yearning to drive. Texas laws relating to a driver's age were lenient. At age twelve, I learned to drive by backing our Dodge pickup out to the street and returning to the front of our garage. That back-and-forth driving eventually resulted in me throwing caution to the wind one day and taking the truck down the street. The act led to an unexpected surprise meeting with Mom and Dad on their way home.

Among the relatives on my mother's side were the Pittmans. My Uncle Raymond and Aunt Edna had four daughters, each more attractive than the other. Included among the group and closest to my age was Jane. Jane qualified nicely as a reasonable version of a tomboy, so Jane and I spent a lot of time together when they came to town for a visit. But one experience stood out.

My contact with Cecil Culpepper's son, John Cecil, was infrequent since John Cecil was a few years older than me. But once, when the Pittmans were visiting, Jane and I were out for a walk in the woods and ran into John Cecil, who was out having target practice with his Daisy Red Ryder BB gun. I was enough of a twerp at the time that John Cecil wouldn't have given me the time of day, but Jane was a cute blonde and about John Cecil's age. So, with little encouragement necessary, John Cecil joined us.

In the course of our walk, we crossed a bridge over a shallow creek that, on that day, sported a large water moccasin, stretched out and sunning itself along the creek's edge below the bridge. As John Cecil's BB gun was conveniently available, it was decided that we should shoot the snake. We took turns shooting with no apparent result; the snake just lay there as though every BB had bounced off.

Under most circumstances, one would not expect a snake to hold still while being peppered with BBs. But that's what happened. After probably fifty BBs, the snake rolled over and was dead, or so it seemed. No one volunteered to go down the creek bank to confirm that the snake was, in fact, incapacitated and not just really pissed. Water moccasins are a creepy enough snake that it was best to avoid checking on even one that appeared dead.

Just about every household in Brazos County had a dog. Our cocker and chow mix, Freckles, had come with us from Los Alamos, and, like every other kid in town's dog, Freckles mostly ran free. But there was a problem: like a lot of dogs, Freckles had an apparent congenital issue with postmen, requiring that he be tied up when mail delivery was scheduled.

But, even so, he became so Cujo-crazed when the postman came around that, after a few weeks, we were informed by the post office that "the dog had to go," or there was not going to be any more mail delivery. I don't know where Dad took him, but I had a feeling that Freckles didn't last much longer.

My dogs were my buddies. When it was decided Freckles had to go, we acquired Pat, a fox terrier who was a dead ringer for the RCA Victor dog and tagged along with me wherever I went.

## Summer Jobs

It didn't take long after our return to College Station to convince Dad that life as a college professor wasn't workable for him. Through a prior relationship with Cecil Culpepper, he picked up a summer job in 1952 supervising a single-family housing project Cecil was developing. When school was out in June, I began cleaning up construction debris around houses as construction progress required.

The work was seriously sweaty, but at thirty-five cents an hour, the pay was better than a paper route, as were the hours. It was the first of several jobs I would have because of Dad's influence. I worked in construction for three summers, mostly cleaning up around construction sites.

During the summer of 1953, Dad's summer job was as superintendent on a large single-family home development in Grand Prairie, a town located between Dallas and Fort Worth. The job required spending the summer in a rental house in Denton.

Initially, with nothing to do because the Grand Prairie project wasn't far along yet, I found comfort as a couch potato, watching whatever was on television. Then came opportunity; my uncle Raymond Pittman needed a helper.

Uncle Raymond was a well-regarded electrician and electrical contractor in Denton, but his preferred reputation was as a superb livestock farmer raising Duroc hogs. And for that, Uncle Raymond was formidable. He was a tough competitor at the Texas State Fair's "Fat Stock" Show, having the Grand Champion Boar and Sow of Texas for several years running.

Typical of a Texas farmer, he was physically a "man's man;" milking cows had given him a set of forearms like Popeye's. Working for Uncle Raymond was one of my most enjoyable summer jobs, but a couple of incidents made the work more interesting than usual. One event occurred when wiring a service station.

Late Friday afternoon, Uncle Raymond had finished pulling wires through the conduit previously installed for electrical service. We were to install the switches and receptacles Monday morning before the city inspector approved activating electrical service. But the inspector was early, or we were late. I don't remember which.

What I do remember is that when I reached into a service bay J-box to pull out the wires, to my surprise, the city inspector had approved the job before we arrived, and the city had turned on electrical service to the station. A 110-volt electric current will shock a person, but the service bay, wired for 220 volts, provided a phenomenally painful shock just shy of that required for a frontal lobotomy. I didn't make that mistake again.

The second incident, and what finished my work experience with Uncle Raymond, resulted from wiring for a stove receptacle in an older home. I had to crawl through a darkened attic to drop a line down the inside of a wall, where Uncle Raymond was waiting below to pull the wiring. I ignored the spider web I had disturbed along the way.

When I removed my jeans that night, it was readily apparent that the black widow spider whose web I had insulted had crawled up my pants leg and, in my moment of vulnerability, had taken revenge, biting me inside my upper thigh. A coal-black spot about three-eighths of an inch in diameter was in the center of a large swelling.

The only immediately negative effect was throwing up in the doctor's parking lot the next morning. A permanent pit in my leg resulted from the venom's work, ordinarily reserved for liquifying houseflies to be enjoyed later at the spider's leisure. The doctor ordered me to spend the next twelve days in bed.

By the time the twelve days were up, it was time to be on my way to the Irvine Ranch Boy Scout Jamboree in Orange County, California.

### The 1953 Boy Scout Jamboree

When we returned to College Station from Los Alamos in February 1952, I joined Boy Scout Troop 102. My final scouting event, 1953's Irvine Ranch Boy Scout Jamboree, overlooking the then-sleepy little village of Balboa, was as memorable as my Los Alamos scouting experience.

I traveled with another Troop 102 member to Houston, where we joined up with the Sam Houston Area Council Scouts. Our transportation to California was a 1900s vintage steam engine with classic train cars, one of eighty trains that had been dusted off to be put back into use carrying Scouts to the Jamboree. While crossing West Texas, the monotony was broken by the lonely presence of tornadoes, which could be seen doing their thing at a proper distance out on the prairie. When we reached Arizona, we stopped at the Grand Canyon for a few hours before moving on to Fullerton, California.

When it was necessary to stop to take on coal and water, the train's brake system often locked, resulting in the engineer having to rock the train backward and forward a few times. The brakes unlocked, and we would continue. The trip took us through the deserts of Texas, Arizona, Nevada, and California; temperatures were seriously warm, but turn-of-the-century air conditioning—fans blowing air over blocks of ice—was reasonably effective until the ice ran out. The ice running out usually occurred in the middle of the night, leaving interior temperatures to once again reach whatever the outside temperature happened to be.

During that trip, I had my only sleepwalking experience. I awoke standing in the aisle of what I thought was our train car. But when I returned to the chair where I thought I should have been sitting, the seat was taken. That began my private "twilight zone" experience.

It was like a surprise party; I had no clue where I was or what I was doing there. It took a while to sort out that I was in the wrong car. But why? And how? I had walked through the vestibule between cars—which was noisy—without waking. When I finally made my way back to where I was supposed to be, it took a while to get over the weird feeling of what had just happened.

Our arrival at Orange County's Fullerton Train Station on Friday, July 17, was greeted by Girl Scouts passing out California oranges. Few of us Texas kids, especially those of us from small towns, had experienced that sort of energy and excitement. Buses took us to the jamboree campsite where over 25,000 tents and kitchen equipment units were waiting to be installed by 45,000 Scouts, all arriving almost simultaneously by trains and buses. Most were from the United States, but some had made their way there from other parts of the world.

The jamboree site was bounded by MacArthur Boulevard, Palisades Road, and Irvine Road, an area that today is occupied mostly by Newport Beach's Fashion Island regional shopping center. But, for the jamboree's purposes, those boundaries enclosed eight miles of roadways, a hospital with 164 doctors, a parking lot for 16,000 cars, and 150 police officers.

On Sunday morning, July 19, 45,000 Catholic, Christian Science, Latter-day Saint, Jewish, and Protestant Scouts attended church.

Our camp was located adjacent to the Minnesota Council, and the Minnesota kids would drop over at our camp to hear Southern accents spoken. It was the first time I was aware Texas speech was that apparent. Other than the use of "y'all," it seemed to us like we sounded like everyone else.

Almost immediately during free time, we began trading badges with Scouts from other parts of the country, some of which later became valuable. Events were nonstop, including archery, beach time, shooting, a trip to Hollywood, a trip to Catalina Island, another to the Griffith Park Zoo and Observatory, and Knott's Berry Farm.

Transportation to Catalina was by water taxi, a flat-bottomed, slow-moving, diesel-propelled boat that pitched and rolled with every wave. For most of us, the closest we had been to a boat prior was a bass boat on a Texas lake. The seasickness that came on was sudden, rendering many of the passengers catastrophically ill as they rolled around in the bottom of the boat until our arrival at Catalina. Most recovered enough to enjoy the island and its diving bell, glass-bottom boat, and a trip out to see the buffalo. Then they discovered that what they had experienced while on the way to the island was to be repeated on the return trip to Long Beach.

A mile stretch of beach had been set aside for Scouts' use for the week. Sixty-eight buses shuttled swimmers to the beaches, which were watched over by thirty lifeguards, helicopters, and offshore boats. Results were impressive—92,000 swims with no injuries for the week.

Nighttime entertainment was professional, staged by an impressive array of celebrities. One event, a show fit for Broadway, had an all-star cast that included Richard Nixon, Bob Hope, Debbie Reynolds, Danny Kaye, Mitzi Gaynor, Dorothy Lamour, and Montie Montana, along with an array of lesser-known, but just as appreciated, entertainers.

Then, on Thursday, July 23, after a nonstop, action-packed week, 25,000 tents were broken down and repacked. To return home the Scouts boarded buses to whatever transportation had delivered them to California. Looking back at the logistics required to conduct such an event seems to lead to a reasonable conclusion—there will probably not be another like it. How that much activity for that many people was packed into one seven-day period can only be explained by exceptional planning and execution by a large and devoted group of adults.

When I returned to Denton, I began working at the Grand Prairie housing development Dad was supervising for Rodgway Construction Company. I was back doing construction cleanup. Then, one morning, I experienced an awakening.

This was what happened. The project's developer requested that I accompany him to his recently completed Dallas home to do some sort of menial task. I have no recollection of what I did for him, but I do remember the car I rode in—a new air-conditioned 1953 Buick Special. I had never seen such a car, let alone rode in one.

Topping off the impression, the shoes the developer was wearing were ventilated on the sides and obviously expensive. I know now they were probably Italian. But, at that moment, I was overwhelmed. And a decision was quietly reached: I was going to have a Buick and a really nice pair of shoes one day.

Dad had begun allowing me to scoot over in the front seat of our pickup to take the wheel as we drove down country roads. Now, with our work on the Grand Prairie development, Dad would usually meet with his foremen at the end of the workday and would let me drive our 1953 Chevy around the de-velopment until he was finished. I acquired a lot of driving ex-perience before it was time to return to College Station and school.

In November, I became eligible to apply for my learner's permit, which allowed me to drive on the streets, provided I had a licensed adult in the car with me. I was a reasonably experi-enced driver by the time my fourteenth birthday came around, so I was able to qualify for my driver's license. Texas allowed licensing at fourteen for those located in a rural area and who could help out on the farm. I don't recall anyone asking me when I got my license what sort of farming we did. I guess our Chev-rolet pickup gave a satisfactory enough impression.

When school started in September, The Texas State Fair, one of Texas's highlights of the year, was soon to begin. In addition to an impressive array of animal husbandry in the Fat Stock Show, Texas had the only state fair in the US to include a full auto show. Detroit brought their concept cars and new mod-els to be placed on display, and the midway rides were cutting edge. The whole package was exciting to the extreme.

A&M Consolidated arranged for two busloads of kids to travel to Dallas to spend the day. It was there I experienced my first sideshow. *Massive* was not a reference most women would prefer to have applied to their physical proportions; *large* was usually adequate. But I encountered a woman requiring such a formidable description as the sideshow's fat lady attraction. Her claimed weight was a then-phenomenal 450 pounds. As a smart-mouthed thirteen-year-old, I challenged her no-way-possible claim.

In response, she graciously invited me to join her on stage to participate in a live demonstration. She would sit on my lap while I disappeared beneath a quarter of a ton of loveliness. Hindsight drove me to conclude that the invitation was to demonstrate to the audience how a really annoying kid—and his mouth—could disappear without a trace under her ginormous butt. My decline of the offer was one of the more mature decisions I made at such a still-young age. I will get to some of my less enlightened decisions later.

The Texas State Fair gained some notoriety during one of the first moves to overturn some of Texas's outright prejudice. A protest was organized against the policy of limiting Black fair-goer attendance to only on "Negro Achievement Day."

Sometime during the 1954 school year, I decided to build a doghouse, not so much because Pat needed a doghouse but because I felt momentarily inspired. About halfway through the building process, I stopped working on the project and just left it aside. It remained partially built for several months until, one day, I had what I suppose was an epiphany—a realization that I had a habit of starting a project, then not finishing. When Pat's new doghouse was complete, I was proud of the accomplishment and more so of my newly acquired awareness.

That summer, I was back working on a College Station construction project developed by Cecil Culpepper and, once again, supervised by Dad. The project was a series of duplexes and a few single-family homes, one of which was for Bear

Bryant, who was moving to College Station to become Texas A&M's head football coach.

The work, consistent with prior construction jobs, was mostly dedicated to cleaning up around construction sites, but that time, I did get to do some carpentry work on roofing and installing Rockwool insulation. I enjoyed the carpentry but learned quickly that installing Rockwool was considerably disagreeable work. The minute we touched it, Rockwool particles tended to hold to the skin, then proceeded to itch like crazy.

That summer, inspiration struck again: this time, to build a tree house in a massive oak behind our house. I enlisted the help of a few friends to build what turned out to be an excellent tree house. Hernando's Hideaway was six by six feet in size, equipped with screened-in sidewalls and a hip roof finished in canvas. A trapdoor opened to a ladder. We often made good use of that treehouse on Saturday nights.

Occasionally on weekends, I would set pins at Texas A&M's Memorial Student Union bowling alley. The pay was ten cents a line, a line being ten frames. To make any money, it was necessary to set two bowling lanes at a time for ten frames each.

Setting two lanes required jumping from one lane to the other to reset the pins after each ball was thrown. The activity was kept interesting as occasionally, a bowling novice would launch the ball down the alley before I had completed resetting the pins. I was usually able to leap out of the way during those times but didn't always escape the occasional flying pin caused by a seriously large guy tossing the ball down the lane like it had been shot out of a cannon, making the pins leap into the air as though intent on leaving the building. Setting pins didn't pay a lot, but free bowling, a perk when I wasn't setting pins, made it okay.

Texas football starts early in junior high, and by high school, it gets taken seriously. My first year of junior high school football was in the eighth grade. I loved the game. When I moved on to high school the following year, I was 115 pounds and slow. But I went out anyway and found that I wasn't, at that moment, up to it. It was a condition that applied to most of us freshmen.

But 1954 was an exciting year for Texas A&M football. Bear Bryant had recruited the best high school football players in Texas and other states in the South. Most notable was Kenneth Hall, who had played high school football for Sugar Land, a Houston suburb, and had carved his name in stone in Texas high school football. As a running back, Kenneth was virtually unstoppable.

At a time when a high school football player was big if he weighed 200 pounds and was usually a lineman at that size, Kenneth was 210 pounds. He was also the fastest kid in the state of Texas at the hundred-yard dash when he was a junior. Many of the records he set in football remain unbroken.

Kenneth was one of that famously unwilling A&M freshman class's losses when Bear drove his team so hard during his first year that a good part of the freshman class quit football for good, leaving coach Bryant with a team roster barely large enough to play that season's schedule. Several who remained from that freshman class went on to win the national championship four years later. The same group of freshman players, including John David Crow, Bobby Joe Conrad, and Charlie Krueger, continued on to become professional football legends. John David Crow was 1957's Heisman Trophy winner.

When high school began, I had several classes with my cousin David. During a test, David stood up to go ask a question of Mr. Orr, our algebra teacher. When he passed by, I reached over and snatched the tag off his Levi's. A magnificent ripping sound caused David to slam himself against the wall. In total confusion, David felt I had ripped his pants, causing him to exclaim loudly, "Ronald, you son of a bitch."

The commotion caused Mr. Orr to order David to go to the principal's office. But David saved the day by explaining that I had ripped his pants. The statement was too much for me; I couldn't stop laughing. It was my turn to be sent to see the principal, Mr. Skrivanek.

Since it had been only a couple of weeks prior that I had been to see Mr. Skrivanek over a homeroom fight with Bill Brezeal, I felt a better choice was to skip Mr. Skrivanek—swats from his paddle were of the sort that made me not want to return for more. So, instead, I decided to mosey up to the cafeteria for lunch. Apparently, Mr. Orr had not seen a need to check with Mr. Skrivanek to ensure I had received the attention I deserved.

One fall day, I experienced a transformative moment. One of Dad's Texas A&M students was doing some work on terracing our backyard and had a readily apparent, impressive set of arms. I engaged him in a discussion, which went something to the effect of, "How did you get those guns," or some such thing.

His response, "Sixty push-ups twice a day," seemed reasonable enough.

Inspired, I went straight into the house to begin my new workout routine—sixty push-ups twice a day. Only, my first attempt to push myself off the floor didn't work—not once. But the moment had been sufficiently motivational. I did eventually get myself off the floor and began doing push-ups. I even bought a pair of dumbbells to supplement the new exercise regime that more or less stayed with me. I owe a debt of gratitude to that A&M Cadet.

Along with a couple of pals, we occasionally would camp in the woods outside town. Sounds at night mostly included birds, chirps of crickets, and croaking of a multitude of frogs, forming a kind of eclectic background symphony.

Once while camping, we received a bonus: the scream of a panther in the dark of night. I have never heard a sound more capable of making every hair on my body stand straight out. I was exposed to that sound once in an area where there were supposed to be no remaining panthers. Among unforgettable experiences, it sits in my top five.

Among my favorite high school teachers was Mr. Boone, a descendent of the Daniel Boone of woodsman fame. Mr. Boone had been a medical school student, bound for becoming a doctor, when he concluded that what he really preferred in life was music, prompting him to drop out of medical school to teach his passion. And he was a very good music teacher.

I learned to appreciate the music from Broadway shows, particularly those by Rogers and Hammerstein, thanks to Mr. Boone. But he had one other talent: he recruited some of the more important football players to join the school chorus. With the presence of the big boys, I was a pushover when he recruited me to join the chorus.

A highlight of the year was staging the musical adaptation of Shakespeare's *As You Like It*. We also sang at churches and won a prize in a statewide high school competition staged in Houston. Mr. Boone was ultimately recruited by Texas A&M as choir director.

It was 1954, two years after leaving Los Alamos, and Dad's restlessness had begun to show itself more definitively:

*For a number of reasons, we couldn't adjust to the salary of a full professor.*

But there was more. In Dad's memoirs written years later after his retirement from what had turned out to be a brilliant career, he confessed that he was not well-equipped for the day-to-day routine. He wanted to be more on the cutting-edge of science, and the life of a college professor, while prestigious, lacked the stimulation he needed.

It was very likely he had been looking for something else to do for some time, as he and Mom sold our house on Ashburn, and we moved into one of the rental duplexes Cecil Culpepper had developed and Dad had supervised.

My suspicion was that Dad may have invested in the Grand Prairie development. I was aware the developers had been required to declare bankruptcy when Gray Construction Company, the earthmoving contractor on that job, had declared bankruptcy due to problems on a highway construction job they were doing somewhere in West Texas. Under Texas law, Gray's financial problems extended to any other contracts they were attached to. The Grand Prairie project had experienced the misfortune of being tarred with that brush.

Over the Christmas holidays, Dad and Mom took a trip with the Lee Thompsons to Phoenix. Dad's notes about that trip implied it was just a getaway, but it seems more likely there had been a discussion with Doctor Lee Thompson, also a Texas A&M professor of engineering, suggesting that there might be an opportunity at an emerging college in Arizona:

> *December 1954 found us with the Lee Thompsons, of the mechanical engineering department, on a Christmas vacation in Phoenix, Arizona. The return route took us through Tempe, Arizona, and we discovered this town to be the location of Arizona State College.*
>
> *We decided to stop at the campus to see what was going on at this college. The president, Doctor Grady Gammage, talked Lee and me into coming to the school to build an engineering college. We both saw the area's potential and decided to accept the positions.*

And so, they did.

## Chapter Six

# Transition

It was late summer 1955 when we left Alamogordo for Tempe, Arizona.

Dad and Lee Thompson had been temporarily employed at Holloman Air Development Center. When he was recruited to stay, there was a considerable temptation for Dad to remain. The truth was, the work was likely more stimulating than the position he had accepted in Arizona:

> *We first stopped off for three months in Alamogordo, New Mexico, to do some consulting work for the Holloman Air Development Center. The work was exciting, and I was comforted by the fact that the Air Development Center tried, in many ways, to get me to stay and work for them, but temptation aside, we had made a commitment to Arizona State.*

On the way to Alamogordo, I had spent a few weeks as a wrangler on my Uncle Mac and Aunt Kathleen McWilliams's Big River Guest Ranch at Wagon Wheel Gap, Colorado. Similar to a paper route, the work kept me occupied. There was no time off.

Work was seven days a week, ten to twelve hours a day. Early each morning when it was light enough to saddle up and ride out to bring the horses in from the mountain pasture, either Robert, another high school kid my age, or I would make the trek.

The ten-by-ten-foot bunkhouse Robert and I shared was heated by a potbellied stove when we were ambitious enough to fire it up, which happened only once. There was little value in doing it since the bunkhouse's walls that served as exterior cladding were also the interior walls, meaning the outside temperature was also the inside temperature. Early mornings when it was time to roll out of the sack and get to work, temperatures ranged between twenty-eight to thirty degrees.

Included in the bunkhouse was a resident nest of field mice, which provided an excellent entertainment substitute for TV. One of our pleasures before turning out the single bulb hanging from a ceiling rafter was watching our little roommates skitter back and forth on the overhead rafters, betting on which would fall first.

Early morning temperatures required working quickly to catch the lone horse that had been kept overnight in the corral and get saddled up. Too much delay resulted in hands becoming too weak from the cold to cinch the girth tight enough. In such a circumstance when the horse let his breath out after the cinch had been tightened and the rider had mounted, the result was the rider being dumped. The oversight wasn't necessary to be experienced more than once.

Pat was with me at the ranch and would join me when it was my turn to round up the horses, hopping down from the chair he had been occupying on the lodge's front porch to trot along with me to search for the herd, then join with me to return the horses to the corral.

Pat was a particularly congenial pup, so he had easily adjusted to the role of "camp dog." He learned how useful that characteristic could be, so he made friends with cabin occupants and took advantage of their generosity with meal leftovers. When refrigerators were cleaned out before returning home after a week of roughing it, the leftovers Pat received improved.

Once, I observed him searching for a suitable location to finish off a rolled roast he was carrying that looked to be half his size, an apparent gift from someone packing up to leave. Pat ate considerably better than the rest of us, as did most of Beirut.

Once the herd had been corralled, mostly maintenance activities—replacing fences, cutting up fallen trees, hauling logs to be reduced to firewood—occupied our time. But cutting and hauling logs dominated. A winter storm had knocked down hundreds of aspens that had to be cleared, then cut for firewood.

A secondary, more enjoyable job was saddle breaking a couple of horses—Dolly and Paint, both cow ponies—which required working with them every couple of days for an hour or so. And when a ranch visitor wanted to rent a horse, our job was to catch a suitable match out of the corral to be saddled for the rider. Dolly and Paint were being groomed to one day become part of the rental pool.

The scope of work was limited but full-time. Other than for meals, while it was still light, no time was allowed for breaks. But one day, after working Dolly and Paint and still full of adrenaline and testosterone, Robert and I were sitting on the corral's top rail, taking an unauthorized break.

A young stallion named Skeeter was coming in our direction, trotting along the corral's inside perimeter. Robert's casual ponder of, "I wonder when we're going to start breaking Skeeter," was answered in a manner attributable only to the truly brain-dead.

My response? "How about now!" Then came the circus.

My launch from the corral fence, targeting Skeeter's back, was still in midair when my senses returned. But it was too late. Bareback was not an easy way to ride, but the inconvenience magnified when attached to a crazed stallion. His leap high in the air was followed by a hard landing on all fours. A drop of his head was followed by him kicking his hind feet nearly straight up, launching me over his head like I'd been shot from a cannon. My landing halfway across the corral finished in a full face-plant.

To my advantage, the corral had never been cleaned. What could have been a catastrophically disagreeable landing was made less destructive than it might have been otherwise. And after a few cups of river water, the lingering taste of what I had unintentionally taken in was nearly gone.

A particularly enjoyable part of the job, one I still reminisce over, was riding out alone in the early mornings when animals were active. The ride was along the old stagecoach road that had at one time connected Creed and South Fork and, for me, called endorphins into play. Early mornings in the mountains can be like that. I would occasionally see bears down in the river, a porcupine working on a tree, or a startled prairie hen, and there were always small animals scurrying through the brush.

It might be thought that the unusually rigid work expectations were at least offset by decent food, but that was not so. My time ended at Big River when the staff members had lingered over what had been a late breakfast one morning to express thoughts about the menu. Food rotation included a steady diet of greasy ribs flavored with liquid smoke, beef tongue, and beans accompanied by greasy ground beef. The discussion had been overheard by Uncle Mac, sending him into an intolerant huff. He summarily discharged the entire ungrateful staff.

I went on to Alamogordo with Mom and Barbara to join Dad, who had been working at Holloman Air Development Center along with Dr. Thompson. The Thompsons were also moving from College Station to Tempe, where Dr. Thompson's position was to be Arizona State College's dean of the new School of Engineering.

For the summer, Craig Thompson had picked up a job as a construction laborer in the mountains below Ruidoso with Mr. Glenny, an El Paso school teacher who spent summers building crude cabins to sell. He needed additional help, and I was glad for the work, which required the same skills—using a garden rake, shovel, and sometimes a pick—I had already been acquainted with firsthand.

New ventures often included learning experiences of some sort. For that one, I neglected to bring work gloves on my first day, and when Mr. Glenny pointed to a spot where he needed a septic tank dug, I set to work in what was no ordinary soil—it was near-solid rock. By the end of the day, the tank was dug, and my hands were a mass of broken blisters. The following day, I had gloves when I showed up for work.

I finished the summer with Mr. Glenny and his Ruidoso-area mountain cabin developments, then prepared for the trip to Arizona.

## CHAPTER SEVEN

# Tempe High School

*So here we are, just three years out of Los Alamos, on our way to Tempe.*

We left Alamogordo for Phoenix early on a Saturday morning, Mom and Barbara in one car and Dad, me, and a cage full of parakeets in our Chevrolet pickup. Dad and I had enthusiastically latched on to an idea to raise parakeets for sale—or maybe just raise them as a hobby—so we had acquired a few in Juarez, Mexico, as starters.

Our Phoenix arrival was on the sort of August day that stimulates wondering what one is doing there. The weather in Tempe, Arizona, was considerably different than in College Station. Natives claimed it was a "dry heat." True enough; it was also hot as hell.

The motel we checked into on Van Buren Street was pleasant—it was air-conditioned and had a swimming pool! The location on what was then called "Motel Row" was close to Tempe and the Arizona State College campus. First impressions of Phoenix by a small-town boy from Texas were mixed.

Most impressive were the palm trees that seemed to be everywhere. I'd been exposed to palm trees during the California

235

Jamboree, but this was my first time seeing them in such abundance. It was the most exotic landscape I'd ever seen—nothing like East Texas's forests.

It seemed every other block had a fruit stand selling everything, including dates and cherry juice by the glass or gallon jug.

But nothing seemed as unique as the prevalent irrigation ditches with running water along most streets. I was told some were once part of the Hohokam Native American Salt River Valley culture, used in irrigating their crops. Now, a supplemented canal system delivered water to citrus orchards and residential housing developments throughout the metropolitan area. Even more impressive, commercial and residential landscapes were mostly watered by irrigation. Flood watering citrus groves made sense. But flood watering lawns? That was new.

Most disconcerting was Tempe's water. Compared to what we had left in Texas, a high alkali content made Tempe's water seem nearly undrinkable.

Open ditches with running water meant mosquitoes. To mitigate the problem, city employees in Jeeps with fogging machines mounted on the back would drive along canals, pumping out dense clouds of insecticide, which affected everyone, including the mosquitoes. The fogging formula was DDT—later abolished in use for its frightful effect on the environment.

The Phoenix metropolitan area was about to become the first town of substantial size we had lived in. Los Alamos had a population of 10,000; College Station's was 4,500. Phoenix was going to take some getting used to. Then, I discovered the cities of Mesa and Phoenix were only of fair size—not particularly large as cities went. The rest of the metropolitan area was a mix of thirteen loosely connected small towns that, added together, had a population totaling 353,000.

We moved into a recently completed home one block from the Tempe Union High School campus; almost immediately, I was registered and attending classes. And shortly after, I signed up for football. Six weeks into our schedule, I broke my leg and was one of three who broke their legs in practice that week.

The break was low, near my left ankle, but the cast extended from near the tips of my toes to near the top of my thigh. For four months, crutches were an inconvenient substitute for walking, but I wasn't prepared for the appearance of a seriously shriveled leg when the cast came off and wasn't sure what to do about it. Physical therapy had not yet come into significant use. We were simply on our own to work back into our previous physical condition the best we could.

What I wanted at that point was a car. That required means. And for that, I needed a job. Dad was head of Arizona State's physical operations. Consequently, he was able to pull some strings for me to get an after-school and weekend busboy job at Arizona State's coffee shop, the Devil's Den. Before long, I was a soda jerk, then grill man. And I was saving money.

Then, I spotted a car to covet—a 1934 Ford five-window coupe. The coupe was no ordinary 1934 Ford. This one had red-and-white Naugahyde-covered seats, Studebaker moon hubcaps, teardrop taillights, and a shocking pink paint job. The car really stood out. It was owned by a mechanic who needed money, and I had just enough to satisfy his price—$350. But its distinctively notable appearance had its downside.

Shortly after acquiring my prize, I was pulled over by a Tempe policeman. In looking over my Texas driver's license and discovering my age was fifteen, he confiscated the license, informing me that Arizona's driving age was sixteen. I recognized that since it wasn't legal for me to drive, I would have to be more careful.

The next time I drove, to avoid attracting attention, I remained on side streets until I turned into an alley to turn around. When I turned to look before backing onto the street, a police car was stopped, waiting innocently in the street with a clear plan to ambush me as soon as I backed out. I used a wave of the hand for him to move on, and he, in turn, motioned for me to come out.

In another of my less-than-fine-moments, the fateful decision I made was to become Burt Reynolds as the Bandit and run from the officer like he was Sheriff Buford T. Justice. The surprise move when I took off down the alley was decidedly to my advantage. Before the officer could get off the street and after me, I was making excellent time down the alley toward a car coming from the opposite direction.

Backyard fences along both sides of the alley left no room to pass—except for one. The other car and I arrived simultaneously at the only house on that alley without a backyard fence. I took the opportunity and drove around the other driver into the convenient yard and back into the alley, leaving the startled driver to deal with the now thoroughly aroused officer to work out his next move while I was putting some distance between me and the problem.

By the time the policeman recovered pursuit, I had doubled back on the next street over and was traveling in the opposite direction. When the policeman saw where I was going, I turned into the next alley and doubled back on that one. I was near home and had lost the officer. The chase ended when I pulled into our backyard and covered the car with a tarp.

Having achieved instant notoriety, I decided to keep the cover in place for a while before driving again. But after giving some thought to my options for a few weeks, selling my high-profile '34 to a classmate, Dave Carraway, seemed the best. The sale money was applied to the purchase of a 1950 Ford. Carraway was left to deal with whatever the circumstances might become. I felt that was okay; Dave's father worked as a dispatcher at the Tempe Police Department.

The 1950 Ford was a rolling money pit. During much of the rest of high school, I was required to work just to keep the car running. Henry Ford's cars were not built to accommodate a teenager's enthusiastic driving habits.

Among my first actions was installing a set of Smitty steel-pack mufflers. In combination with the Ford flathead V-8 engine, excellent sound was achievable with proper attention to the rate of acceleration. For this Ford, I did have a valid Arizona license and was driving legitimately, if still more to the liking of a sixteen-year-old driver than traffic law enforcement preferences called for.

My junior year of football proved my left ankle still wasn't up to taking the stress. After a few weeks of bench-warming, I went back to work at the Devil's Den after school and on weekends. During that time, my pal Ralph Flores and I sanded down my car to prepare it for repainting. Ralph's father's occupation was painting cars, and he graciously offered to paint my car at no charge. The Cadillac color I chose combined a sky-blue appearance with a pinkish tint. I loved that color.

Meanwhile, Dad was working directly with Doctor Gammage as the president's right hand. And Doctor Gammage had continued to expand Dad's role in managing school affairs as they related to the physical plant until they eventually became more than seemed reasonable. Dad's frustrations were clarified when looking back at his role with the school a number of years later:

> *The Arizona State College (which in fall 1958 became University) assignment was ever-expanding. I hardly knew what the president really wanted before he placed me in charge of university planning (along with my other assignments, including new dormitories development and oversight of all buildings and utilities.) And he continued to add new responsibilities that he wanted me to supervise.*
>
> *And finally, it was decided that he wanted me to move onto the campus next to him so that I could "assist him with the campus's pressing needs" and "really have a feel for what the University's building program needed."*

The house we moved into was built in 1895. A basement of the sort that in scary movies housed unspeakable creatures of malevolent intent was included, along with an only slightly less creepy attic. The creepy attic became my room on one side and an ironing area for Mom on the other.

Doctor Gammage was getting his money's worth from Dad; then came what was probably the final straw:

*And shortly after that, I became responsible for liaison with the student council, pom-pom girls, and chief of the campus police, etc.*

One benefit of the move to that house was that it prompted us to build a backyard aviary for the parakeet-breeding venture. I joined the American Budgerigar Society and was banding the chicks as they hatched. For what, I'm not sure. While my experience as an entrepreneur was limited, I enjoyed working with those colorful little birds.

I often drove out to the Hi Jolly bird farm in East Mesa and another breeding facility on Phoenix's west side. Both had a wide variety of colors and types of parakeets. The west side facility was owned by a disagreeable character who raised birds for sale through pet stores and wouldn't give me the time of day when I offered to buy any of his birds. During that period, I took one of the parakeet chicks I had raised into the house to make a pet.

When acquired sufficiently early in their development, parakeets can be considerably affectionate little characters. And that one became my little buddy. He lived in an open cage in my room upstairs, leaving him free to come and go. When I walked into the room, he would fly over and land on my shoulder and often stay there until I had to shoo him away. If I tried to nap, he would stand on my ear, chirping to wake me up.

Then, one night when I was out, he was attracted to sounds downstairs. It was dark, and he ended up on the stairway, drawing my dog Pat's attention. It was a sudden ending to my little friend.

I did sell a few of that little bird's brothers and sisters, but sales were mostly limited to our next-door neighbor, who gave them to her grandchildren. I found that I resented selling the birds, ending the idea of it being a business venture. It was a hobby.

The house included an ancient, dirt-floored, tin-covered, free-standing garage, which served for me to have a place to pull my car's engine to be rebuilt. With the upgraded engine, the car was quick, but the Ford's drivetrain was notably inadequate to the task. Along with assorted other mechanical issues, three transmissions were dropped, actually destroyed, along with one broken axle over the next couple of years. There was more.

The Ford's crushingly apparent quality deficiency reached its zenith on a Saturday night. Three of us were in the front seat, and the car was stopped on a slight upward grade leading onto Apache Boulevard, Tempe's main traffic thorough-fare connecting with Mesa. We left the stop sign in a no-more-impressive-than-usual manner, but the well-executed second gear resulted in too much strain on the front seat mounts, which let go, dumping the three of us into the backseat.

With six legs pointing at the ceiling in the backseat, the car barreling down Apache Boulevard with no driver was in need of immediate attention. In such a moment, the need to discuss how to coordinate the effort for getting righted isn't necessary. Following that act of self-preservation, my driving for the rest of that night was more subdued and, at times, downright athletic.

In hindsight, awarding a driver's license to sixteen-year-old animals full of raging hormones was probably not a good idea. There were mitigating factors. One, and probably most important, being that relationships between teenagers and police officers during the '50s were remarkably different from today's police interactions. For the most part, police in the '50s were formerly tough kids who became policemen after having been a bit rowdy themselves. That often worked in our favor.

An example occurred one afternoon while leaving school when I was in a line of cars behind two friends. My buddy Gilbert in his 1955 Ford Fairlane left in a particularly excellent fashion, followed by Allen White in his 1950 Mercury's equally impressive departure. None of us had seen the perfectly apparent police car parked directly in front of the school. As a result, when Gilbert then Alan roared by, the thoroughly agitated policeman came flying out of his car, furiously waving his arms for me to pull over. Adding to the moment's drama, I had just achieved breaking the tires in high gear, following having also achieved an impressive second gear.

"I ought to *kick your ass!*" The greeting was clear enough but was made more so by the fact that the policeman was Benny Hinds. Officer Hinds was a Tempe high graduate from several years prior and was known to have been a real badass. I was contrite.

After a scorching dressing down, I left, having given Officer Hinds my assurances that I would not trouble him like that again. I became friends with him a few years later when he was an assistant bank manager and I was managing a pizza parlor nearby while I was in college.

In 1955, Phoenix's only indoor theater was the Paramount. The Paramount had originally been one of a former chain of ornate theaters created for the vaudeville circuit under the Orpheum name.

Completed in 1927 as a 1,364-seat palace with elaborate interior features, including murals, carved moldings, and a vaulted ceiling with twinkling stars and a moving cloud bank, it created a feeling of watching a film outside. The Orpheum was the sort of place I could imagine a pipe organ entertaining theatergoers in past times. Phoenix's Paramount didn't have that sort of luxury, but the Paramount maintained dominance as Phoenix's only theater until 1956 when the Palms Theater was added.

A few other theaters were scattered around the metropolitan area: Scottsdale's Kiva theater had the latest in art films such as *The Immoral Mr. Teas* and *Deep Throat*; Mesa and Tempe each had theaters, both of which were small, old, and mostly tattered; and if those theaters didn't appeal, there was the Northern Drive-In Theater on Seventh Street.

I don't know if there was a time best described as film's heyday, but we did have some splashy musicals, crazy-fun kinds of comedies, a few romantic films, some excellent mysteries, science fiction, and, like in College Station, lots of Westerns starring John Wayne. Some of the more memorable science fiction movies included *The Blob*, *The Day the Earth Stood Still*, and one of my all-time favorites, *Forbidden Planet*, starring Walter Pidgeon.

But going to the movies in Tempe was not social, except on a date. Instead, on Friday or Saturday nights when I wasn't working, a group of us were more likely to get a card game going. We became so hooked on playing hearts that card activities often extended to both weekend nights and even sometimes Sunday afternoons. The games we played were whatever came to mind. I don't remember the names of all of them, but, in addition to hearts, smoke, smear, and rummy come to mind.

Often the game would be at Esther Mariassy's house. Esther and I had become friends through a former girlfriend I had dated who was best friends with Esther at St. Mary's High School. There would sometimes be five or six of us at Esther's on a Saturday night. Likely more than once, we overstayed our welcome. Thanks to a tolerant Mrs. Mariassy, we were never kicked out.

Most of us had occasional dates, but a card game of just about any kind was just as much to our liking. Once, when the night of cards was at my house in my room, I'd had all the cards I could handle and went to bed around midnight. I awoke at

6:00 a.m. to find that the game was still on. Like eating peanuts, there were times when it was hard to quit.

Then, sometime during our senior year, folk music at Scottsdale's Baboquivari coffeehouse caught our attention. Loy Clingman, a former cowboy singer, owned the Baboquivari and was the featured singer most of the time. But Dolan Ellis, who later became a member of Randy Spark's New Christy Minstrels folk singing group, was our favorite. There was no cover charge for the Baboquivari; we just bought a fruit juice of some kind and could stay all night.

Scottsdale's motto during that time was "The West's Most Western Town." To celebrate, the town held an annual rodeo along with a parade and Saturday night closure of Scottsdale Road for a street dance. Plenty of Coors was served up, flowing particularly freely at the Pink Pony, then located at the corner of Scottsdale Road and Stetson Drive.

The Pink Pony bar was ten-deep with celebratory types, so ordering a beer only required passing the request, along with a couple of dollars, through the crowd to the bartender, who then passed the beer back to whoever had placed the order. I had not yet developed a taste for beer, but the opportunity to give it a try was too enticing; I took advantage and decided to return to the dance.

Coors in hand, I left to return to the street and walked straight into a deputy sheriff. I don't know which was more surprising: a direct encounter with bad news written all over it or the deputy's order to "get back in there with that!" Turned out, I liked Coors.

In 1955 when Walt Disney opened Disneyland on sixty acres in the town of Anaheim, its success was immediate. And I wanted to see it. My first Disneyland trip was with a friend in the summer of 1957, between my high school junior and senior years. Disneyland was a primitive but recognizable version of the wonder it was to become: Main Street, Sleeping Beauty Castle, Fantasyland, the steam train that encircles the park, the Jungle Cruise, and more were all there.

Having used up our "A" ride tickets, we were still looking for something to do that didn't cost money. Then came inspiration! There it was; there were no impediments to entering and exploring the Jungle Cruise's jungle. And our jungle exploration naturally led to assisting Disney creatures by making jungle sounds to increase the passing boat rider's pleasure. The activity lasted for a few minutes before we were invited by a couple of security types to join them on a trip to Disneyland's security office (to this day, still located near Disneyland's main entry above Main Street). Our visit with security, consistent with what one might expect of Disneyland, was courteous but concluded with a pointed request not to do that sort of thing again.

Work that summer, extending to Saturdays during the school year, was with Arizona State's maintenance department, doing whatever was needed but mostly cleaning and preparing dorms for when school started again. It was a time when air-conditioning was not a luxury attributed to Arizona State's buildings. Use of swamp coolers required an annual changing of excelsior cooler pads and scraping accumulated mineral deposits from cooler interiors.

I worked on swamp coolers for several weeks without encountering any difficulties until, one day, I encountered a third-floor unit on "Old Main," which had once been the administration building when the school was Arizona State Teacher's College. OSHA was not yet dealing with rules relating to job safety, so the cooler was reached through opening a window, then leaning out to grab a platform composed of a two-by-six plank on a metal frame.

My respect for heights enhanced the struggle to position myself on the platform. Then, when I leaned forward to scrape the cooler's interior, the unsecured two by six rocked forward, dumping me off and leaving me hanging from a cooler frame three stories above the ground.

It's surprising the kind of strength such a circumstance gives a person. I pulled myself up and repositioned myself more carefully on the two-by-six platform nearly instantly, sporting a heart rate something near the maximum allowable limit. I serviced the unit and returned to the building's interior intact. The experience remained with me for several days.

That fall, General Electric installed a computer center on the college's campus, and Dad coordinated the installation. Looking at Dad's notes regarding the timing of the computer center's installation, it was entirely serendipity. Inspiration was once again redirecting his enthusiasms:

> Then, in early 1957, I was asked to assist General Electric in setting up its on-campus organization until its Deer Valley plant was completed. Setup included an IBM 704, the

*latest in computer technology and which had just been intro-*
*duced to the market. I had particular interest as a result of my*
*activity at Los Alamos, then at the Holloman Air Develop-*
*ment Center.*

Helping with General Electric's campus setup was clearly another very lucky break for Dad, and he had taken full advantage to both pick the IBM installer's brains and also impress GE's computer people with his knowledge and likely his enthusiasm for what they were doing:

*My work with the General Electric group ended up being*
*very close, resulting in their offer of a position to join their*
*new computer manufacturing department. I felt the salary*
*and new challenge could not be overlooked, so I accepted Gen-*
*eral Electric's offer.*

With the move to General Electric, we returned to our house near the high school, and Dad began his second career in a new technology.

During my senior year of high school, I was the senior class's boy representative to the student council and volunteered to be chairman of the March of Dimes' Teens Against Polio events at Tempe High. For one fundraiser, we received permission to block off the Tempe Bridge, requesting drivers to donate to the March of Dimes to pass. The activity was a considerable success.

Then, suddenly, it was graduation time. And graduation called for a celebration—a road trip that included Disneyland. That time, the trip was with two other graduates: Fred Weber and Larry Bartlett. We did it all—flying Dumbos, the Monsanto all-plastic House of the Future, Jungle Cruise, the Riverboat, all of Main Street, and all of Fantasyland, including the teacups. For three eighteen-year-olds, the teacups called for spinning fast enough to make the other two sick. It worked. We each managed to get the other two sick.

What was most remarkable then about Disneyland was the park's exceptionally like-new appearance. During the sixty years following, my trips to Disneyland have numbered something over fifty times as Carolyn and I have returned with our family—children and grandchildren—then back to just the two of us. The park has transformed itself into one incredible, super-slick, high-tech iteration after another over the years. And, through it all, Disney magic has continued to present a like-new condition every morning when the park reopens for another day of pandemonium.

The trip covered five days, during which we took in just about all that Southern California had to offer. With college to begin in the fall at Arizona State, I needed work, but the 1958 summer job market was limited. After a few days of job searching, I stopped at the Orange Julius, where I was a frequent customer. That Orange Julius was owned by Bernie and Rose, and a short conversation with Bernie was successful; I had a job. Not the sort of job I had hoped for, but it was "good enough."

I worked either in the morning to open or evenings until closing. The work was not what I would have preferred, given a choice, and was not challenging most of the time. But what became apparent was that Bernie and Rose both worked long hours and tended to let their hair down at the end of the day with a few longnecks. Near-nightly top-of-one's-lungs discussions reverberated through the walls of the mobile home they occupied a few yards behind the Orange Julius.

When it sometimes became necessary to summon help when restaurant activity became too busy, a button connected to a buzzer in their trailer would inform them, most often summoning a fully relaxed Rose.

I had been employed for about a month when I was made aware that Bernie had worked a partnership arrangement with an investment group that was going to sponsor two additional Orange Julius locations. But the agreement was made on short notice, and they didn't have enough employees to staff the three locations.

As a result, what began as a forty-hours-a-week job became a seven-days-a-week marathon at twice the number of hours. Days often started with me opening the Phoenix location at 9:00 a.m., followed by driving to the Mesa location where I worked until closing at 12:00 p.m.

When it was time for Arizona State's registration to begin, I was grateful.

## CHAPTER EIGHT

# College—The Single Years

College! It was time to start. Arizona State orientation and registration consumed two weeks of intense activity.

There was a freshman mixer, a rally for changing the name of Arizona State College to Arizona State University, an assembly describing how to find our way around campus, and orientation sessions with professors in our majors. The engineering orientation was held in a chemistry lecture hall, during which we were instructed to look first to the right, then to the left: "Those individuals will not be with you when you graduate." So much for pep talks. "Go get 'em, guys. You can do it!"

Class registration was in alphabetical order except when the order was reversed like this time. Names beginning with "A" were last to register; "Bs" were second to last. Lynn Adams and I had agreed we were going to get some classes together, but, as first-semester freshmen, we were left with slim pickings for classes available to us.

Two years of ROTC, Army or Air Force, were required of all incoming freshman men. Lynn and I both selected Air Force ROTC and left registration to be fitted with our uniforms, where we were instructed about proper maintenance. Shined shoes? Seriously, shined shoes! And properly pressed uniforms? Yes, that too.

Lynn and I did get a couple of classes together, including ROTC. Because we had been last to register, I ended up with two night classes. Engineering drawing was with Lynn, and college algebra wasn't. The rest of my classes were scattered randomly throughout the week. ROTC drills were scheduled on Tuesday and Thursday mornings at 7:30 a.m. On Tuesday morning, while lining up for our first ROTC drill, I met Larry Wilson, my drill element leader.

College was mostly little changed from high school; I was still living at home, a condition that applied to most Tempe High graduates who decided to give college a try. Saturdays still included getting together with high school friends to play touch football. Esther Mariassy had pledged Gamma Phi Beta sorority, so, in place of cards at Esther's house, I now had access to Esther's pledge sisters for Saturday night blind dates.

I had been used to getting by with little attention to study time in high school; college placed a penalty on that behavior. Chemistry had been a favorite high school subject thanks to Mr. Kennedy, a former World War II B-17 pilot and an outstanding teacher. As a result, I found college chemistry to require less study time to get by.

Two weeks after classes began, freshmen were required to write an essay on an assigned topic in English class, though now the subject escapes me. The test exempted eighteen incoming freshmen students from taking English 101 as a requirement. I was among them, so I moved on to second-semester

English. I later learned that a couple of courses during that first semester were designed to weed out freshmen who "weren't meant to be students." Introduction to business was one of those courses.

As an engineering major, I looked down my nose at liberal arts or business school classes, so I mistakenly assumed the course would be a piece of cake. Along with college algebra, introduction to business was one of my first semester's most significant challenges. So much for unsupported hubris. But, despite seriously questionable study habits, I got by. My grade average was a little better than a "gentleman's C," which was one of the more useless terms I learned in college.

While standing in line with Lynn for second-semester registration, I wondered aloud if an exterior door to a classroom included in the basketball gym building where registration was held might be unlocked. I walked over, gave the door a tug, and strolled into registration unopposed. That led to a friendlier second-semester course selection.

Freshman year did not provide a flood of memories, but a couple of ROTC incidents are worth mentioning. I volunteered for the Air Force ROTC Drill Team. I still don't understand what I must have been thinking, but my lack of commitment resulted in me skipping the required number of practices and being summarily dismissed. Then, for a reason equally never understood, I was briefly made a flight leader but found that not particularly to my liking either. My experiment with doing little more than sometimes simply showing up for drill ended with me having no future plans of my own for the military.

Moments of hilarity generally result from spur-of-the-moment surprises. One of those moments came one second semester day. ASU's campus landscaping was, like most of Phoenix, watered by flood irrigation. In an effort to avoid being late for our ROTC class, Lynn and I decided to hop a planter median between the sidewalk and the street curb. It worked for me, but Lynn slipped and stepped into the well-watered median, sinking into ankle-deep mud.

The sucking sound as the mud removed his shoe was accompanied by muddy water instantly rushing in to finish the event. The laugh-out-loud moment as Lynn retrieved the shoe was too much for both of us. We ditched ROTC class.

The rest of the second-semester experience was reasonably bland until Dad mentioned a new turn of events:

*I was with GE for a short time when I was moved into management. It brought about a number of things of which I had been unaware: first, GE had a policy of moving its management from one location to another when they felt the move was a good one. This was evidenced to me in 1959 when I was sent to Redstone Arsenal, the big space facility in Huntsville, Alabama, on a temporary assignment as manager of their contracts. This included the Redstone Arsenal Space Center computer operation.*

Dad's work impressed Wernher von Braun. Doctor von Braun had been the director of Germany's World War II rocket development program at Peenemünde and was now at Redstone Arsenal as director of rocket development for the United States:

*The assignment was to have been for a thirty-day period. But then Doctor von Braun, director of the Space Center, notified GE that he wanted me to stay as manager of the General Electric contract and would not accept a negative response. I really did not want the position because I felt the Huntsville area's lifestyle was too different from what we were used to and the move would be too extreme. But I lost the discussion, and we moved to Huntsville. Turned out, the experience gained there was invaluable.*

It was during the semester's last two weeks when the move was initiated, leaving me to remain in Tempe until I finished the semester. Dad's logic was simple: "Why don't you try to find someplace to stay until school is out." Okay, but where? Through Fred Weber's family's generosity, I finished the semester—term papers and finals—with Fred's family before heading to Huntsville.

Before they left, Dad gave me a Texaco credit card. The consideration had not crossed his mind that I might be overcome by the urge to eat or stop for the night along the way. I mentioned that possibility to him in a telephone call when I was getting ready to leave Tempe. His suggestion was to "add to the charge when you stop to buy gas at a Texaco station to get a little extra cash." A sort of "you'll work it out" answer that more or less implied, "see you when you get here."

Huntsville was 1,638 miles from Phoenix. It was sometime in the afternoon when my last final was over. I left Phoenix soon after and drove until around 11:00 p.m., then I pulled into a down-and-outer motel that looked like it might take the five dollars extra I had added during my last fill-up somewhere in New Mexico. I had the feeling the motel owner would have taken less if I had pressed the issue. That's right; it was that kind of place.

The next morning, I was up early and on my way to Huntsville. The day's travel extended to something over 1,000 miles. And I was about to be provided the sort of *Twilight Zone* experience Rod Serling used to speak of. Somewhere in Mississippi, I noted a road sign indicating the next town of significance to be 154 miles away; then, five minutes later, or so it seemed, I was there. I had no recollection of what I had seen or what had transpired between the two signs. That was my first experience with road hypnosis.

Around 10:00 p.m., I arrived in Huntsville, my cognition meter pegged on empty. While stopped beside the road, trying to make sense of instructions describing how to get to our house in Jones Valley, I was aware a car had pulled up. There was Dad and a friend; they had been out looking for me. Sleep that night came easy.

## Summer in Huntsville, Alabama

The next morning, Dad stuck his head in my room and asked, "Would you mind mowing the backyard after breakfast? The mower is inside the garage." I was happy to do it. When I finally worked up the energy, I confronted what I expected to be a lawn. As a small boy in Texas, a favorite play area had been the "long weeds." Now I was looking at a grown-up version of my old playground.

It was apparent that a few weeks prior, when Mom, Dad, and Barbara had moved into the house, it had been sitting for a while without anyone having fretted over maintaining the backyard. As a small boy, the long weeds had been about up to my waist; these weeds were close to my height. Only now, my height was six foot two.

Proper equipment more nearly required a flamethrower or John Deere tractor; the small rotary mower I found in the garage didn't rise even to the level of "barely adequate for the job." I was just finishing up as Dad was pulling in from work at the end of the day. I had spent most of the day reducing very tall weeds to short weeds, in the process having run over and killed mice and a snake and stirred up a yellowjacket wasp nest.

Yellowjacket wasps were aggressive even when one hadn't disturbed their nest. But add that insult, and they assumed an insect version of going berserk. I can confirm their sting to be vicious and better to be avoided.

Dad had arranged a summer job for me at Redstone Arsenal's Marshall Space Center in their summer intern program. When I showed up for work, I was informed I would be working with the Static Test Tower group, which included the Jupiter and Saturn rockets. The Static Test Tower operation was headed by Eric Kauschig, a German engineer who had worked at Peenemünde, Germany, in Hitler's rocket program, headed by Wernher von Braun. Along with Doctor von Braun, Eric Kauschig had been recruited, along with other former Peenemünde engineers, to work on the United States' rocket program.

The Static Test Tower was the most interesting of my summer jobs during my college years. That summer, I participated in several thunderous Jupiter rocket engine test firings, followed by evaluating the engines' performance. The Static Test Tower included an internal elevator to the top. There, a door opened onto an open metal grating that provided a clear, straight-down view of the ground 176 feet below. That sight, followed by walking out onto the grating, always resulted in quite a thrill, no matter how many times I experienced it.

I was, along with the engineers and technicians, in the safety of the blockhouse control center for all but one of the Jupiter's firings. The mechanics who worked on the Jupiter had invited me to join them as they stood thirty-five yards in the open from the Jupiter while it completed a firing cycle of the big Rocketdyne F-1 engine. There are no adequate means to accurately communicate how devastating the sound of one of those engines firing can be.

The engine started with a small flame ignited by a hypergolic (self-igniting) solution, which appeared to drop quietly from the flame screen, followed instantly by a monstrous explosion as the five-thousand-horsepower liquid oxygen and rocket propellant pumps powered up and the engine hit "mainstage," its maximum output. Decibel levels reached an ear-damaging extreme; the pressure from the shockwaves vibrating my chest felt equivalent to being directly next to a bomb detonation, extending in an explosive stream lasting forty seconds that seemed like five minutes until engine shutdown.

Once, a tour of the facilities and test demonstration of a Jupiter firing was conducted for the initial astronaut group, some of whom were to one day make a moon landing. I didn't know the group since they had only recently been selected. But Doctor von Braun was acquainting them with the Saturn first-stage rocket, which was mounted on the opposite side of the test tower from the Jupiter.

On July 20, 1968, the Saturn would boost three of them on a trip that would have Neil Armstrong and Buzz Aldrin land on the moon.

I was at the top of the test tower when three of the Mercury Seven astronauts came up. Gus Grissom's eyes were saucer-sized when the door opened and he was asked to step out onto the metal grating. Turned out, not even the astronauts were immune to the respect for heights.

For weekend recreation, I developed friendships with a couple of other student interns that summer. I spent several Saturdays with one of them at Guntersville Lake, one of the TVA lakes near the Tennessee border. We would swim across the lake and back, then work on a tan. It was a little freaky swimming among snapping turtles and water moccasins, both of which could be seen swimming nearby as just their heads poked out of the water's surface.

The other Static Test Tower office intern was attending Georgia Tech on the quarter system and worked at Redstone Arsenal during alternating quarters with school. We also got together occasionally on weekends and once dropped into a curiosity shop where we were attracted to an unusual delicacy of insects—ants, grasshoppers, and caterpillars—encased in milk chocolate and pleasingly wrapped in gold foil.

Dick tried a couple of those delicacies and acquired a box. I turned down his offer to try one. Insects, even of the chocolate-covered variety, hadn't yet risen to a level required to be included among my food preferences.

On Monday morning, out of politeness, Dick offered our office secretary, Nelly, one of the chocolates. To my surprise, she took one. I was impressed; Nelly was a seriously good sport! Then, without explanation, she flew out of the office like a startled covey of quail. Half an hour later, she returned to provide Dick a top-of-lung explanation of her displeasure for such a gross act of trickery. Turned out Nelly had not included chocolate-covered bugs on her list of delights either.

To Nelly, insects covered with chocolate weren't real. That was until she saw the other half of the chocolate-covered morsel she had just crunched. Nelly's impressive gag response had launched her out of her secretarial chair and down the hall to the girl's room. Having barely made it, the caterpillar and everything else she'd had that morning and probably the past week were hurled violently into sweet oblivion. The process had required several repetitions of bug regurgitation during most of the half hour she was away. I was glad not to have tried one or to have been the one who offered her the sample.

In mid-August, it was time to return to Tempe for ASU's fall semester and my sophomore year. My intent was to drive the 765 miles to Houston in one day, where I would stay with my cousin Buddy and Aunt Louise and spend some time with my grandparents, who now lived in Houston. Pa had been diagnosed with late-stage prostate cancer, and I was happy to be able to spend some time with him and MeMama, as well as with Buddy and cousins David and John Brock, before tackling the 1,175 miles to Tempe.

### Return to ASU—First Semester, Sophomore Year

Houston to Phoenix in one day was a challenge; my second encounter with road hypnosis was near El Paso. I was driving on what, by then, was automatic pilot when a near-miss with a car traveling the opposite direction woke me from my trance. The drive to Tempe was finished with a feeling of gratitude for having arrived in one piece.

Sophomore year began with a new experience—dorm living. Check-in was enlightening. My roommate was a decent guy, but we had little in common other than we would be sharing an eight-by-ten-foot room for a semester. "Want a shower?"

"Down the hall."

My view of the whole thing was grim, made more so by near-nonstop hallway noise, adrenaline-fueled by my fellow dorm dwellers' excitement for returning to school after being off for the summer. The effect was immediate: I wanted out of there.

I had made friends the year prior with Larry Wilson, my ROTC Element Leader. Larry had then invited me to drop by the Delta Sigma Phi house, but living at home had stanched my enthusiasm for fraternity life. Now, there I was, enthusiastically signing up for the fraternity rush.

I indicated an interest in Delta Sigma Phi on the rush sign-up form. Then, while attending my first Delta Sigma Phi rush event, I ran into Bill Druke. He had handled my application at rush sign-ups and had already, along with Larry, put in a few words for me.

I liked the Delta Sigs immediately but also was attracted to Alpha Tau Omega, which included my high school classmate Harry Mitchell. Harry pressed me to pledge ATO, and I enthusiastically agreed. But, during my discussions with fraternities, I had insisted that if I were going to pledge, I would like to have a room in the fraternity house—I still can't believe the arrogance—when only five fraternity houses on what was called "fraternity row" had that option. I liked two of them—ATO and Delta Sigma Phi—so I was on the right track.

The next day, Delta Sigma Phi called; they had a room for me. The room I was to share was large in comparison to my dorm room, and I shared a bathroom with the room next door. Even better, Von Dutch, a California legend in custom car striping, had pinstriped the room while he had been a Delta Sig pledge. Von Dutch had returned to California without having become active, but the room came with the custom striping he was famous for, along with bright-red bedspreads and a custom gray wall color.

The challenge of pledging a fraternity and carrying an engineering class load at the same time was quick to assert itself. Every Saturday was a workday, requiring that pledges were obligated to clean the fraternity house. Most distractions were entertaining and unending, and pledge participation in intramural athletics was mandatory. And there were parties. That semester, I participated in intramural football, ran in a cross-country event, and placed third in the shot put in intramural track.

A disadvantage of living in the fraternity house as a pledge was that our hindquarters were available for any active member in the mood to give us a swat, prefaced by, "Go get me a paddle."

A swat required the receiver to enthusiastically shake the swatter's hand while gratefully requesting, "Thank you, sir. May I have another?"

During my pledge semester, the adjacent room was occupied by two actives—Mike Tiffany and Dave Moynahan. Moynahan was a part-time Turf Paradise horse racetrack pari-mutuel clerk; consequently, he came in late several nights of the week, often after a few beers. One day, the opportunity was too much to resist: I short-sheeted his bed. That evening, when attempting to crawl into bed, Moynahan discovered the alterations to his comfort; his howls of displeasure were followed by every pledge in the house being lined up in the hall for swats.

Moynahan was short-sheeted a couple of times more before my pal and pledge brother Ray Taylor grabbed me after one of our swat sessions and said, "Brock, dammit, cut it out. I'm tired of being drug out of bed in the middle of the night to have my ass beat." To my pledge brothers' credit, no one ever ratted me out.

My grades that semester were insufficient to allow me to transition from pledge to active status. Fortunately, my prior semester grade point average qualified. That led to hell week—four days and nights of no sleep and nonstop harassment as we participated in one sadistic activity after another. On the second day into hell week, after a sleepless night, I awoke in calculus class hanging upside down out of my desk. The professor's perplexed expression as he gazed upon my pathetic position convinced me to skip the rest of my classes until we were through with initiation.

Hell week involved a collection of interesting experiences, one of which was a "square meal" during which initiates were seated in our fraternity house dining room at a long table, each initiate directly across from a pledge brother. As we were all reasonably starved, the meal, prepared especially for us, seemed agreeable—meatloaf, mashed potatoes, and green beans. We were instructed to look directly into the eyes of the person across the table while raising the utensil straight up and then straight toward our mouth in a suitably squared-off fashion.

The particular meatloaf we were served deserved an honorable mention. Louie, the fraternity's female cook, made her version of meatloaf on Thursdays, resulting in excellent savings in food costs to the fraternity. Louie's meatloaf was borderline inedible and so well-known, it was given a name: "Louie loaf."

Most of the brothers found some other place to have dinner on Thursdays.

When instructions were over, we were invited to eat. And we were all so hungry that even Louie loaf sounded good. Then, *wait!* The active member standing behind each of us took our plate and, with overstated exclamations about getting things correct, dumped the plate's contents into a baby potty, then thoroughly mixed the contents with the wooden spoon that had now replaced the silverware.

Once again, looking directly at the person opposite, we each reached straight out, then down to the potty for a spoonful of the new supper, then raised the spoon in a proper straight line to return it to our mouths, all the while keeping our eyes locked with the person across. While the square meal was in process, actives were assisting us, adding A.1. Sauce and plenty of Tabasco sauce as additional flavorings to add to our dining pleasure but leaving several participants gagging.

Ron Tankersley, my dinner partner, was performing in proper square meal fashion when, suddenly, his eyes doubled in size, and, in one spectacular event, all that he had managed to choke down up until that moment he blew lunch across the table and into my face. Not a drop was wasted on anything else. Hell week had other interesting events, but the square meal's dessert provided the most lasting memory. I would never touch lard topped with A.1 Sauce again.

Initiation finished early Sunday morning; at breakfast, we became Delta Sig active members. The semester ended shortly after that.

A few days later, Ray Taylor and I were having lunch when a couple of the brothers returned to the house after completing their second-semester registrations. They had each acquired an empty cardboard box imprinted with "IBM" from the trash. Each carrying an empty box on his shoulder, they entered registration, set down the boxes, and completed registration in a few minutes. Classic! Ray and I headed straight for registration.

Since the box thing had already been done, we went next door to the Memorial Union Center, picked up a long table, and carried it out the front door and into the registration center next door. The table was left in an aisle, and we registered for our classes.

When student political elections were scheduled toward the end of the second semester, I was a candidate for Associated Men Students vice president and was elected. I was to begin my position in the next year's fall semester.

During my second year in ROTC, Tom Currier, a Delta Sig brother, was my squadron commander. Thanks to Tom, I seldom attended drill and spent even less time on my uniform's fastidious appearance. When the end of the semester came, I only had to participate in "Honors Night," and I was through with ROTC. Honors Night was held on a Friday when pomp and circumstance required ROTC participants to pass in review to recognize individuals receiving their commissions.

My presence in the ranks was notable: shoes with an unmistakable appearance of having been shined by a wire brush, a shirt missing a button, and a uniform that had not been pressed for the entire semester. Then came news that the review was delayed.

Not to miss an opportunity, an ambitious military-type decided that since we would not be marching soon, we would use the time for one more inspection. It was bad news. Demerits counted against our final ROTC semester grade, and I was a walking demerit factory. With options limited, there was only one thing to do—leave.

An inspection required a flight's back element to take two steps backward to open ranks. I added a third step, executed a proper military right turn, and left the field, saluting all in authority I encountered as I left. When I reached the Delta Sig house, I removed my uniform for the last time. It was a good feeling.

Kemp Biddulph became engaged in March; a celebration was naturally in order. A punch of the sort capable of floating sledgehammers was served. Early in the evening, I squatted down with a cup of Green Fog in hand, conversing with Larry Wilson and his girlfriend, Binky. I'd had a couple of cups prior but felt nothing—until I attempted to stand. Instead, falling forward, I spilled most of a half-full cup of Green Fog into Binky's lap. I was then aware I'd had too much, a condition meaning only that I would be having more.

The next morning, I awoke to a cheerful Ron Tankersley's puppy-dog enthusiasm as he said, "Let's go get some breakfast!" I had already determined that most Maricopa County hospital patients felt better than I did at that moment. My protests—my teeth itched, and I was too near death to get out of bed—were insufficient. Tank's insistence won out.

I don't recall what I ordered, but Tank chose pancakes. And when they arrived, he buried them in blueberry syrup. Before he could begin to attack his breakfast delight, I was on my hands and knees in the parking lot. Anything that might have been left in my stomach after the engagement party now belonged to the Huddle restaurant's parking lot.

The engagement party wasn't my last experience with Green Fog, but I was more careful after that. Green Fog, a creation of our resident mixologist, Dave Mecke, was a creative combination of Everclear (95 percent pure grain) alcohol, Oso Negro Mexican vodka, and limeade concentrate. It was as deadly a comparison to Kickapoo Joy Juice as likely has been outside a *Li'l Abner* comic strip.

Fraternity life definitely included parties. But there was also dating and just spending time with the brothers. One Saturday night, four of us without dates were discussing what we could do that we hadn't done before. The topic of Miami bordellos was raised: had anyone seen one? It was decided we should go see one for ourselves. Ray Taylor had an Olds '98 and a preference for fast driving. Dick Kilpatrick (Killer) was four years older, a result of a stint in the Navy prior to coming to ASU. As the only one of our group who was the legal age of twenty-one, he acquired the obligatory case of Coors needed for the trip.

Racing through the switchbacks on the two-lane road from Apache Junction to Miami was suitably raucous when, about ten miles outside Miami, we took advantage of an unpaved traffic pullout. The stop turned out to be fortuitous. While standing around the car, taking relief with beer bottles in hand, a highway patrol car came flying around the corner and into the pullout in a blaze of red lights and a cloud of dirt and rocks. Beer bottles went flying.

The 1950s were a time when police were not as concerned about their safety as more current circumstances require. When I ran up to the officer's window, I greeted him with "Hi!" for lack of anything better to say.

The officer responded, "I've been chasing you guys for ten miles."

"Really? We had no idea we were driving that fast."

"Where are you guys going?"

"Oh, just up to Miami."

"You going to the whore house?"

After a slight hesitation, I said, "Yeah."

Then he reached over to his dashboard microphone and said, "You can call off the roadblock. I've got things under control." Then he said to us, "You've got to take it easy on this road, guys. It's really dangerous." He left in a cloud of dirt and rocks as he peeled back onto the road to Miami. It was a time when truly macho types were cops; we had just met one.

We had heard there were two houses of ill repute in Miami—the Keystone Hotel and Top of the World Ranch. The Keystone was easily found as soon as we entered town; it was the only house we saw with a red porch light. Ray led the way. When he knocked, the door was answered by a grandmotherly type of the sort who always won the blue ribbon at the county fair's cake decorating contest. We were at the wrong house! We were already running when she called, "Come in, boys. You have the right place."

There in the living room of the old house was as frightful-looking a group as any Playboy cartoonist ever dreamed up. Okay, that was plenty for Hansen and me. We thanked them and returned to the car to wait while Killer and Ray made some new friends.

The rest of the semester was mostly uneventful. My cousin Penny Roberts was living in Phoenix, and my Aunt Louise had joined her for a few days' visit. When it came time for me to leave for the summer, Aunt Louise decided to keep me company on the ride to Houston. So we could get an early start, I slept on the floor of her motel room that night.

We left at 6:00 a.m.; at 10:00 p.m., fifteen hours later, we pulled into another cheap motel with two rooms available. We had covered something over 1,000 miles; our arrival in Houston was during the next morning before noon. When asked how the trip went, Aunt Louise's response, "I'll never do that again," summed up the answer.

After a brief stopover in Houston visiting cousins and MeMama and Pa, I finished the 765 miles to Huntsville the following day.

For the second summer, Dad had lined up an intern position for me at the Arsenal. This time, I was assigned to the industrial engineering group, where I discovered engineering was not a suitable career move for me. In hindsight, my disillusionment was unreasonably influenced by circumstances. It was government work, and I was working in an office staffed with low-level government engineers. I was informed when I met my new boss that the Redstone lead engineer had recently resigned and that I would fill the vacant position for the summer. The prospect sounded promising.

Then, I discovered that the full scope of the work was to investigate the results of testing a Teflon O-ring in the Redstone engine's hydrogen peroxide system. Aside from the disappointment in not doing something worthwhile, I was informed by other members of the industrial engineering group that I shouldn't worry about not having anything to do; they didn't have anything to do either. I was to make the best of it—a really boring "best of it."

What was worse was, not only was the job totally undemanding, there was nothing else for me to do other than hang out with the other intern, Eike Heuter. Eike was the son of another German engineer who had come to the US from Peenemünde with Wernher von Braun to work on the rocket program. Eike and I joined a gym, and most days after work, we would lift weights for two or three hours. Eike had never done that sort of thing, so he was a good workout partner. He got pretty buff over the course of the summer.

When I had arrived for the summer, a surprise from Dad was that he had acquired a 1956 Chevy for me and would be taking my 1950 Ford as the car he would drive to work. That was a considerably generous and unexpected gift. I guess there must have been some sentimentality attached to it; on the morning I left to return to school, Dad hugged me with tears in his eyes.

I had never seen that from him, and it caught me so off guard I couldn't stop thinking about it for quite some time. Worse, I have often regretted that I didn't say to him, "I love you, Dad." But that wasn't our way, as it had not been Dad's way when growing up. It wasn't that we didn't feel it; it was just that the words were never spoken. And I didn't get used to speaking the words until I met the love of my life, who was to change everything.

### First Semester Junior Year

My return to school from Redstone Arsenal's summer of enlightenment had been a near straight-through drive.

The fraternity house was filled with a lot of *glad-to-be-back*s, so getting celebratory was a requirement. A few pitchers with a few bros at Little Lulu's resulted in Lynn Cereghino wiping out the side of my car with the impressive quantity of Coors he had enjoyed through most of the evening. No problem. Lynn's brother, Warren, did even better a few months later.

The next day, I was interrupted in the middle of a game of ping-pong on our fraternity house patio by an urgent telephone call. John Sampson, Associated Men Students president, was nowhere to be found; I was needed at the freshman men's orientation assembly as the vice president of AMS. When did they need me? "In forty-five minutes."

On my way to the assembly, I was drawing a blank. What to say? What *could* I say? I arrived in time to be ushered to the stage and seated along with Doctor Gammage, the university's president; Gary Walker, the student body president; and the senior Army and Air Force ROTC officers in charge of those entities. Gary was at the podium, wrapping up his comments to the couple of thousand freshman men present when I heard my name being introduced. Showtime! "Wait, I'm not ready!" At least that's what I wanted to say. But no. It was my turn.

Resorting to a stream of clichés, I informed the freshmen that upperclassmen were there to assist them in answering questions they might have as Arizona State's newest class. A "big brother" would provide advice when they needed help. Big brothers were simple enough to find; they would be the ones hustling the little sisters. A couple of laughs loosened me up, and I was able to finish without incurring unnecessary embarrassment.

The freshman men's assembly was my first and last official act as AMS vice president. As titles go, it was a less-than-nothing job. My other nothing organizational position was Interfraternity Council representative for Delta Sigma Phi. Nothing was accomplished in those meetings either.

By prior arrangement, I was to be admitted to fall semester registration as a Pershing Rifles member, the Army ROTC's honorary society. Bob Hanson was a Pershing Rifles member and would vouch for me if challenged. So when a suspicious registration monitor challenged me by surprise, instead of stating I was a Pershing Rifles member, I claimed membership in the Arnold Air Society, the Air Force equivalent to the Pershing Rifles. Oops. Too late for "What I meant to say was . . ." I was escorted to the Arnold Air Society desk, where my former ROTC instructor saved the day. He vouched for me; my early registration string remained unbroken.

Fraternity rush was, as usual, time-consuming, but when completed, we had a decent pledge class and were ready for school to start. Delta Sigma Phi's first social exchange of the new school year was with the Alpha Phi sorority. As usual, a "pig pot" made certain that no girls were left unattended. But the Alpha Phis were an attractive group; the pig pot was unnecessary. Our guests were not shamed by being ignored.

That exchange included an attractive Alpha Phi pledge who caught my eye: Carolyn Bennett, from Fullerton, California. We spent just long enough for me to show her around the fraternity house, including my Von Dutch pinstriped room, and have one slow dance.

At an October Four Freshmen concert, I ran into Lynn Adams while on a date. Lynn was on a double date with Rhett Wilbur and Sue Tanner, also former Tempe high classmates. Lynn introduced me to his date, but I didn't speak with her beyond "nice to meet you." I didn't even pay attention to what she looked like.

Later reminiscences disclosed Lynn's date had been Carolyn Bennett, the girl I had met at the Alpha Phi exchange. I only learned that later when Carolyn mentioned she had been at The Four Freshmen concert with Lynn. She didn't remember me either. So much for love at first sight.

Not long after, Warren Cereghino and I went on a double date to a Delta Sig party and were dropping our dates off where both were staying for the weekend. I had said good night to my date and waited for Warren to complete his more thorough good nights. When he returned to the car, he, in an inebriated state of cluelessness, climbed into the back seat again.

Warren was an early morning disc jockey on radio station KPHO under the pseudonym of Ken Warren. While driving back to the fraternity house, I asked him if he would be doing his usual 6:00 a.m. disc jockey show.

His muttered "you never let your work get in the way of your fun or your fun get in the way of your work" was a considerably more advanced response than I would have been able to agree to at that moment. Then came a telltale retching from the back seat as Warren puked the night's celebratory intake into one of the two depressions in my '56 Chevy's backseat floor.

When we reached the fraternity house, Warren insisted on needing to clean up the puke. He was meticulous; he was also hammered. There was no reasoning with him. It was 2:00 a.m., and I'd had more than enough of an evening. I started toward the house, but Warren had already pulled a garden hose from the side of the house and was in my car, hosing it out.

My first thought when I woke at 9:30 a.m. was picturing Warren in my car with a fully involved garden hose. Warren was cheerfully on the radio, sounding like his usual perky self. His work in my car had dried, and it was totally clean.

### Providence and The Epiphany

Providence struck one October Sunday afternoon.

I was in my room studying when Dave Sorensen, a current Delta Sig pledge, stuck his face in the door and said, "We're going to play touch football with the Alpha Phi pledges. Let's go!" My insistence that study time had already been too lacking for the week fell short of resolve. His persistence, combined with my weakness, won out.

The touch football game was just a ruse to overcome the boredom of a Sunday afternoon. It was all fun; contact beyond playful touching would have been a bad idea. But when I lined up like I was going to knock the two girls in front of me down, each grabbed one of my feet, causing me to land on my knees. Fall was intramural football time, so I had two impressively skinned knees that, until that play, had been scabbed over. Their trick left my knees bleeding profusely down my shins.

"Oh, your poor knees."

It was the redhead who had spoken.

Where had *she* been?

Later, back at the fraternity house, I was told her name was Carolyn Bennett. The Carolyn Bennett I had met at the Alpha Phi exchange. Only now, I had experienced an epiphany and was suddenly smitten.

When I called her for a date to our party that Saturday, she was already busy. No problem. How about Friday? No? Next weekend? No? It was getting frustrating! I decided maybe I would try later.

Friday night, a couple of us decided that the Phi Delta Thetas and the American Standard flush toilet party punch bowl we had heard so much about deserved a visit. We found the Phi

Delt house to be mostly empty, except for one individual who was conveniently occupied with his girlfriend in a back bedroom. In the process of taking the punch bowl, we also discovered what seemed to be a ceremonial sword. We left with both.

The question became how to return them properly with optimum enjoyment. I know! A halftime presentation at next weekend's football game? Perfect! Costumes made of bedsheets were fashioned into something too much like KKK costumes. The concept was in bad taste then and worse today.

At halftime, the toilet/punch bowl was carried in, preceded by me holding the sword upright in proper ceremonial fashion. We had barely entered the stadium when we received a satisfying raise from the crowd but also alerted the Phi Delts, who poured over the wall separating the fans from the track surrounding the field. Abandoning the sword and toilet, we cleared out of the stadium, stopping just long enough to turn and deck one of the Phi Delts in hot pursuit. The rest had remained to guard their treasure until the game was over.

In my continuing pursuit of the reluctant Carolyn Bennett, it was late October, and she was still booked. Maybe it was just that she didn't have time for me. Friday? Tied up. Saturday? Ditto. Next weekend? The same. It was not going well.

I had experienced an epiphany; as a result, I was obsessed with Carolyn Bennett. There was no way I was quitting; I was *going* to get the girl's attention. Then, the indifference barrier was broken; she agreed to let me pick her up when she returned to school from Thanksgiving break.

Our first date was for a Coke at the Huddle restaurant near where Greyhound dropped off passengers. Her return from Thanksgiving break was the opening I had hoped for to slide into her schedule. But it was only a teaser. I was once again rebuffed for further weekend dates but did convince her to be my date to the Delta Sig Christmas formal.

I was so thoroughly hooked by then that the hard-to-get thing was energizing instead of off-putting. A reasonable conclusion for anyone would have become a clear message by then: "Hey, sport, the girl has no interest in you." But my obsession for this girl from Fullerton, California, had only grown stronger.

My sister, Barbara, was in Tempe to finish her high school senior year, living with a friend and her family. As a result, with both of us there, Mom and Dad came to Tempe to spend Christmas. I convinced them that, as long as they were there, it was a good time for us to take a trip to visit Mom's brother, Harry Wood, in California. They agreed, and we surprised Uncle Harry and his ultra-disagreeable wife, Britta, in Sherman Oaks, imposing on them for a place to stay.

Traveling from Sherman Oaks to Fullerton was a distance of forty-two miles. It took seventy minutes of driving time during the best time of day. Since I was on a mission, I saw that as no problem whatsoever. The call to Carolyn was made almost as soon as we arrived. And, staying true to character, she waffled: "I have a term paper that I haven't started, and I can't take any more time off before getting to it. I don't have time to go out."

My mind went into crisis mode. *What?* "No" as an answer was not an option; we *had* to get together. At least, that's what was in my mind. I went into full selling mode, relying on adamant insistence to win out. I picked her up at seven for a seven thirty movie at Fullerton's Fox Theatre. At 11:00 p.m., we said good night.

On rare occasions, Southern California experiences nighttime pea-soup fog; that was one of those nights. When seeing much past the car's hood ornament was out of the question, the condition led to a choice—pull over and spend the night or open the driver's-side door and follow the pavement's white line for navigation.

The return to Sherman Oaks passed through the LA freeway interchange's maze of freeways, which during the day was confusing; when signage was obscured, taking the wrong turnoff to follow the wrong white line was all but guaranteed. I followed the white line until it was apparent my direction was compromised.

At 3:00 a.m., I was parked on the freeway's shoulder, reading a map and trying to assess just how truly lost I was. A deep voice in the style of James Earl Jones said, "Need help?" Startled is the only active word that springs to mind. The time of day, dense fog, and disembodied voice walking along the roadway's shoulder called attention to just how unusual that was.

Regaining composure, I responded in a voice an octave higher than usual. "Why yes, as a matter of fact . . ." The voice turned out to be very helpful, pointing out that I was heading out of town toward San Bernardino. It then directed how to get back in the direction of Sherman Oaks. I never saw the voice's source but assumed it to have been from a guardian angel. I reached Uncle Harry's at 4:00 a.m., five hours after dropping Carolyn off.

It had been worth it.

That was our third date.

Did she have to make it so hard?

I returned to Tempe and the fraternity house the next day.

During my two years living in the fraternity house, I had a couple of roommates, but Dick Kilpatrick was my most memorable. Killer was a part-time pari-mutuel clerk at the Turf Paradise horse racetrack, which often meant his return to the fraternity house was around midnight. Killer had two annoying habits—one was related to his late weekday working hours, and the other was a lazy streak.

Possibly, what appeared to be Killer's laziness was more just being congenitally obtuse. Whatever it was, in the morning, he would remove a shirt from his closet, drop the hanger on the floor, and leave it. A buildup of several days' hangers meant attention to picking them up was often left to me. His late arrival from the track involved turning on the lights with no concern about keeping down the noise. The combination inspired a payback.

After one of his more impressive accumulations, I gathered the hangers and placed them between the sheets at the foot of his bed. Arriving that night in his usual manner, Killer flipped on the lights, got ready for bed, and turned off the lights. I could hardly contain myself. Anticipation of Killer's probable reaction had me ready to explode.

Then, Killer's feet touched the coat hangers, and his response nearly drove him through the wall at the head of his bed. Restraint was over; I erupted. Killer turned over my bed with me in it and began kicking both the bed and me around the room. I was too weak from laughing to do anything to protect myself.

On another occasion, several of us were sitting around in our room making small talk when Killer came in, having imbibed a few brews first. After removing his shirt and pants, he flopped onto his bed on top of the covers and proceeded to snore like a bull. The jockey shorts he was wearing had a slightly open fly, leaving no doubt among the group about what had to be done: half a can of shaving cream filled his shorts, and he never woke. The next morning, Killer must have had a certain curiosity about the event, but nothing was mentioned. He probably thought he'd had some sort of weird but pleasurable dream.

But, once again, I was back to my Carolyn Bennett quest. When we returned to school from Christmas break, an unexplainable change in circumstances had remarkably occurred. I don't have any recollection of how our third date might have made an impression, but Carolyn was now my willing, frequent date to our fraternity parties. And we took a Saturday to go to Flagstaff with my buddy Ray Taylor and one of Carolyn's sorority sisters to play in the snow. Progress was picking up.

Delta Sig parties were often epic. Several years before John Belushi and his *Animal House* costars hit the theaters, Delta Sig had toga parties, desert parties, pajama parties, luaus, parties at the Pulaski Club, parties at the Phoenix Women's Club, and events at any other venue we could pick up. Our favorite band, the Swingin' Blazers, would have made Chuck Berry proud. They were late for one party and, upon investigation, were bailed out of jail after only a forty-five-minute delay. The Blazers never failed to entertain.

A party at Rustler's Rooste, a South Mountain venue, was made more memorable when I engaged in seriously poor judgment and equally poor behavior. I had refreshed Carolyn's drink with bourbon every time she was distracted. I guess I thought it was funny until I panicked when she became near falling-down inebriated. Fortunately, I was able to walk her around and sober her up some before she had to get back to the dorm. She paid a price for my error: she was placed on forced study tables for a week.

One unlucky fraternity brother had passed out at that event, leaving his apparently lonely date to make friends with a few of the brothers in the men's room. For the most part, our parties were nearly always memorable.

That was mid-February, and the two competitors for Carolyn's attention who had given me such grief, a Sigma Nu and an ATO, were history. By mid-March, Carolyn and I were inseparable. In addition to Friday and Saturday night dates, we now shared a bean burro on Sunday nights at Chico's Mexican Restaurant.

Easter was on April 2, and Carolyn invited me to go home with her over Easter break. I accepted. Then, a seriously bad case of cold feet attacked. I wanted out of my commitment. But she was having none of the feeble excuses I made in my attempts to bail on her invitation. Now it was Carolyn who wasn't going to take no for an answer; I went to meet the parents.

Mr. and Mrs. Bennett were down-home, unpretentious people, and I was taken by both. Carolyn's close relationship with her parents, particularly with her father, was apparent. He really loved his daughter. And so did I.

Every hour that could be spent with Carolyn that week was spent with her showing me her favorite Orange County spots during the day. Her overly generous parents took us out to dinner most nights. A tour of their favorite restaurants included The Water Wheel in Anaheim; their favorite Mexican restaurant, La Chiquita; the Charter House in Anaheim; and The Palms, a Polynesian restaurant in Fullerton. The Palms had a particularly capable rum drink: the Lapu Lapu, served in a large snifter with two straws. Carolyn and I left the restaurant in agreement that one of those was plenty.

When we returned to school after that week, I was more hooked than ever. I loved that girl, and she loved me. I wanted to spend every minute with her. Near the end of April, the fraternity serenaded Carolyn and her Alpha Phi sisters as I gave her my fraternity pin. In May, it was mutual; there was no one else. The whirlwind had been just over four months from when we returned from Christmas vacation until we reached a serious conclusion: we were going to be married.

Dad had satisfied Wernher von Braun in that the General Electric computer organization he had built in his two years in Huntsville was satisfactory to the new space program's needs. They had done work in several new fields, including numerical control and flight stimulation, which were primary concerns of the new plans for going to the moon. Conveniently, Dad had now returned to General Electric's Phoenix operation, and Mom and Dad had moved into a home in Tempe. I moved home for the summer.

*In 1958, General Electric sent me to Huntsville, Alabama, to manage their contracts at the space center there. We stayed in Huntsville until GE transferred me back to Phoenix in 1961 to manage their new data processing center.*

A scheduled September wedding left the summer for Carolyn to make plans and for me to find a job and a place to live when school started. The perfect apartment was in an eight-unit property located on the edge of the ASU campus. When I called Mr. Jones, the property owner, he stated his reluctance to rent to students, but I convinced him to meet with me. Our meeting at his impressive central Phoenix home worked; he agreed to rent the available apartment to us.

I had also found a job as a warehouseman at Montgomery Ward's distribution center loading dock. I had the job I needed.

In June, I drove to Fullerton with an engagement ring. A couple of other trips to see Carolyn were made to Fullerton during the summer. Then, it was time.

## CHAPTER NINE

# College—The Married Years

In a perfect rendition of a ceremony spoken in a Scottish accent, Reverend Edward Cadigan presided over our wedding on Friday, September 8, 1961.

Carolyn had chosen the Fullerton Presbyterian Church, and Ray Taylor, Dick Kilpatrick, Bob Hanson, and Doug Gherman—all Delta Sig brothers—and Fred Weber from high school stood up with me. Carolyn's bridesmaids included her pals Judy Lake, Suzanne Streech, Joni Peterson, and my sister, Barbara.

In a stark departure from more current wedding magnificence, the church foyer cake-and-coffee reception completed formalities. Then, we were on our way.

Married life began with a celebratory whiskey sour in the Anaheim Charter House hotel bar. Our first night was spent at the Tropicana, an inexpensive but acceptable motel across from Disneyland's main entrance. The next day, we drove to Santa Barbara's Miramar, a quaint seaside hotel Carolyn had booked based on recommendations from friends who had spent their own honeymoons there.

The Somerset House in nearby Montecito was our first dinner at a nice restaurant. It was also the last dinner at a nice restaurant for several years. Three days later, we returned to Carolyn's parents to spend a couple of days, gather up wedding gifts, then drive on to Tempe. Carolyn's first impression of 102 E. Tenth Street was that she had found "a little playhouse" in Mr. Jones's furnished three-hundred-square-foot, one-bedroom apartment.

My parents had stocked our refrigerator, including a cube steak. Carolyn had not yet achieved status as the excellent cook she was to become, so I cooked the cube steak in proper Texas style—chicken fried—for our first dinner together. It was a reasonable introduction to home cooking as I knew it.

Following registration for classes the next day, I returned to the role of a Montgomery Ward warehouseman, and Carolyn found secretarial work for Doctor Jelinek, a member of ASU's education faculty. Our new routines initially limited social events: we both worked, went to school, and took inactive status from fraternity and sorority life. We tried to continue socializing with Ray Taylor and his girlfriend, Diane Smith, but the chemistry wasn't the same with our change in interests.

My new schedule required classes to begin at 7:30 a.m., followed by time in the library until 11:30 a.m. Work was scheduled on weekdays from 1:00 p.m. until 6:00 p.m. and all day on Saturdays. Study time was shifted from evening hours when I discovered my best results came early—from 4:00 a.m. until time to get ready for class, where I met new friends.

Andy Ryan was seated next to me in my Corporate Financial Management class. His wife, Janet, was a schoolteacher and recent ASU graduate, so rapport as couples was instant.

Andy had attended the University of Arizona a few years prior, had dropped out for a few years, but had returned to ASU after marrying Janet. Through Andy, we met Ed Edwards and his wife, Jane. An old friend of Andy's, Ed, had also returned to school to finish a degree after several years in the Air Force.

Both Andy's and Ed's return to school was supported by their schoolteacher wives. We all had similar positions—we were married to women who were teachers or soon to be a teacher, and all of us were subject to limited economic circumstances.

When I returned to my warehouse job, my new wage was $1.50 an hour. That worked until the end of the Christmas season when a combination of events occurred. First, there was an accident involving a coworker who lost several fingers on his right hand as a result of a faulty forklift safety guard. The problem was that I was the one driving the forklift, and I had no knowledge of the safety guard having been removed earlier in the day.

I wrote up the accident report, but when it was submitted, I was asked if I would like to amend the language, removing the company from responsibility. I chose not to. At the end of the holiday season in January 1962, warehouse crew layoffs included me.

Andy was working as a waiter in Tempe's Pizza Hut and recommended that I speak with the manager regarding a job. I spent the next few months as a waiter, opening the restaurant for business and having pizza for lunch each day.

Carolyn's graduation with an elementary education degree in June came with a second-grade teaching position at

Broadmoor Elementary School, where she had completed her student teaching. The new job had us feeling flush and looking at new cars. A seriously attractive canary-yellow 1961 Chevrolet Impala hardtop was our first big purchase. The car had no air conditioning, resulting in profuse sweating as we drove around Phoenix and when we crossed the desert to visit Southern California. But the look? Attractive.

Our largest prior purchase had been our first television set from a shylock operation presenting itself as a discount appliance store. That acquisition was the most expensive television set we ever owned. We were sold on the fifteen-dollar monthly payment; the length of the contract period was not of concern. We were still paying on that television years later.

My promotion to Pizza Hut's manager in June included a promised bonus in an amount based on a percentage of sales but no less than fifty dollars per month. The percentage bonus never materialized; it became a straight fifty dollars per month regardless of how well we did. But things worked out. The management experience was of considerable value, and I never got tired of eating pizza. When I worked late, I would often take a pizza home to share with Carolyn and sometimes with our neighbors Oscar and Joyce.

Oscar had flunked out of an Eastern school in spectacular style after the first semester, prompting him to spend three years in the Army to regroup. When he returned home after completing his service obligation, he discovered that the once-tomboyish teenage girl next door had grown into an attractive young woman. Oscar married her and decided to take another crack at school. This time, he was a straight-A engineering student.

When the apartment adjacent to ours became available, it was rented by Ted and Sue Bredehoft. Ted was ASU's wrestling coach and needed jobs for his wrestlers, which I accommodated at the Pizza Hut. I didn't realize it at the time, but the Tempe restaurant, as the first Pizza Hut west of the Mississippi, was historic.

One of ASU's wrestlers was the national collegiate champion in the 157-pound class, and he gave me some helpful instructions on wrestling that I took to the intramurals. I pinned my first opponent, then spent the rest of the tournament making my opponents look good.

Ted provided my last registration boost when he arranged for me to enter early under the name of Alex Henderson, who was, at the time, ASU's premier track star in the two-mile event. Alex was tall, had a strong Australian accent, and wore glasses. We couldn't have been more different. But it was my last time using subterfuge to register, so I figured, why not? I went into registration unquestioned for the last time and registered with the privileged group.

With the final semester before graduation coming up, I discovered an available opportunity to work in the Market Research Department of GE's computer plant on Black Canyon Freeway. It was the plant where Dad had recently served as the data processing center manager.

The position sounded like a reasonable resume builder and allowed flexibility to pursue job interviews. The possibility of a sales position in GE's Computer Division was raised by our manager, Pete Scola, but the timing wasn't working out. For the most part, I found the opportunities through Arizona State not suited to what I preferred, and the GE people were dragging their feet in concluding an offer. I learned why later: GE was in the process of closing the division.

During my final semester, I interviewed with several companies, but my enthusiasm for finding a marketing position was contrary to what the companies were looking for. My interviews were for sales positions; consequently, I wasn't enthused about them, and they felt the same about me.

Of the sales positions I considered, IBM had shown the most potential, taking me through several levels of interviews and testing for their computer division. But that didn't work out. A few weeks later, IBM called me regarding an opening in their office products division, which I declined.

In my work in the GE Market Research Department, I discovered that, while IBM was a highly regarded company, they were also highly regimented, dictating how to dress and what sort of car to drive and possibly going to the extent of pressuring wives to uphold the IBM image.

In another interview time waster, I was flown to Los Angeles for an interview with United California Bank, but when I engaged them in conversation about the potential for a marketing position, that wasn't of interest either.

In June 1963, graduation settled it: my ASU on-campus job search had not worked out. My enthusiasm was for marketing, and most positions in sales were well outside the realm of marketing, even for future possibilities. We packed everything we owned into a small U-Haul trailer and headed for California.

CHAPTER TEN

# The Fast 10

In 1961, Congress passed a $1.7 billion 1962 National Aeronautics and Space Administration (NASA) appropriations bill, which included $60 million for a "manned spaceflight laboratory." Under the direction of Robert Gilruth, the new facility was to occupy 1,620 acres of land in an undeveloped area twenty-five miles southeast of Houston, adjacent to Clear Lake near Galveston Bay.

NASA had begun recruiting Dad almost immediately to participate in the manned spaceflight program. As Dad had only recently returned to Phoenix with GE from Huntsville, he was reluctant to make another change. This time, the change was not only geographic but involved a return to government employment:

> *NASA was expanding rapidly, and its space program had grown beyond anyone's imagination. They were going to build a new facility in Houston and began to make contacts with me to manage their data processing and production facility. General Electric management felt that opportunities with GE were considerably better than a position working for the government. But NASA personnel were convincing—*

*what I was being offered was probably the best assignment anyone could ever have the good luck to come by.*

Enough said. The arm-twisting had worked; Dad was convinced:

*We moved to Houston in February 1962.*

Center construction began in April 1962, and it was officially opened in September 1963. By an act of the United States Senate, the center was renamed the Lyndon B. Johnson Space Center (JSC) on February 19, 1973, in honor of US President and Texas native Lyndon B. Johnson.

*My position was director of the computation and analysis division of the manned spacecraft center, and all of us headed for the moon.*

Times were as exciting as anyone might have imagined.

Dad, Mom, Carolyn, and I were beginning ten very active years. For Carolyn and me, there was no letup in life during a time of continual change in careers, family, interests, and personal growth. And Dad's boyhood dream accelerated beyond anything he had ever imagined:

*As a boy, I dreamed of the many things that I wanted to be—an artist, a violinist, or perhaps an archaeologist. But most of all, I wanted to be someone other than the head of a*

*small East Texas farm family. Every step I would take in the
future would be away from that responsibility.*

Realizing his dream had, at every step, come with demands he could not possibly have considered, but, just as assuredly, he would not have changed anything, given the opportunity:

> *The assignment turned out to be the most challenging of
> my professional career; responsibilities of a division chief in
> the computer field include interface duties well beyond that of
> a normal position. One must be responsive to requests for
> speeches, papers related to the computer field, and consulting
> work with the academic community.*

And he would do those things before finally deciding he'd had enough of the demands of such a high-profile position. But that would be a few years from then.

## Graduation and the Move to California

We moved in with Carolyn's mother and father in June 1963. The plan was to "stay a few days" while I found a job; the few days turned out to be a full month.

For Carolyn and me, the living arrangements were stressful. But giving fair consideration to Carolyn's parents, describing the time as stressful for their part had to have been considerably understated. Their small, 1,250-square-foot house was not built to accommodate a crowd. It had been just fine for

Carolyn and the two of them while Carolyn was growing up. But my addition created an imposition, one that almost certainly must have prompted at least a few bedtime discussions between the senior Bennetts, whispered in hushed tones: "How much longer do you think they'll stay?"

My job search had been without a positive result. My objective was a job in marketing, but no one had such a position available—only sales jobs. I wasn't ready to give in to what was being made clearly apparent: aside from the fact I wasn't qualified for a marketing position, I was looking in the wrong places anyway.

I had avoided contacting Hunt-Wesson Foods since my father-in-law, Carol Bennett, was a long-term Hunt-Wesson employee, and I felt the need to avoid potential conflict. But after speaking with a variety of companies, none of which were of interest to me, I decided to at least speak with Hunt.

The Hunt-Wesson interview went well. For the first time, I was informed, "Do well in sales, and, possibly, you can be considered for a marketing position." Good enough; that worked for me. My position improved when I set a high score for applicants on the Wonderlic test.

Interviews with several territory sales managers resulted in me being offered a sales trainee position by Wally Monett, a crusty fifty-two-year-old World War II veteran and no-nonsense type. Wally would one day become one of my most effective mentors as well as become a close friend, but things almost didn't work out that way.

The Fullerton sales office was an open format, and I was seated in a cubicle filling out employment forms when another sales manager came in. Wally stated, "We got Mr. Brock."

The other manager, Ken Smith, said, "What did you get him for?" The silence that followed was deafening as I visualized Wally frantically waving his arms at Ken not to say anything more. But it was too late.

I had been too eager to accept the job at the salary offered. The feeling then was instant dissatisfaction, but I had resolved when I left college that I would not voluntarily leave my first job for at least one year. At that moment, I knew when I would be leaving Hunt-Wesson: exactly one year from that date.

A few minutes later, Al Crosson, Hunt-Wesson's dynamic young national sales manager, came to the district sales office from his office down the street in Hunt-Wesson's corporate tower to introduce himself. I didn't realize the significance of Al taking out time for that until several years later.

My first two weeks as a trainee were spent observing four experienced Hunt-Wesson salesmen. Each had occupied their sales territories for many years and, in the process, had built excellent rapport with their accounts. Watching them in action was entertaining but of little value other than learning a sales call's procedures. Executing a selling presentation was another matter, and I soon found just exactly how much of another matter sales call execution would be.

My first day to begin sales calls started with meeting up with Wally to review what we were going to do that day. My first sales call was on Bandini Market in the City of Commerce.

The store owner listened patiently while I delivered my pitch in a monotone reeking of a hostage tape message. When I was finished, his response was a terse, "No."

I thanked him and returned, actually slunk, back to the car to fill out my call report. Wally held back to apologize for the call's embarrassing ineptness. After what seemed like several minutes, Wally returned to the car and got in without a word spoken. Then, after what seemed like several more minutes of looking straight ahead—it was probably more likely twenty to thirty seconds—a sudden long, noisy inhale through his nose was followed by an explosive, "*Boy, have you got a long way to go!*" So much for the Earl Nightingale school of motivational sales training.

After a proper dressing down for the things I did incorrectly—and there were a lot of them—we moved on to the next sales call. And I improved. In the following call, I improved even more. By the end of the day, I had found a groove, selling to everyone. Wally had fallen asleep after lunch and slept through the finer parts of my first day on the job. But he liked the orders I had written in from some of the afternoon's calls.

By month-end—probably much to my in-laws' delight, though they were too polite to show it—Carolyn had found a job teaching second grade at Garden Grove Elementary School, and we had located a small, 350-square-foot, two-bedroom, one-bath house to move into.

The training territory I was assigned was composed of a collection of small stores, all located in the worst parts of Los Angeles. Watts and East LA were the most challenging, but there were more. When I placed first in the district's sales contest, Wally was chastised by the other sales managers for having sandbagged my quota. He defended vigorously against the accusation.

I was promoted to a full territory that extended from Hollywood into several beach cities. Meanwhile, I also initiated a search for a suitable location for a pizza parlor. I don't know what possessed me, but I began to pursue the goal of opening one almost as soon as I started with Hunt-Wesson. I found a vacant building at the corner of Cherry and Carson in Long Beach. *So now what?* What had seemed easy enough before that point became complicated. And that had not been my only goal—my intent was to be president of a major corporation one day. Both objectives were fueled by the purest of naive audacity.

As soon as I began work in my trainee territory, I found selling in Los Angeles to be as stimulating as I had first discovered it to be with our fifth-grade office supply store. That same enthusiasm continued in my new sales area. My task in the new area was simplified by having followed salesmen who had left behind more than a few unhappy customers in key accounts.

It took a while, but I overcame unhappy account animosities and placed first in the district's sales contest again. This time, it was without grumblings that I had too soft a quota. The outcome once again resulted in a promotion to a larger area focused in the San Fernando Valley.

I was selling during the day and working nights planning the pizza parlor. In the process, I discussed what I was up to with a manager of one of the stores I was calling on and also disclosed to Wally what I was doing. Dick, the grocery manager at Hughes Market, wanted to be part of the venture, as did Wally. Our venture was formed with me, Dick, and Dad as founding shareholders in Seabrook Enterprises, Inc. Wally bought the building and rented it back to us.

Dick quit his job with Hughes to manage the pizza parlor. To assist him, I contacted Bill Vining, who was still working at the Tempe Pizza Hut, and convinced him to join us. Portofino opened for business in November 1964. I was working two jobs: I was selling on weekdays, Monday through Friday, then I was at Portofino on Friday and Saturday nights from 6:00 p.m. until 2:00 a.m. Saturday daytimes were for bill paying and marketing planning and execution before going to work at Portofino again at 6:00 p.m.

Sunday afternoons were spent with Carolyn's parents in Fullerton.

Promotion to the San Fernando Valley territory prompted district sales management to require that we move from Fullerton to Glendale. Carolyn was pregnant, and available apartments were near-nonexistent. Taking the only option we could find, we moved into an apartment community with almost no redeeming qualities except for turning out to be socially interesting. We made acquaintances with several couples, one of whom remained in contact for a lifetime.

On January 25, 1965, a tiny, five-pound-eight-ounce redheaded baby girl, Kimberly Suzanne, was born at Glendale Adventist Hospital. Birth complications resulted in Carolyn hemorrhaging a substantial amount of blood, leaving her too weak to care for herself or a new baby. When she was released from the hospital, she and Kim moved to Fullerton, where Carolyn's mother provided the needed support. I remained in Glendale to deal with work requirements.

At the end of that month, I was thirty pounds lighter. Between my sales job and Portofino, time to see Carolyn and Kim was limited to Sunday afternoons and some Saturdays before going to work at Portofino. That spectacularly brutal month caused me to rethink what I was doing. I still wonder what I had been thinking.

When Carolyn and Kim returned to our Glendale apartment, what had been a considerable challenge before had grown out of proportion. I left for work at Portofino on Fridays and Saturday nights, leaving behind a very unhappy wife in tears. Carolyn was spending time alone in a drudge of an apartment with only Kim to keep her company.

Before leaving for work in my sales accounts every morning, I fed Kim her bottle, often accompanied by some interesting moments, as she was inclined to throw up some of the bottle she had just finished when I placed her on my shoulder to be burped. A couple of times, the result went down my shirt collar. No problem—a cloth diaper draped over my shoulder solved the issue most of the time.

One morning, I left the apartment thinking I was still smelling sour milk, but, checking over my shoulder and seeing nothing, I assumed I was remembering what I had just left. Still, I kept thinking I was smelling sour milk all day, but continual checks to confirm that what I thought I was detecting was only in my imagination revealed my assumption to be correct. Then, I removed my shirt that night: Kimmy had outdone herself that morning.

A diaper had captured a portion, but the rest of her bottle was down my shirt, mid-back to almost my belt line. It was a strange feeling to know that I had spent the entire day on sales calls without anyone saying a word about the unusual cologne I was wearing.

I was still on a roll, placing first in that year's sales contest ending in February. And once again, the success resulted in transferring to a new sales territory. That time, the new area was an experimental format that didn't have a manner of classifying accomplishment. The first sales manager in the new area lasted less than six months before he returned to Northern California, where he had been promoted from salesman to manager. The second manager didn't do much better or last much longer. Both had been newly promoted from salesmen and had some rough edges resulting from management inexperience, a condition that left them both ineffective.

It was soon after that I was presented with a dilemma: I was offered the San Diego territory sales manager position. It was decision time. *Do I continue with the prospect of growing Portofino? Or ante up for a future with Hunt-Wesson sales management?*

Several factors made the decision easier: Dick and I were both burned out on managing Portofino, Carolyn had had more than enough by then, and my little Kim was growing up. There was an opportunity to sell the business to a pizza operator who had another location near the UCLA campus and ambitions to expand. The sale was completed in October. Carolyn, Kim, and I moved into a rented house in the San Diego suburb of Lemon Grove.

My first sales management experience was with two salesmen who were extremely disenchanted with the prior manager and the company and were engaging in long nightly telephone calls, complaining about everything Hunt. The problem partially resolved itself when one of the two resigned to accept a new job three weeks after I arrived. My position reverted to one of calling on accounts as a salesman and acting as a manager over the remaining salesman, a circumstantial equivalent to a violin and harmonica duet. But things worked out.

In May, I was promoted to managing a territory headquartered in Orange County. The new sales area's geography absorbed the San Diego territory and included Orange County and a geographic area extending north into Nevada's Clark County and east to Arizona's border, including Mexican border cities extending from Calexico to Tijuana. Our duration in San Diego had been six months, and it was time to move—this time, to Orange County.

In the meantime, Dad had been building the world's largest computer center for the manned spaceflight program. During a visit to see Mom and Dad in 1966, Dad gave us a tour of the NASA computer facility. I had read about supercomputers and their capabilities, so I was impressed by the names included in the center's array—Cray, CDC (Control Data

Corporation) 6600s, and IBM 7094s. Not just one or two of each but seemingly dozens.

**Center:** Gene Brock in Building 12 - Manned Spacecraft Center 1964

All were programmed to make use of distributed computing, a form of functional programming that allowed a problem to be described mathematically, then let the computer system's components determine how to break up tasks and run them in parallel, allowing all of them to be working at one time on the same problem. I would remember that tour years later when I began my own flirtation with computers.

When we returned from our visit with Mom and Dad we moved from San Diego to Tustin in Orange County. Our Tustin move was to a townhouse, ending our experiment with single-family home rental.

The townhouse was considerably more socially attractive than our Lemon Grove rental had been. The Lemon Grove single-family home was an experiment that sounded good at the time but turned out to be lonely for Carolyn. In Tustin, there was considerable social activity for Carolyn and Kim during the day. We made friends with several couples, all of whom became close and who remained long-term friends.

The new territory's challenge was declining sales and chronic turnover. Those were fixable. But circumstances included another more challenging aspect: a member of the Orange County sales group, Harry Kentopian, had been one of my trainers just over three years prior. And Harry was not happy with the announcement that I would be his new manager.

In a lame attempt to mitigate the problem, I acknowledged Harry's professionalism, experience, and leadership value, emphasizing that I would only expect him to be the area's top salesman. It took a while for him to develop trust in me, but Harry eventually came around and became one of my much-appreciated advocates.

Within a short time with the new sales group, it became evident that two of Orange County territory's salesmen had not been doing their job. Their replacements, a couple of young guys in possession of the enthusiasm I was looking for, were quick to pick up the slack.

In March 1967, our sales group was announced to have placed second nationally in the annual sales contest. In August, I was transferred to San Francisco as Northern California territory sales manager, and we moved into a Walnut Creek townhouse community.

I had been warned that declining sales and excessive sales organization turnover were issues, exactly as I had encountered in the Orange County territory. Only this time, my attempts to identify where the problems were located were met with considerable frustration. It seemed that whatever I was going to discuss with a salesman, such as a performance review, was already known ahead of our meeting.

A key account salesman left the company during the annual sales contest, so I once again took on key account sales along with managing the territory's sales organization. With some coaching, sales activity picked up among most of the others. I discovered a partial answer to the turnover issue when I found that one of the old hands with the company, a salesman in the adjacent sales territory covering central California, had made a point of pulling aside new recruits to warn them: "Get out of here while you can. We're stuck, but you don't have to be."

This individual should have been terminated long before since he was notable for his lack of success in his own sales activity. But that disclosure didn't seem enough to account for the turnover rate in the territory I was managing. There had to be something else.

Then came a breakthrough. I was spending the day working with one of my salesmen who clearly seemed to have something on his mind but was reluctant to say it. With a bit of cajoling, he disclosed the problem: a salesman in our group had been ostentatiously living with the office's secretary. She was passing along confidential information to him, and, in a display of self-importance, he was keeping the other salesmen informed.

I had not found pleasure in terminating individuals before, but that time was different. Sending this individual on his way was so satisfying that my comment after informing him that he no longer had a job was, "The only thing I regret is I can't fire your ass twice." The office secretary was next. Between the two of them, they had made my life a nightmare for several months. It was a pleasureful day.

At the end of the sales promotional period, our territory had increased sales against objective from the prior year's last in the Western region position to finish in first place.

In January 1968, I was offered a marketing position at the company headquarters in Fullerton. My introduction to Al Crossan when he had dropped by the office the day I was hired four and a half years before came back to me. Al had since been promoted to vice president of marketing and sales, and the promise discussed as a potential prospect on the first day I interviewed had become a reality. "If you do well in sales, there is a possibility you may be considered for a marketing position."

Now I wasn't as sure. Did I really want to give up selling? I was uncertain. Selling was as much avocation as vocation to me, and senior sales management was attempting to dissuade me from leaving sales. But after a short consideration, I chose marketing. I knew I could always go back to selling if that became my preference.

Carolyn had been pregnant during our time in San Francisco, and Kim had been adamant that she wanted a sister, not a brother. When Ron Jr. was born on February 22 at John Muir Hospital in Walnut Creek, Kim was so excited she kept exclaiming, "I always wanted a brother!" She became a little mother immediately, posing for a snapshot of her holding Ronnie on her lap. Three days later, after putting Carolyn, her mother, Kim, and Ronnie on a plane to Fullerton, I finished cleaning our apartment and drove to Fullerton that evening.

My new position was responsible for marketing Hunt commodity products: canned vegetables, fruit, and tomato juice. Then, I was assigned a new product—an enhanced version of Hunt's pork and beans—and was provided an insider's perspective on corporate dirty tricks. The individual who had developed the product owned a small chain of fried chicken stores in which the beans had attracted a following.

Several meetings with the chain's owner led to a decision to enter into an agreement to make use of the formula in a new Hunt-branded product. But during the process, it was suggested that I request the Hunt-Wesson research department to fabricate paperwork that illustrated how we had been working on a product of a similar type so, consequently, we would not need that individual's formula.

To preempt that move, I made an appointment with Ed Gelsthorpe, Hunt-Wesson's president, to review with him where we stood in our discussions, to explain expectations for the product, and to say that I planned to proceed with an agreement with the seller. With his approval, we developed a product called Big John's Beans 'N Fixins to be sold under the Hunt label. And the owner was paid his royalty.

When we moved to Fullerton, we decided to rent a single-family house again. The backyard came in handy, and we had a next-door neighbor who had a little girl Kim's age. I received another life lesson. Kim was animatedly describing something she had experienced with Suzanne, her little playmate. In her excitement, she lisped while describing what Suzanne had done, referring to her as "Thuthanne." Thoughtlessly, I smiled and chuckled. Kim was quick to ask, "What was funny?" When I mimicked Suzanne's name with a lisp, Kim responded with, "You know, Dad, sometimes I don't say things so good." I never underestimated a small child's intelligence again, most particularly this one's.

In December 1968, David Mahoney, chairman of Norton Simon Inc., Hunt-Wesson's holding company, imposed a 20 percent reduction in Hunt-Wesson's corporate staff.

When department layoffs began in early 1969, I assumed that the marketing organization, already a sufficiently small group relative to the total organization's size, was unlikely to experience a personnel reduction. I was wrong. Marketing organization size had been reduced by half by the second quarter's beginning. As part of the process, the Ohio Match Company was spun off as a separate division.

I was offered the position of Ohio Match Company's marketing manager, which was to be headquartered in Wadsworth, Ohio, a village a few miles outside Akron. We had never lived in the East, so we figured, why not? I accepted, and our seventh move in six years took us to Akron, Ohio.

Before the move, a week was spent with Mom and Dad, doing some trout fishing at the Blue Creek Lodge fishing camp across from Big River Ranch, where I had worked for a part of the summer of 1955. On the night of July 20, we stood on the lodge's front lawn, looking up at the moon like probably most of the world was doing. We were listening to Neil Armstrong's narrative as he stepped from the landing vehicle onto the moon's surface for the first time.

It was disclosed later that difficulties with the lunar lander's computer had rendered it useless for the landing.

What had not been considered in planning was that the landing capsule's analog computer was unable to calculate, transmit, and receive data from Houston at a speed sufficient to support calculating autopilot landing coordinates. Fuel usage was nearing depletion sufficient for a landing to be made and still leave enough to return to the orbiting vehicle that would return to earth. Neil Armstrong had been forced to make a critical decision: he would have to return to the orbiter or force a landing. He turned off the autopilot and, taking a chance on location, set the lander down.

When he overrode the computer and landed the vehicle manually, his heart rate was reported to have been 150 beats per minute. An incorrect decision would have left Neil and Buzz Aldrin stranded on the moon forever.

We completed the move to Akron in midsummer. I immediately repositioned the marketing strategy for the Ohio Match line of products from utilitarian to decorative. As a result, the line experienced an explosion of growth, riding a wave of products oriented toward the "turned-on" generation.

*Sales Management* magazine featured our success in a mid-1971 issue, and I hired an assistant to free my time to develop new products.

Reflecting on an excellent marketing experience at Ohio Match, I also acquired useful experience from observing our division president's shortcomings as a leader. He was captive to an ego that was quick to take credit when things went well and just as nimble at shifting blame when outcomes didn't work to his advantage. The resulting animosity was reflected in compromised attitudes among support staff members.

For several months, there had been rumors of a new management position to encompass both sales and marketing. The company's sales manager, Bill Simpson, had assumed he was the logical choice for the position and discussed that prospect with me more than once.

Then, in January 1972, I was promoted to the position of director of sales and marketing. In the discussion of my new position with the company president, I was directed to find a replacement for Bill. The term "caught between a rock and a hard place" likely resulted from exactly such a situation. There was no reasonable way I could comply. My wife and Bill's wife, Chris, had developed a close relationship, and so had I with Bill. More complicating was that Bill had been confiding in me, certain that the job would be his.

When he was informed of my promotion, he was hurt and assumed immediately that I had disclosed his discussions concerning his expectations for having the job. I couldn't tell him that I had been given an order to replace him; it was not going to go well. But an even worse complication was that Bill was well thought of within the Hunt-Wesson sales organization responsible for the sale of our products. I decided there was only one reasonable option—after nine years with Hunt-Wesson, it was time to move on.

An aggressive New York City headhunter had been contacting me for a couple of years about moving me to another company. I had rejected the idea but now was convinced that the timing made sense; I agreed to look around. I interviewed with a few Midwestern and Eastern firms, but none were of interest.

Then in May, I interviewed with Dallas-based Frito-Lay and accepted a position to begin managing Cheetos brand marketing in June. But when I arrived, I was informed I would be managing Doritos tortilla chips marketing instead. The introduction of the new Doritos Nacho Cheese Flavored product was my priority. When I asked how much time I had to get ready for the introductory date, I was informed that the introduction was to be one month from that point. I hadn't moved yet; my family was still in Akron. We began immediately scrambling.

On the way out of the door to organize getting the family to Dallas, I met with the advertising agency to review plans for the first ad and with the media buyer to set the television schedule. I wrote a sales brochure copy on the airplane returning to Akron. Loading the moving van lasted until early evening, resulting in us driving most of the night to find that the motel room we had reserved in Terre Haute had been sold a few minutes before we arrived near 4:00 a.m.

Our arrival in Dallas the next morning was in time to check the family into the Marriott hotel and for me to catch a flight to Los Angeles to shoot the first Nacho Cheese Flavor Doritos commercial with comedian Avery Schreiber. I then met with the sales organization when I returned to Dallas to discuss introductory meetings.

And the most excited about Nacho Cheese Flavor Doritos were Kim and Ron, who enjoyed the position of being among the first kids in the country to sample what was to become one of the most successful new product introductions of the 1970s. Nacho Cheese Flavor Doritos were that good.

When Frito-Lay's senior vice president received my sales forecast for the next quarter, he called me to his office to confirm the numbers, as they were going to considerably exaggerate company sales revenue expectations. I assured him the numbers were correct. Then, it was purchasing's turn for a meeting. My forecast would require the acquisition of the world's supply of tomato powder for the next year. The order was placed.

On October 1, an ASU marketing classmate contacted me regarding a marketing job in the family-owned business he was managing. I explained that I had no interest, but he prevailed on me to stop by Phoenix on my next trip to Los Angeles, which was in a few days. That was an offer I couldn't refuse. Chuck had been president of the company since shortly after we both graduated from ASU in 1963 and had also been responsible for the company's marketing. From what I could see, he had done a very good job.

I was curious about why he would be interested in having me join the company in the marketing position he had been occupying. He explained that his plan was to free up time to pursue acquisitions of other companies in the animal health industry.

It was a difficult decision. My experience with Frito-Lay proved that it was an outstanding company, and I had thoroughly enjoyed my experience. But after considerable thought, Carolyn and I concluded the move would allow us to transition into our own business within three years and live in a city we had said we would like to return to.

I accepted the offer with a couple of provisions: one being that I would be purely responsible for marketing with no interference; the other was I was to have a three-year guaranteed contract in the event things didn't work out the way he thought they would.

The company I associated with on January 1, 1973, held a dominant presence in retail animal health care products. But my transition from a corporation to a family-owned company was quite an eye-opener. An in-house advertising agency created collateral materials and print advertising layouts, a condition raising immediate skepticism.

The agency was supervised by a commercial artist, who turned out to be one of the most creative characters I had ever met, and I had met some very capable people in my experiences. Elmo Sears was at first standoffish, but we earned each other's trust, and, in addition to making an excellent right hand, he became a lifelong friend.

The eye-opener about a family-owned business was the function of family dynamics within the company. A domineering mother gave the impression of keeping her distance, but she spied on her son through the cooperation of two individuals responsible for opening each morning's mail. She was being provided direct knowledge of everything Chuck was receiving. There was also his sister who, while maintaining a reasonably hands-off position, had her own say regarding company operations.

The problem for me came when Chuck realized that plans to acquire other companies in the animal health field were not working out; he was left having little more to do than read industry magazines. Toward the end of the year, we had a disagreement regarding the direction of a planned promotion with Dale Robertson, the actor, culminating in my decision to move on, citing the no-interference clause in our agreement.

During the guaranteed salary period, I took advantage to pursue my own interests. It was the beginning of 1974.

## CHAPTER ELEVEN

# Commercial Real Estate

Considerable thought had been given to what I would do when I decided to strike out on my own. My sales experience had brought to mind three options that seemed to make the most sense: insurance sales, residential real estate sales, and commercial real estate sales.

But a discussion with an architect friend resulted in him suggesting, "Why don't we develop a condominium project together?" Condominium development? Why not?

In mid-1974, after several intense months dedicated to site selection, design, planning, and predevelopment requirements, lender discussions began. Then, a disaster of the sudden-death kind upended our ambitions.

Our near-ready-to-develop project's timing coincided with a real estate market downturn that struck with the intensity of a category 5 hurricane on a mobile home park. What had been a robust condominium market ended suddenly and violently.

It seemed that overnight, every Phoenix-area condominium project reverted to being bank-owned. And real estate developers couldn't get out of town fast enough for the calming effects of a better-than-average European vacation before returning to Phoenix to declare personal bankruptcy. So much for our condominium development plans. But the time spent on the exercise had its value.

Experience with our project's predevelopment had influenced my opinion that commercial real estate brokers, in general, seemed to be infected with the desire to do very little for what was often an attractive paycheck. I was certain I could do better. And I was eager to prove it.

Commercial real estate brokerage was to be my new career.

A few weeks later, real estate license in hand, I sought the advice of Cecil Lawter, a venerable Phoenix real estate market participant. Cecil knew everyone and was quick to make two recommendations—Coldwell Banker, which later became CB Richard Ellis, and Russ Lyon Realty Company—one corporate and the other locally owned.

I had had enough of corporate life; Coldwell Banker wasn't a good fit. A few days after I began work with Russ Lyon, I overheard an enthusiastic discussion between two agents in the commercial real estate division regarding an ad to be placed in the Sunday newspaper offering an apartment property for sale.

What I heard was a near-sleep-inducing description, prompting me to interrupt their discussion to comment on how I thought the ad might more effectively attract interest. That was my first conversation beyond "hello" or "good morning" with Ron Button, the property's listing agent.

Expressing gratitude for the unsolicited advice, Ron insisted on including my name in the ad as a contact along with his. I thanked him, declined the offer, and thought no more of it. Then, on Monday morning, Jeannie, our office receptionist, buzzed me. "I have a telephone call for you about an apartment property you advertised in yesterday's newspaper."

As the call was obviously in error, I stated that I had no knowledge of why someone would be calling me. Then I remembered—*the ad*! My insistence there had been a mistake fell on Jeannie's rigidly deaf ears, responding that it was not her concern.

The next sound was a dial tone, followed by a man's voice. "Hello, I'm calling about your ad for an apartment property in yesterday's paper." The circumstances did not need clarification. Button had left me to respond to requests regarding a property I knew nothing about while he had elected to go missing.

I was stuck and said, "Good morning, sir. May I ask who is calling?" Avoiding several questions, I suggested making an appointment to see the property that afternoon. I assumed by then Button would have gotten out of bed or at least finished whatever it was he was doing and could take over.

But the caller was motivated and was having none of that; he wanted to see the property—now! Attempts to delay further discussion until I could round up Button fell on deaf ears. At 10:00 a.m., we would meet at the property. I was obligated.

With continued attempts to reach Button going unanswered, all that remained was to make a frantic search of the listing files to determine where the property was located and a description of what it was. I arrived at the property just as Vic Love pulled up in his Mercedes 450. In a theatric display of bravado, I whipped out my newly printed business card while simultaneously suggesting that we review the property.

My first-ever apartment property showing was of one I had not seen and had only the cursory knowledge provided by a one-page flyer procured only a few minutes prior with the helpful assistance of an associate. To my astonishment, the prospect's impression after a brief tour was sufficient. He liked what he saw.

We moved on to spend a few minutes at a coffee shop to discuss a form of contract to purchase, which was another totally new experience to me. When I left the client to return to the Russ Lyon office, a realization swept over me. So this is commercial apartment sales? I had no idea it could be this easy.

The following morning, our meeting with Mr. Love's lawyer gave instant meaning to the designation of "shark," as, following a cursory introduction, he shouted out, *"MY CLIENT AND I AREN'T SIGNING ANYTHING!!"* Mr. Love had employed a litigating rather than a real estate attorney as his lawyer, a decision as inappropriately equivalent as keeping a caged cobra as a house pet.

Litigators live only to crush the opposition. In fairytales, they are known as shapeshifters, capable of instant transition into a form even more sinister. In this case, it was one of literature's fabled "hounds of hell." My first sale dissolved in a cloud of sulfurous hyperbole.

Still, I left the devil's sanctum hooked. The challenge had me; I *liked* apartment sales. Button was quick to attempt to persuade me that we should team up. He had a plan: he would list properties for sale, and I would sell them. My immediate reaction was that I was not obligated to anything else currently; maybe a partnership with Button could work. But the proposal came with a few rough edges, beginning with my new partner's less-than-stellar reputation as a non-performer. And I had already experienced his leaving me hanging once.

When I told Jim Tubbs, Russ Lyon's commercial division manager, of my decision, his reaction was the verbal equivalent of a bucket of ice water administered to my jockey shorts. Speaking in confidence, Jim informed me that Button had proven himself remarkably ineffective during his brief tenure with the firm. And his flaky non-performance had landed him on a short list to be drummed out of there. Jim further added, "There is no known instance in which a commercial real estate sales partnership has succeeded."

The response was not what I had visualized as a beginning. My new partner was a loser; it was a partnership concept that hadn't worked anyway. But fair warning aside, I judiciously ignored Jim's comments. Until I had acquired some understanding of apartment brokerage, I would take my chances with Button.

I discovered soon after that A. Ronald Button II, a University of Southern California electrical engineering graduate, was acutely interested in computers. The interest was a carryover from his prior employment in General Electric Company's Phoenix-based computer operations, where Dad had been a manager before his recruitment by NASA.

Button's diversion to commercial real estate sales was prompted by GE's corporate decision to exit the computer business, close its Phoenix manufacturing facility, and lay off division employees. While associated with GE, Ron had acquired several computer design patents; they were impressive credentials for electrical engineers but bore little relationship to forecasting commercial real estate brokerage success.

But having no Phoenix electrical engineering job alternatives at the time and a pressing need for continued funding of the family's grocery bills, he had joined a group of apartment brokers. The group had cataloged a modest three-by-five card catalog of mostly small Phoenix metropolitan area apartment properties. When the group disbanded a few months later, Ron took the property card catalog with him and landed at Russ Lyon's commercial division.

Our partnership was hardly up and running when Ron's brilliant, quirky, multifaceted, eccentric personality made itself apparent; his interest in computers was consuming. Regardless of whom he was speaking with, the discussion would inevitably transition to the subject of computers. The diversion was catastrophic to a sale transaction, a nuance was seemingly lost on Ron, clarifying beyond any doubt whatsoever that, while brilliant, he was also characteristically imperceptive.

While I was engaging a prospective buyer in conversation with Button sitting in as an observer, I frequently found that he hijacked the conversation to divert the discussion to computers. My admonitions to resist the temptation to bring up computers during sale conferences fell on deaf ears: "I don't bring up computers, they do."

A more direct approach, stating, "Keep your thoughts about computers to yourself, or client meetings will not include your face," made a more effective impression.

Still, as odd personalities are inclined, Button would regularly find ways to enhance his Exhibit A position as an eccentric. The Lincoln Town Car he drove would have been unremarkable if he hadn't equipped its exhaust system with Smithy glass pack mufflers, eliciting the deep, throaty sound expected of a teenager's street rod but one not at all consistent with late-model luxury sedans.

While on a property tour with Ron driving and me speaking with clients, I frequently had difficulty making myself heard over the Smithy's melodious tones. Combined with a nerdy obsession to ramble on about the many delights of computers, it was apparent there was more than a little weirdness there.

But, overlooking those distractions, Ron's nose for locating apartment properties to sell was satisfactory. The partnership seemed workable; Button would keep his commercial division desk for now.

I began apartment brokerage within reasonable, clearly defined circumstances. During the 1960s, 1970s, and extending into the early 1980s, Phoenix apartment development was near-universally committed to the viewpoint that: "People live in apartments out of necessity. Given the choice, renters would rather live in a house." Apartment ownership among smaller properties was dominated by individuals. Among larger properties, ownership was dominated by organizers of limited partnerships, principally focused on tax shelter benefits and relatively short (three to five year) holding periods. The industry was unsophisticated; participants needed little research support for their activities.

As a result, commercial real estate brokerage firms specializing in serving Phoenix developers or investors were no more concerned with excellence in their client services than they needed to be.

A commercial real estate agent's value was mostly underwritten by the ability to identify a property for sale, then facilitate the sale with as little further input as possible. By any reasonable standard, the commercial apartment industry was primitive. The opportunity for a more service-oriented apartment brokerage firm focused on larger private investors seemed apparent.

Descriptive material for a property listed for sale by a commercial real estate agent of the time typically relied on a single-page flyer, minimally illustrating an apartment property's features in a sort of *Reader's Digest* form. Information related to current apartment market conditions was anecdotal, based on an agent's or appraiser's opinion, and primarily supported only by hearsay. "Oh sure, the Phoenix apartment market is very strong, everyone says so."

We set out to change that. To distinguish our partnership from the competition, these changes to the then-current equivalent of a third-grader's approach to market research were made:

- The single-page summary was upgraded to a several-page descriptive summary.

- Anecdotal representations of market conditions were replaced by a historic macro-view of Phoenix apartment market development and vacancy and rental rate cycles.

The change was enabled by a stroke of exceptionally good luck. A formerly active market research firm had compiled Phoenix property and market-level information. Our acquisition of their data placed a proprietary advantage on our position as a knowledge-based commercial apartment brokerage. The timing was fortuitous.

The economic downturn that had so thoroughly thrashed the Phoenix condominium market was coincident with a change in Canada's province of British Columbia's political climate. The former conservative government had been displaced by socialists, prompting concerned Canadian investors to turn their thoughts to Western United States markets, including Phoenix.

It was a triple hit: Canadians wanted out of an unsatisfactory political climate, the calamitous US economic downturn made Phoenix real estate appear bargain-priced, and the exchange rate was favorable to the Canadian dollar. It was our lucky day—or so it seemed. There was a hitch.

Around the turn of the century, the Arizona Legislature had passed the Alien Land Act, prohibiting foreign entities from owning Arizona real estate. The avowed intent was to discourage Chinese immigrants from moving to Arizona. Clearly unconstitutional, the problem was soon resolved through some work by a few aggressive Phoenix attorneys. And our partnership, finally able to deal with Canadian investors, closed among the first Phoenix-area apartment transactions with that group.

A new level of sophistication had been added to our services, but our equipment for investment analysis still hadn't left the Stone Age. Investment analysis relied on hand-held calculators, pencils, and fourteen-column spreadsheets as tools for describing an investment property's pro forma operating projections. The activity was inefficient and labor-intensive to the extreme. Many weekend days were spent preparing for an out-of-town customer expecting to discuss investment options on Monday.

As our partnership had found considerable success in the business of large apartment property sales, Kim and Ron were growing and active in youth sports. And Carolyn had discovered a knack for interior design. It was a busy time for all of us.

As for me, in addition to putting in some serious hours in apartment brokerage, I coached Little League Baseball during that season, then followed with Pop Warner football coaching in the fall.

And Carolyn, in addition to her newly discovered career, found time to be available after school to Kim and Ron.

Our added services had been successful, resulting in our partnership developing a high profile as apartment sales agents among Canadian investors. We each qualified for our broker's licenses, then formed a legal entity, Brock, Button & Associates, which still maintained a close relationship with Russ Lyon Realty Company. The partnership with Button had worked out well. In addition to business activities, the Brock and Button families had developed a separate social relationship, taking ski trips together and generally enjoying a cordial social relationship.

I discovered a year or so after we had become partners that Ron was a member of the San Francisco-based Bohemian Club. In addition to club headquarters in downtown San Francisco, the Bohemians maintained a retreat in a Sonoma County redwood grove on the Russian River. Each year, club members and guests assembled at the Bohemian Grove for two weeks and three weekends for a gathering of mostly cultural events. The Grove was organized into a series of camps, each with a relatively small number of individuals. Club membership was exclusive, composed of prominent figures in politics, captains of industry, writers, musicians, high-level military, and entertainment celebrities of all sorts. Several former presidents have been members.

My question naturally was how A. Ronald Button II had been admitted to such an exclusive organization. Turned out, the camp adjacent to the camp in which Ron and his father, Ron Button Sr., were members included Bill Hewlett and David Packard, the founders of Hewlett-Packard, one of whom had sponsored Ron for membership.

Ron's father had been an influential mover in California politics, serving at one time in former Governor Pat Brown's administration. But Ron and his father had become estranged when Ron, having taken sides with his mother during a contentious divorce, incurred his father's enmity. Father and son later reconciled to an uneasy truce.

I attended the Grove a couple of times as an invited guest. I found it fascinating to spend time in an atmosphere with so many high-profile people coming together in such a relaxed manner. The club's motto, "Weaving Spiders Come Not Here," was clear: enjoy the experience, but, whatever we saw or heard, keep it to ourselves. And any attempt to make business contacts was strictly unacceptable.

It wasn't that business discussions were not held. But they were private and were only among members or important invited guests. Among the Grove's thirty-six camps, everyone was gracious, and, for at least the time there, it was just a gathering of guys having a relaxed, congenial time. The club had no female members.

Food was excellent, the outdoor pipe organ concerts were thrilling in their majestic setting, and there was always music among camps—played by some of the better musicians of the time. Musicians were given a special place at the Grove and, for that, were expected to display their talents. One of the camps, named The Aviary, was composed entirely of musicians. But musicians were scattered throughout and made their skills available every night.

A steady stream of revelations related to my curiously quirky partner had included the discovery that Ron was a late-night ham radio denizen. The activity frequently left him sleep-deprived. It wasn't unusual for him to suddenly drop off for a ten-minute chin-on-chest nap at his desk, still sitting bolt upright in his chair. Then, like a bobblehead doll, his head would just as suddenly, as though there had been no interruption, pop up to resume whatever he had been doing prior.

The radio hobby was supported by an impressive array of high-powered equipment, all constructed from kits acquired through Radio Shack. That lust for assembling electronic gadgets from kit form coupled with an undiminished dedication to the cult of the computer was soon to be rewarded.

### Commercial Real Estate's Introduction to Computers Begins

The December 1975 issue of *Popular Electronics*, a publication principally subscribed to by avid electronics enthusiasts, advertised the IMSAI 8080, described as a "hobbyist computer," which was made available in kit form. The ad had its effect: Button was a trout; the IMSAI was a willow fly.

Fifty IMSAI 8080 computers were shipped the following month, among which was one sent to A. Ronald Button II of Paradise Valley, Arizona. Within a few weeks, our partnership became the country's first computerized commercial real estate brokerage partnership. While there may have been bragging rights, the condition was marked more by flamboyance than substance.

The IMSAI's central processor was based on a 2 MHz 8080 Intel chip, among Intel's first. But as clunky as it was, the IMSAI provided the advantage of electronic storage of three-by-five card technology and was the beginning of real estate computer applications. A rudimentary electronic sort capability of a reasonably complete Phoenix-area apartment inventory gave Brock, Button & Associates added competitive cachet. A previous void of Phoenix apartment market conditions information availability was filled by a now more comprehensive apartment inventory source.

Real estate computer applications for small firms, while not necessarily raging out of the gate, began with our partnership occupying, for a very short time, a first-in-market competitive position. To the extent there was an advantage to Brock, Button & Associates, it was brief.

Steve Wozniak assembled his first Apple computer in mid-1976 and proceeded to make the Apple II in 1977, revolutionizing the personal computing business. IBM followed with their model 5150 PC in 1981, but Apple had preemptively established PC market dominance, and competitive real estate agents were actively acquiring the Apple to get their own technology stake firmly planted.

By 1985, Apple and IBM's desktop computers, initially introduced as novelties, had become seen as useful for activities beyond recipe storage. Commercial real estate brokers began making use of property storage, then spreadsheet programs for financial analysis. An enterprising Phoenix-area commercial real estate agent, taking the thought further, introduced a new service to the Phoenix commercial apartment industry under the name RealData.

RealData included an individual full-page printout of all Phoenix-area apartment properties of fifty-plus units in size. The RealData product was comprehensive, updated quarterly, and delivered by mail. Our brief flirtation with a clear-cut competitive advantage was crushed.

Introduction of RealData's product caused us to consider offering a service of the same type in competition. But further thought resulted in concluding that a product offered as a Real-Data alternative would only be a commodity in competition with all of a commodity's limitations: extreme susceptibility to destructive price competition, limited ability for product differentiation under current circumstances, no barrier to entry for other services of similar type, and excessively high cost of production and delivery.

We remained interested in a competitive product to RealData. Floppy disc technology provided the possibility of offering property photographs in color and a more efficient manner of distribution. But investigation proved that prospect to be as impractical as developing a competitive notebook had been; floppy disc technology was simply not up to the task.

Photographic images, even when compressed under then-current technology, were notorious electronic storage hogs. Numerous floppies would be required to store what was at the time a still relatively limited base of the Phoenix area's fifty-plus unit apartment properties.

Floppy disc technology limitations aside, the concept was further complicated by computer hardware limitations. Even the best desktop computers would have crashed after downloading the information held on only a few floppies. The idea was right, but technology timing still wasn't up to it.

Data manipulation—moving an item of data from one location to another—had not yet become a reasonable possibility; the best database software was limited to simply storing data with relatively simple access. Data standardization, the concept of making an objective apples-to-apples comparison of one property with another, was an occasional topic of discussion, but no one had come up with an answer to that question either.

In late 1985, we were informed that Russ Lyon Realty Company was to be sold to another commercial real estate firm. The result was to combine Russ Lyon's and the other company's commercial divisions, a move we determined not to be in our best interests.

Activities were set in motion to form a new commercial real estate brokerage entity. In mid-1986, a group of former Russ Lyon commercial agents formed Rand Commercial Brokers, moved into new offices, and began an odyssey of frustration related to computer system realities.

Our first error involved an untried Wang word processing software package, which was installed on our office secretary's computer. The IMSAI was still clunky but had been upgraded to a networked format and included spreadsheet software capable of performing investment analysis tasks, just painfully slowly.

The Wang software proved a constant source of irritation that was further aggravated by service providers, one for software and the other for hardware, each pointing a bony finger at the other whenever there was a problem: "It's not a software problem; it's a hardware problem," or the reverse when it was the software contractor doing the speaking. Between the two, problems with the Wang software were constant.

The combination of a word processing system that seemed dedicated to making roadblocks to getting anything done and a laboriously slow IMSAI system created a new set of frustrations every day.

In 1988, having had enough of the Wang software and still working with a painfully slow database, a fully integrated Wang system was acquired. The new Wang was more versatile, but the central processing unit made use of an Intel 286 chip supporting dumb terminals. System speed was less laborious than the IMSAI but still irritatingly plodding when too many users were online at once.

But technology continued to improve, and by 1993, the Wang system was in urgent need of an upgrade. Discussion with the Wang sales representative disclosed a system upgrade would attach an exorbitant cost. The Wang was a closed system, meaning that it was incapable of interacting with other manufacturers' cutting-edge components. That left us with a choice: scrap the Wang and convert to a networked PC-based system or acquiesce to Wang's predatory pricing. We opted to scrap the Wang.

The Wang had been purchased five years earlier at a cost of $140,000 and was now a victim of functional obsolescence.

We sold it for $300 and an agreement with the purchaser to haul it away. The networked system we acquired solved the aggravations of slow system speeds and had the added advantage that it was simple to upgrade as needed.

And technology was gaining new momentum.

## CHAPTER TWELVE

# Pierce-Eislen and the World Wide Web

Serendipity struck one day in 1995.

Kim, our little redheaded daughter born in Glendale, California, was now grown up and employed by our commercial real estate brokerage firm. One day, she burst into my office, saying, "We need to do this!" The flyer she was waving promoted a seminar introducing a new concept—the World Wide Web. My reaction was disinterest; I had plenty to occupy my time. But her enthusiasm was infectious: "We *need* to go!" Okay, let's do it.

The presentation was riveting!

The speaker had hardly begun describing the new concept when it became apparent that what we were seeing was so cutting-edge that the creative thoughts being stimulated were conjuring all manner of possibilities. The ability to expand delivery of an apartment property's description in a format allowing computer storage capable of being easily manipulated, then transmitted electronically, was an idea we had explored without success as each new technological innovation had been introduced. And that was just the beginning. There was more! Where had it been?

The answer we had been waiting for was here!

## The World Wide Web

In March 1989, Tim Berners-Lee, a British software engineer employed at the CERN particle physics laboratory in Geneva, Switzerland, had quietly submitted a document modestly titled "Information Management: A Proposal" to his boss, Mike Sendall.[1]

This was the proposal's background:

Tim's graduation with a degree in physics from Oxford in 1976 had been followed by several computer industry stints in software design. In part, he had come by computer talent naturally. His parents, both computer scientists, had participated in developing the Ferranti Mark 1, which was among the earliest stored-program computers.

During the period extending from June through December 1980, Tim had been employed as a software consultant at the CERN large particle physics lab outside Geneva, Switzerland.[2] While at CERN, he developed a personal program he referred to as "enquire." Enquire could store information in files containing "links," a new technology providing access from one file to, and within, other files. Links technology later became known as "hypertext."[3]

In 1984, CERN requested Tim to work on a new assignment, this time for developing procedures that would allow diverse computers to communicate with each other. CERN scientists had come from universities worldwide, arriving with computers of all types—PCs, mainframe, and medium-sized— each running its own variety of software. The result was a cumbersome inability to exchange information readily.

Tim commented, "Well, I found it frustrating that in those days, there was different information on different computers, but you had to log on to different computers to get at it. Also, sometimes you had to learn a different program on each computer. So finding out how things worked was really difficult. . . . Can't we convert every information system so that it looks like part of some imaginary information system which everyone can read?"[4]

Two components important to Tim's concept were already in use: the internet network and hypertext technology. Tim recognized hypertext's capability for providing the needed shared commonality missing among computers.

The internet, at the time, was a system of interconnected computer networks; hypertext was text highlighted on a computer display with references allowing immediate access to other hypertext.

The proposal Tim had submitted to Mike Sendall was unclear but sufficiently interesting that there seemed to be something to pursue. It had taken a year and a half for Mike to get around to it, but in September 1990, Mike Sendall approved Tim's proposal document and gave him time to work on his project.

Before the end of October, while working on a NeXT computer developed by Steve Jobs during his brief forced separation from Apple Computer, Tim had written the three primary technologies that were to become the foundation of today's internet:[5]

- **HTML** (Hypertext Markup Language) is the standard language for documents designed to be displayed in a web browser.

- **URL** (Uniform Resource Locator) is a unique "address" used to identify each resource on the Web.

- **HTTP** (Hypertext Transfer Protocol) allows for the retrieval of linked resources across the Web.

When these were combined with the existing internet and hypertext language, they became the World Wide Web. To place the World Wide Web in perspective, it's widely acknowledged as the most significant communications breakthrough since Johannes Gutenberg invented his movable type printing press in 1439.

In possibly history's most magnanimous decision ever made by an inventor of such proportion, Tim committed his invention to open-source status; anyone anywhere would be allowed to use the new system without paying a fee or even having to ask for permission to use it. And CERN agreed that the underlying code would be made available royalty-free, guaranteeing open-source use forever. When it was announced in April 1993, the decision became known as the World Wide Web.[6]

Tim moved from CERN to the Massachusetts Institute of Technology in 1994 to cofound the World Wide Web Consortium, an international community devoted to developing open Web standards.[7]

## Rand Commercial Brokers and the Web

And it was soon after that, thanks to Kim's alert enthusiasm, we were exposed to Tim's ideas.

For our need, it was immediately apparent that the World Wide Web was a highly evolved tool for distributing real estate data at a considerably reduced expense. Characterizing the difference between the then-existing technology and the Web was like comparing a 1931 Model A Ford to a new Ferrari Testa Rossa. No more waiting to print out changes in data until quarter end; no more cost of mailing bulky printed materials. But that was just the tip of that iceberg. Our thinking was still stuck at the shallow end of the possibilities pool where conventional thinking happily dominates.

Our initial perception, a simple transition from one database format to another, was to become a tar baby as the term *simple* evolved into a steadily increasing stream of complexity. Every obstacle and moat monster that anyone could have conceived was included if we had been looking for the sort of challenge that lying awake at two a.m. was made for.

What had seemed a sophisticated but simple data distribution solution at first exposure had become a prickly new opportunity. Now, adding detail to the data provided could include reporting on property sales, new properties in development, color photographs, and more.

It was also apparent that the Web opened the ability to store and freely manipulate data. And that opened a new potential: the elusive real prize was the ability to differentiate one property from another on a basis other than simply the property's age or location address. Our excitement was accelerating. What by then we had begun calling the internet had the clear potential for revolutionizing real estate market sophistication light-years beyond what was currently accepted as state-of-the-art.

Our thinking was expanding. The problem was that apartment communities were treated relatively uniformly even though they ranged considerably in desirability of either physical characteristics or location. There had been discussion over the years among sophisticated real estate organizations concerning the need for a system capable of objectively setting one property apart from another, but no one had yet bridged that gap. The opportunity was apparent: why don't we do it?

We were committed to solving the problem. But first, more urgent needs had to be addressed.

The initial assumption was we would simply sign up for Web access and begin using it. But no. There was a full set of new requirements. At first exposure, the most apparent need required conversion from a Visual Basic database format to an internet-compatible format. Okay, it seemed we should be able to do that.

We were a "Microsoft shop," and Microsoft's internet software solution was Sequential Query Language (SQL), so our existing database would have to be reformatted into SQL.[8] The solution seemed simple enough—hire a software developer competent in SQL to write the code needed to accommodate the conversion. But wait! As it turned out, we weren't the only ones to see opportunities in new Web applications.

In fact, there was no end to the flood of new product ideas being dreamed up to be served by the Web, all named "dot-com something or other." In an every-man-for-himself frenzy, each was dedicated to their product achieving first-to-market position, and all needed SQL or similar software developers to make it work. Only internet-compatible software, as the new sheriff in town, left nearly everyone flat-footed. The Web was a vastly complex new technology; a series of complicated hurdles had to be jumped by a then-largely clueless support and prospective user industry.

Metaphorically, someone had yelled the equivalent of *Fire!* in a crowded room, and all who had been exposed to the World Wide Web and thought they saw potential of their own were trying to leave the building through the room's only door. Placing our company's future on the line, we went to work. A bet-the-ranch condition threw one roadblock after the other over an intense period in which solving one problem uncovered two more of even more formidable size.

Programmers had been working on a wide variety of other software but not, as our interests were concerned, on SQL. For the few software developers who did have SQL capability, demand for their services was extreme. The condition left the door open to bogus software developers claiming SQL capability. But that didn't seem to bother any of them; all were eager to charge what had become a going rate of $185 per hour ($336 in current dollars) for internet-related programming.

The resulting high-tech gold rush was just as frenzied as had been the original Klondike version. This time, high-tech opportunists hawked shares in companies with no readily apparent product or prospect for profitability to unsuspecting individuals. Rather than discuss a demonstrable path to profitability, a frequently spoken mantra for these new internet-driven products claimed "driving eyeballs to the site" was the ticket. "We'll figure out how to make money from that later." Maybe.

It was a circus, and the effect was devastating to our plans.

We stepped back to determine what could be done to solve the problem.

We couldn't just walk away. We needed to see if our ideas could be developed. But how? We went through the process of engaging several imposters, each claiming to be SQL developers. Some even had the barefaced audacity to request a copy of our SQL manual when they arrived at our office to do the work.

Several failed tries with profound incompetence proved economics were not remotely going to work. To be fair, even if these individuals had possessed excellent SQL capability, our new enterprise would still be bankrupt before the product visualized could be made available.

It was apparent that circumstances had us attempting to compete in a fool's game, one in which we were not equipped to field a team. What had been seen as a simple adoption of internet capability for our apartment brokerage firm was not practical, sunk by a complexity that required a much-too-substantial speculation in new capital.

We had to decide: developing an internet product had to be shelved, or we would have to try a new tack. But which to choose? We had been dealing with individuals falsely claiming SQL expertise anyway; could a starving-student sort be a workable alternative? Brainstorming led to a solution: we could pay a bright Arizona State University student to learn SQL. And if successful, that individual could develop the software we needed.

An Arizona State University electrical engineering student, a young-genius type whose hobby was computer programming, turned out to be the perfect answer. As a bonus, he had acquired basic capability in ColdFusion, an Adobe programming language with SQL similarities.

An offer of fifteen dollars per hour (a current twenty-seven dollars per hour equivalent) for what was part-time work was made to Sheldon to learn SQL programming. We would provide the training materials needed to learn SQL programming and pay him for his time spent on the learning process. The assumption was that he would then apply what he learned to our needs. The problem was solved.

What had been a nearly insurmountable roadblock was cleared. SQL programming was water; Sheldon was a duck. When he came up for air, results were refreshing—he was capable! And before long, our brokerage product began to spring into life.

Then, one day over lunch with a client, I was enthusiastically explaining planned improvements to our capabilities when the client asked, "Why not expand into other markets besides Phoenix?"

What an obvious thought. Why not?

There was a business here!

Just like that, our thinking expanded from filling a currently unfilled Phoenix real estate industry niche to a national scope. Two components were essential differentiable qualities:

- **A searchable database:** This would identify all apartment properties of fifty-plus units in size and be capable of storing and considerably expanding property-related detail: property photographs in color, a property description expanded from a single page to several pages, inclusion of new products planned and under development, and property sales and sales history, all of which were all to be accessed on our server through the internet.

- **A formalized means of property and location classification:** This would enable an objective, like-for-like comparison of one property's relative desirability to another's.

The database format was relatively easily resolved; property and location classification was another matter. For the commercial real estate industry to accept any format as an objective solution to a problem of such long-standing was a challenge extending well beyond anything else we were doing.

But further investigation uncovered several other needs. Implementation began in earnest in 1995, addressing a full range of requirements applicable to an internet-enabled product:

- **A professionally designed website was required.** Everywhere we turned, people who had set up shop to do internet-related things were pricing their services light-years beyond reason. I was informed that a website would cost "at least $500,000, possibly closer to a million."

- **Database software customized to the envisioned capability had to be developed.** How data was to be accessed and displayed had to be determined, and screenshots of outputs had to be illustrated.

- **A high-powered, internet-capable server had to be acquired.** A computer was not sufficient to support internet applications.

- **Phoenix apartment properties had to be digitally photographed.** To be internet-enabled, photography required purchasing digital equipment and engaging a photographer to take multiple color photographs of each property.

- **A company name was required.** It had to be sufficiently distinctive to set our product apart from prospective competitors.

- **A distinctive logo was needed.**

A once-simple planned improvement to our Phoenix apartment brokerage services had evolved into much more. To make it happen, a substantial increase in capital was required.

But there was no need to address funding without having some indication of what the look and feel of the envisioned product was to be.

Fortified with a full load of undisguised chutzpah, I had complete confidence the product I envisioned could happen. How that could be was still to be determined. Sometimes, it pays to be naive.

The list of others interested in doing something with the internet was growing. Some were individuals with ideas for products to be sold through the internet; others were lawyers, software developers, internet consultants, and more who were charging catastrophic fees to advise individuals who were attempting to implement their innovative new product ideas. An organization founded for that purpose held monthly meetings with speakers of interest and served as a useful source of information that was still limited. It was within that group that I learned our project was called a start-up.

## What To Call Our Start-Up

Any new business begins with an idea. We had that. I discussed my thoughts with several apartment industry acquaintances and came away from those discussions convinced that a prototype illustrating the product's look and feel was necessary. It was also apparent that capital to fund the cost of software and transfer of our existing Visual Basic database to the SQL format was an immediate requirement.

After a digital camera was acquired and a few Phoenix apartment properties were photographed digitally, bandwidth—

circuit capacity serving the Web—was a new confounding issue. Network usage was progressing too fast for existing infrastructure to adequately serve needs. As a result, up to three minutes were required for transferring a photographic image over the internet.

We were confident that industry need would stimulate correction of that circumstance. Internet system capacity would grow geometrically, resulting in an acceptable image transfer time when we were ready to introduce our product. The assumption was correct. Within a relatively brief period, what had been minutes to transfer an image was reduced to seconds. In even less time, internet infrastructure development had reduced image transmission time to barely perceptible milliseconds.

Conditions had led to a catch-22 circumstance; we needed capital. I was provided the name of a high-profile Phoenix lawyer who was actively engaged with internet start-ups as someone with whom I should speak.

His advice was cryptic: "Have a management organization in place." Investors who were going to put up capital funds would have to be convinced that a believable management organization—chief operating officer (COO), chief financial officer (CFO), chief executive officer (CEO), and sales and marketing management—had been addressed. That added a few more loose ends to be tied up.

But first, we needed a company name. To present a desired company image, it was determined that the name would communicate the impression of an established research firm; no hint of association with the use of dot-com. By then, the dot-com term had been overused to the point of being worn out. And no one knew what it meant anyway.

We felt our company name should be in two parts. "Pierce" had been decided as a first name, but I was drawing a blank for the second. Then came inspiration while watching *Star Wars: A New Hope* with my grandson, Ben. The spaceport where the characters were really funky was called Mos Eisley. It struck me that Eisley had potential.

After a short time playing with it, Eisley became "Eislen." "Pierce" had been inspired by the 007 film *GoldenEye*, starring Pierce Brosnan as James Bond. When the two names were combined, the chemistry seemed right. The search was over; our company name was Pierce-Eislen. Now a logo was needed.

A brief discussion with a design firm regarding logo cost was convincing; we would do the logo ourselves. I met with one of our firm's junior associates and, with the help of a computer design program, spent a few minutes on a logo design that I would probably have selected if we had paid the $25,000 quoted fee for the graphic design firm to do the work.

Developing a series of reports in formats required to enable the flexibility expected of the new product required providing screenshots of intended outcomes to our boy-genius software developer. The reports he created were followed by documentation describing how customers were to use the software. My nights and weekends became dedicated to cranking out documentation copy.

It had been a struggle to solve an intricate puzzle: What should the service look like? And what should it accomplish? We were getting there. The hardware need was solved when it was discovered that a high-priced server was being made available at an attractive discount from a failed dot-com.

While these other needs were being addressed, progress was being made on solving the question of great value: developing a standard for differentiating one property from another with enough objectivity that it could be accepted as an industry standard. Then, it was done—we had it! Physical characteristics most likely to influence the relative desirability of a property's physical improvements or its location had been concluded.

Under the new system, a truly superior property would be rated as "A" or "A+"; category ratings extended from "A-" downward into the "B" and "C" rated categories, each including a range of three ratings of desirability. A property rated "D" was truly inferior, the apartment property equivalent of a running sore.

And with the rating system, we had what we had been looking for—a proprietary competitive advantage. For the first time, a customer would be able to objectively compare their properties with others. Separate patents were filed on both property and location qualifying systems with the US Patent and Trademark Office.

The initial attempt at developing an executive group resulted in my recruitment of two individuals I knew well: a former brokerage client as COO and an apartment industry acquaintance as CFO. Both individuals came equipped with excellent credentials. Then, almost immediately, both positions required replacement. The COO determined after a conversation with the CFO that we were undercapitalized and, consequently, would run out of money within six months.

It was my intent to raise additional capital funds as required, but that was not satisfactory. My newly acquired COO had had a recent experience with the spectacular failure of a dotcom he had been associated with, prompting his decision to resign from Pierce-Eislen to move on to another start-up. Soon after, our new CFO was offered what seemed a more attractive opportunity as COO of an apartment investment company.

It seemed apparent that I was attached to a tar baby; I could quit what I was doing and write off the investment already made, or I could assume more risk and continue moving forward. The decision was an easy one to make. I was moving ahead.

Personnel changes took a positive turn when I attracted Jim Kunkel as CFO. Jim had been Coopers and Lybrand's Phoenix office's managing partner and was well connected with the Phoenix investor community.

Jim also became an important investor himself and remained as CFO until Pierce-Eislen was sold to Yardi Systems thirteen years later. The COO position turned out to be irrelevant. It was filled briefly by another individual, but that association was brief; the position's function was not required.

By early 2000, the important issues had been concluded: we were wrapping up website development, Phoenix-area property photography was complete, and a Delaware corporation had been formed to become Pierce-Eislen's legal entity.

We had determined not to spend money on a high-priced website developer, a decision enabled mostly because dot-coms had suddenly begun going out of business rather than engaging in new business. A website developer in need of work reduced the expense associated with our initial website to $75,000.

Preliminary funding of immediate capital requirements was satisfied by a limited family and friends round, making stock available at a discounted price to a few people.

Shortly after, Jim and I began pursuing investor funding for an angel capital round. To complete those needs, multiple investor meetings were conducted in a short time. In the process, we learned a lot about potential complications.

Speaking with others who had raised funds for their own activities, I was advised to have a slick elevator pitch—a concise reason for why, in a few words, what we were doing should be taken seriously. "Elevator pitch" was jargon for the brief period between entering an elevator and leaving as the doors opened on the selected floor. The point applied to all private investors but most particularly to the many venture capital funds.

I had been warned about the Silicon Valley venture capital groups: the first question likely to come out of a typical VC's mouth was, "Why the [eff] should we invest with you?" They were flush with successes and had what seemed like piles of money to invest. For those who had dealt with them, many venture capitalists had adopted a childish hubris bloated so far out of reality that a businesslike conversation bordered on the near-impossible.

It didn't sound like a circumstance that would work for me; contact with that group was ruled out. But then, it wasn't quite that simple. Having investors in place was as important as developing an effective product. Our focus was on investment from individuals active in the Phoenix apartment industry.

Our service's expense would be a new line-item cost on any prospective user's operating statement. As a result, initial investor meetings were often characterized by an opening objection: "Why would anyone buy your product when they can get the information free off the internet?"

In response, I turned my laptop over to the individual raising the issue and said, "I haven't seen that availability. Can you show me where you found it?" Since there was no such thing, we moved on.

We learned soon enough how to deal with investor concerns and what answers to objections seemed to work best. It was a challenge to be simultaneously raising money to fund an angel investor round and building a prototype of something likely to solve a problem that was sufficient to prompt people to be willing to buy it or invest in it.

I had heard what seemed a useless premise from other early participants in internet-oriented products: "Bottom-line orientation to profitability forecasts is obsolete." The premise was supported by an equally vacuous premise stating that what was important were "eyeballs to the site." Most dot-com pitches assumed operations would remain flat until five years out when, magically, profitability would occur after eyeballs to the site had been monetized. The approach became a cliché, most investors referring to the forecast format as the "hockey stick."

Still, money was being thrown at dot-coms as though there was no question everyone was going to get very rich on all of them. It was no surprise that by the year 2000, things were out of hand.

Just how much so was shown by one of our monthly Internet Association guest speakers. He described his experience with a Silicon Valley venture capital organization from which he had requested $18 million in funding to launch an online single-family homes auction. The VC stated interest in funding his venture but insisted the investment be $38 million instead of the proposed $18 million. The venture failed after eight months.

It was one of many new organizations funded during the 1995–2000 period that became a casualty when the dot-com category imploded. For a brief period, our discussions with prospective investors had to deal with the issue, but our offering was for a real product, a service to an industry capable of recognizing what it would do for them. The dot-coms had often not had that luxury.

But the most significant problems facing most dot-coms centered on three near-insurmountable conditions: the management teams lacked experience capable of guiding the organization through the development period, most did not have a salable service, and few could demonstrate a believable path to profitability.

To add strength to the Pierce-Eislen investor offering and to the company, angel investors were required to serve as members of the board of directors. The strategy's success was surprising. Our investors were high-powered businessmen, and a very small start-up began its existence with an excellent group of advisers.

Staffing a sales organization turned out to be a more-than-expected challenge. Earlier appearances had made it seem like the dot-coms had sucked up all the sales talent. Now, with the demise of those organizations in large numbers, an abundance of individuals with seemingly excellent qualifications were on the market looking for sales jobs.

We had the pick of individuals who had held what sounded, from their resumes, like high-level positions. It seemed a logical assumption that most held well-supported credentials, but they were no more effective for us than they had been at their prior employment.

It became readily apparent that the dot-coms had populated their organizations with whoever they could get by providing magnificent salaries, stock options, and important-sounding titles to attract a lot of empty suits who had no business ever occupying sales positions to begin with.

I had been directly involved with Pierce-Eislen's sales and marketing until then. Now, conditions led to a reality: I would have to remain a near-full-time salesman until we could develop a sales team. Then, the cavalry rode in to the rescue in the form of Ron Jr. When Ron joined the firm, he had been remarkably successful in selling mobile phones and now could help establish Pierce-Eislen's sales organization.

Between the two of us, the sales need was temporarily satisfied. An objective look back resulted in the conclusion that Pierce-Eislen's success would have been considerably inhibited had he not joined our organization with his sales skills when he did.

During the next several months, sales organization incompetence continued to be an organizational Achilles heel as individuals came and went in the sales department. Still, new customer acquisition was developing as planned: Phoenix apartment market participants were actively building a customer base, the Tucson market was in the process of opening, and the San Diego market was under development.

Then, on September 11, 2001, terrorists flew airplanes into New York City's World Trade Center buildings, and just about everyone stopped to deal with the shock of what had taken place. But within a few weeks, market development and new Pierce-Eislen customer acquisition resumed in earnest.

Consideration was given to the possibility of acquiring smaller existing apartment research companies to speed expansion, but the premise proved unsatisfactory. Smaller information providers were discovered in several markets, but their information was mostly incomplete and near-uniformly inaccurate. That weakness was complicated by a view held firmly by the smaller companys' owners that their operations held considerably more value than we felt they did. And by then, the Pierce-Eislen internal market development function had become effective in developing new geographic areas. We were adding new markets at a rate that resulted in a new need to address.

One of our product's components, a three-times-annual telephone survey of rents, had become too burdensome for our research department to maintain and simultaneously develop new markets. An alternative was needed. To solve the problem, a home-sourced program making use of homebound individuals was created. Individuals within the new organization, acting as independent contractors capable of conducting telephone surveys from their homes, were an efficient solution.

Momentum in Pierce-Eislen's organizational growth by late 2007 required additional office space. Discussions with our existing building owner were not successful. Unjustified chutzpah gave him the feeling that we were in a bind. As a result, he felt time was on his side and held to a position of non-negotiation. We met the challenge, successfully locating an alternative. Then, in another moment of unsatisfactory timing, we moved into our new location on October 1, 2008, a day near-simultaneous with the disastrous derivatives market crash that threatened to break the world's financial institutions and sent the US economy into a crisis.

And suddenly, we were in a crisis mode of our own; the need to substantially reduce overhead was clear. Our most readily apparent options were to reduce organization salaries by 20 percent or lay off 25 percent of our workforce.

It was concluded that cutting salaries would be disastrous for everyone; 25 percent of our workforce was laid off that afternoon. Following that nightmare, I met with our remaining employees to explain the necessity behind the decision. Sleep didn't come well that night.

Two Texas markets under development when the crisis hit were finished. But further market expansion was temporarily halted. Conditions had resulted in our customer base declining by 9 percent, but cash flow from operations remained positive. We had been funding market development with a small bank line of credit but had no other bank debt. As a result, we had not been placed in jeopardy of the insolvency many firms experienced as a result of banks pulling credit lines.

Banks notoriously choose times of economic downturn to make it difficult for businesses. The same bank that may have eagerly pursued new clients until the moment a disturbance in economic conditions occurs suddenly doesn't want to speak with them anymore. In our case, when the downturn came, the bank didn't want to continue our line of credit. But the need for the credit line had already become unnecessary.

Our meeting with our concerned bank's senior management was unsatisfactory. At the bank's insistence, a small credit line balance was paid off. But the clumsy manner taken to inform us we needed to do that left us with the feeling that, when circumstances returned to normal, we would have a new bank.

Before long, that, of course, happened. The other bank swooped in with attractive incentives to entice us to switch our business operations to them. It was a pleasure to leave our prior bank to contemplate why they had taken such a knee-jerk position with us.

Before long, economic circumstances settled down, and we returned to adding new markets. Pierce-Eislen had become a national company and was attracting attention from other companies interested in acquiring ours. Feeling we were better served to continue building new markets and expanding our customer base, we turned them down.

And during that time, after many iterations of our patent had been filed, filed again, and refiled several times more during the ten years following submission of the first requests, the US Patent and Trademark Office issued patent numbers US 7,974,930 B2 and US 8,060,450 B2 to me on standardized methods of categorizing a real estate property's physical desirability and location desirability.

Then came a new dilemma: a major shareholder died, leaving a substantial estate. There was a need to establish Pierce-Eislen stock value for purposes of valuing his estate.

Board discussion concluded that the only reasonably accurate way to settle on a value was to engage a middle-market investment banking firm to offer the company for sale to determine what a qualified highest bidder might be willing to pay. When the process was complete, bids from two qualified prospective purchasers were submitted to the board for approval.

It had been an exciting ride, one complete with every unknown we could have asked for. As the World Wide Web evolved into the internet, we had participated in developing our own little slice of history.

Pierce-Eislen's sale to Yardi Systems of Santa Barbara, California, was completed on July 1, 2013. I remained with

Yardi as an employee to assist with selection, then transition, of a new management team. Two well-qualified individuals were recruited from the apartment industry, and on September 30, 2014, at a retirement event for me, I thanked individuals who had been instrumental to the company's success and said good night.

As had been my experience in the apartment brokerage business, spending many hours at the business of developing an internet product, then a company to deliver it, had been a consuming work schedule. But the time spent developing Pierce-Eislen's Web presence was among the most enjoyable periods of my business career.

# CHAPTER THIRTEEN

# After NASA

In a nostalgic review of his life, Dad reflected on his good fortunes and the challenges he had encountered:

*The marvels of innovations have always been a big part of my thoughts and interests. It's still difficult for me to believe that most of the technology that we now accept as commonplace has happened during my lifetime. Some of the items were invented before my time, but their final development and perfection has been recent for the most part. I refer to such things as the radio, TV, automobiles, airplanes, rockets as applied to space travel, computers, and so many other things that I cannot use the space to name them here. It has been a fortunate time for me.*

His experience as director of the Computation and Analysis Division at NASA's Manned Spacecraft Center was the capstone to an extraordinary career. But the work by then was primarily administrative; the challenge of developing new technology was no longer the focus of his activity. And he was restless:

*The assignment turned out to be the most challenging of my professional career; responsibilities of a division chief in the computer field include interface duties well beyond that of a normal position. One must be responsive to requests for speeches, papers related to the computer field, and consulting work with the academic community.*

Dad's success with NASA had resulted in a notoriety impossible to escape, creating demands for professional organizational participation, papers, speeches, and committee representation well outside his preferred work activities. And Mom and Dad were at an age where the familiarity of routine had taken on increased value:

*We had loved our home in El Lago, and it was really the first one that we had both designed and built. The Space Center, as well as Houston, was nearby, and we became involved in a broad scope of activity.*

Dad wrote of the satisfaction he and Mom felt with the house they had custom built to their specifications in Clear Lake City and for the location's desirability. But boredom with demands associated with the extracurricular activities of the director's position had set in. And whether consciously or unconsciously, he was open to the prospect of a new experience. He just hadn't heard about anything that sounded like a challenge that would appeal to him.

Then, in August 1971, the University of Virginia came calling regarding a senior position they were charged with filling. The timing was serendipitous:

*By the end of the 1970s, most of the basic work of the outer space program was complete. And for me, the challenge associated with the space effort had disappeared. Consequently, when the chairman of the selection committee for a University of Virginia Computer Center director contacted me to request I apply, the timing was right.*

*The committee's chairman, a retired General Electric vice president, convinced me to accept the position as director of computing for the university and the state of Virginia's District II, which included an additional twenty educational facilities. I accepted the position in August 1970.*

*Our move to Charlottesville was a pleasant change. It did not take long to discover the Virginia Blue Ridge Mountains' beauty. The days we spent in exploration of new areas were like holidays. But not long into the new work, I discovered job expectations were more than what I had anticipated. The combined workload between the university and the state was stimulating but overly demanding.*

Dad avoided mention of frustrations associated with an often-immovable resistance from the various state of Virginia and University of Virginia departments. They were a technologically unsophisticated bunch, which was why Dad was there in the first place. But each department head had their own vision of what a computer should be able to do for their department.

Dad was placed in the impossible position of having the responsibility to solve the problems for the state of Virginia and the university but without the authority to make the necessary decisions. Finding agreement within a committee composed of a series of academic agendas was simply too much. It didn't work:

> *In spite of the heavy workload I was handling, we were having a good time. But our stay in Charlottesville was cut short; I suffered a heart attack and was not able to shake off the effects.*

During my visit to see Dad in the hospital, I discovered he was fortunate to have survived. The heart attack had occurred during a flight to Atlanta. Unbelievably, he had checked into the hotel where he was to attend a meeting the following day but discovered he couldn't sleep due to pain. A taxi took him to Atlanta's general hospital, which kept him waiting in the emergency room for several hours.

The pain was so intense that he returned to the airport, boarded another plane, and returned to Virginia, where he checked into the hospital. Whatever he may have been thinking in the process of going through that series of errors was obviously based on mistaken judgment. But whatever it was, he'd had enough of the dysfunction and associated stress with the University of Virginia job.

He spent the rest of 1973 recovering from the heart attack while remaining on the University of Virginia's faculty as a visiting professor of electrical engineering. During that period, he also served as a computer operations consultant for the federal banking system. After a few months of recovery time, it was determined that the university position was impractical. It was time to move on to something else:

> *Both of us felt that travel would be good for us. So began a period of association with the International Executive Service Corps, which places retired executives in consulting positions in developing countries.*

The International Executive Service Corps had been formed in Washington, DC, in 1964 by David Rockefeller and several high-profile business leaders. The IESC's express purpose was the improvement of living standards in developing countries by strengthening private enterprise. It was a perfect way for Dad to contribute his knowledge and expertise and for Mom and Dad to see a bit of the world they might never have experienced:

> *Beginning in 1973 and extending through 1978, our travels and consulting assignments included:*
>
> *1973 – West Africa Examinations Council, including facilities in Ghana and Nigeria; our assignment in Africa was followed by a review of the federal banking system in Belo Horizonte, Brazil.*
>
> *1974 – Most of 1974 was dedicated to projects in Brazil, including three months each in review of the state data processing system in Goiânia, the state banking system in Belo Horizonte, and the cocoa distribution system in Vittoria.*

*1975 – Setting up an audit and control system for the VAM department store chain in Caracas, Venezuela.*

*1976 – Returned to Caracas, Venezuela, for work on the audit and control system of the VAM department store chain.*

*1978 – Consultant on computer planning, Brazilian government in Brasília.*

*When our last project was completed in the city of Brasília, we returned to Houston mostly retired.*

*I finished my career with some teaching at the University of Houston.*

Mom and Dad returned to Arizona in 1982, where they moved to Sun City. Dad continued his enthusiasm for the art that had begun with Georgia O'Keefe while he was in Los Alamos. He had continued painting while he was associated with NASA and, during that time, held numerous one-man shows as well as participated in fifteen juried exhibits. And his art was shown in museums throughout the Southwest.

Thinking back to his boyhood days in the Big Thicket when his overwhelming thought was, *I'm going to be an educated man* stimulated philosophical contemplation:

> *My career does not imply that I am a dreamer by nature, but it was always my feeling that I was attracted to the newest and foremost technological advances as they were being visualized or in the developmental process. I wanted to be part of all of it. I realize that it was outside my nature to simply be an administrator. I would never have been happy*

*with a position, in some effort, that was an ongoing or con-*
*tinuing process without there being some element of newness*
*keeping things interesting.*

*Partly, it may have been because it seemed that my non-*
*professional career lasted for years before I had the oppor-*
*tunity to be a professional person of any kind. The first part*
*can be described as just plain hard labor, and I enjoy the fact*
*that I can still do it without losing my love for the professional*
*environment.*

*But my pride is most activated by the challenge of profes-*
*sional activities associated with the front-end of what is most*
*clearly the newest of technology. Not for monetary compensa-*
*tion but for the sense of achievement that can only be satisfied*
*by the challenges of what can only be brought on by being*
*among the first to find involvement.*

And with that, he expressed regrets:

*I spent a great number of years satisfying my lust for the*
*new and unknown at the expense of the family. So it is with*
*some regret that I expose that trait with the history of my*
*professional career.*

He was reflecting on where he came from and thinking
back to how much history had passed under that bridge since it
was first crossed:

*When you go back to a place and walk down the paths*
*you walked as a boy, every step makes you want to stop and*
*just stand there, remembering . . . But the old ways and the*
*old habits are so etched that one leaves the dreams unrecon-*
*structed and uses these paths as reminders of what once was.*

*And so it is with much of the material covered in this*
*story.*

## A Son's Observations

Dad's unusual competence in so many things was illus-
trative of a creative genius. He was also a very human genius,
flawed in some ways, but not the stereotype of an eccentric often
illustrated by individuals of such highly developed intellectual
capacity.

He could solve complex problems but also was the pos-
sessor of a mind attaching a sometimes-quirky curiosity about a
lot of other things. He never outgrew a childlike desire to see
and do a lot. It seemed everything he did was simply because it
attracted his interest.

Whether it was engineering, art, music, collecting pottery shards left behind in the desert by a once-thriving Native
American culture, or attending Native American dances, coupled with insatiable curiosity, he found it all fascinating. And we
were invited to participate in most of his passions.

Dad, your experience was also our experience. And
speaking for myself, I never felt deprived because of what you
were doing. Despite your many personal enthusiasms and the
fact that you indulged in so many of them, you did a lot of

interesting things that I look back on and realize: what an incredible time we had.

Most probably through osmosis, I learned from you how to lead a more creative and intellectually satisfying life if light-years below your personal capabilities and achievements.

So, Dad, you did it. Just look how much you accomplished—and in only one lifetime.

# Notes

## Chapter 1 – The Big Thicket

1. Abernethy, *Tales*.
2. Britannica, The Editors of Encyclopaedia, "Conquistador."
3. Weather for You, "Climate of the Big Thicket."
4. McCaslin, "Polk County," TSHA.
5. Abernethy, *Tales*, 203.
6. Ibid., 11.
7. McCaslin, "Polk County," TSHA.
8. *Texas Almanac*, "Population."
9. National Register of Historic Places, "Early Logging Industry . . ."
10. Ibid., "Early Logging Industry . . ."
11. Ibid., "Early Logging Industry . . ."
12. texasalmanac.com, "Population History of Counties"
13. Wooster, "Leggett," TSHA.
14. Wooster, "Moscow," TSHA.
15. Ibid., "Leggett."
16. McCaslin, "Polk County," TSHA.
17. Wooster, "Moscow," TSHA.
18. Abernethy, *Tales*, 174.
19. Abernethy, "Big Thicket," TSHA.
20. Abernethy, *Tales*, 173.
21. Ibid., 140: Kleiner, "Sour Lake," TSHA.
22. Wooster, "Saratoga," TSHA.
23. Abernethy, *Tales*, 176.

24. Wooster, "Saratoga," TSHA.

25. Isaac, "Beaumont," TSHA.

26. Etienne-Gray, "Higgins," TSHA.

27. Ibid., "Higgins, Portillo."

28. Wooster and Sanders, "Spindletop Oilfield," TSHA.

29. Ibid., "Spindletop Oilfield."

30. Ibid., "Spindletop Oilfield."

31. Ibid., "Spindletop Oilfield."

32. Ibid., "Spindletop Oilfield."

33. Abernethy, *Tales*, 140; Kleiner, "Sour Lake," TSHA.

34. Kleiner, "Batson, TX."

35. Wooster, "Saratoga, TX."

36. Abernethy *Tales*, 144 and 145.

37. Ibid., *Tales*, 144.

38. Wooster, "Saratoga, TX."

39. Smith, "Humble Oilfield."

40. Hardin, *Life*, 5.

41. Ibid., 15.

42. Abernethy, *Tales*, 110.

43. Hendrix, "Livingston," TSHA.

44. Abernethy, *Tales*. 13.

## Chapter 2 – Texas Tech, Marriage, and the Depression

1. Acosta, Garcia, and Orozco, "Settlement Houses," TSHA.

2. Kever, "Pride."

3. Zepeda, Lone Star Legend, 16.; Wagner, "Sixth Ward," 38-41.

**Chapter 3 – College Station -1941-1948**

1. Odintz, "Brazos County," TSHA; Census, "Census of the Population and Housing."
2. George H. Butcher, "The Electric Home of the Future", Popular Mechanics Magazine, August 1939, 161.
3. O'Brien, "Camp Hearne."

**Chapter 4 – Los Alamos**

1. Hales, *Atomic Spaces*, 71.
2. Ibid.,72.
3. Kelly, *The Manhattan Project*, 24-25.
4. Ibid., 26.
5. Ibid., 29.
6. Ibid. 29.
7. Ibid., 104.
8. Ibid., 45-48.
9. Ibid., 51-55.
10. atomicarchive.com, "Einstein's Letter."
11. atomicarchive.com, "President Roosevelt's Response to Dr. Einstein."
12. Kelly, *The Manhattan Project*, 82-85.
13. Atomic Heritage Foundation, "Glenn Seaborg."
14. Hunner, *Inventing*, 18.
15. Ibid., 19.
16. atomicheritage.org "The Plutonium Story."
17. Hales, *Atomic Spaces*, 44-45.
18. Ibid., 47.
19. Ibid., 44, 215.

20. Hales, *Atomic Spaces*, 43; Hawkins, "The Los Alamos Project Y," 1&2.
21. Ibid., *Atomic Spaces*, 14-17.
22. Hunner, *Inventing Los Alamos*, 13.
23. Ibid., 15-16.
24. Hales, *Atomic Spaces*, 14.
25. Ibid., 14.
26. Hawkins, "The Los Alamos Project Y," 3.
27. Hunner, *Inventing Los Alamos*, 17.
28. Hawkins, "The Los Alamos Project Y," 66.
29. Ibid., 17.
30. Atomic Heritage Foundation, "Los Alamos."
31. Hawkins, "The Los Alamos Project Y," 94 & 110.
32. Michnovicz, Gibson and Michnovicz, *Los Alamos 1944-1947*, 18.
33. Atomic Heritage Foundation, "Los Alamos," 35.
34. Hawkins, "The Los alamos Project Y," 24 and 110.
35. Ibid., 7 and 101.
36. Hawkins, "The Los Alamos Project Y, Vol. I," 6.
37. Ibid., 41.
38. Jogekalar, "What John von Neumann Really Did . . ."
39. Nrc.gov, "Fissionable Material."
40. Hawkins, "The Los Alamos Project Y," 29 and 50.
41. Truslow and Smith, *Manhattan Project Y, Volume II*, 82.
42. Ibid., 126, 186, 1250.
43. Atomic Heritage Foundation, "Electronics and Detonators," 1-9.
44. Atomic Archive, "Design of Two Bombs," 2.

45. atomicheritage.org., "Little Boy and Fat Man."

46. Atomic Heritage Foundation, "Trinity Test – 1945," 1–6.

47. Ibid., 3.

48. Hales, *Atomic Spaces*, 323 and 324.

49. Ibid., 287.

50. Atomic Heritage Foundation, "Tinian Island."

51. National Archives, "Truman's Announcement of the Atomic Bomb On Hiroshima."

52. Atomic Heritage Foundation, "Harry Daghlian."

53. nuclearfiles.org, "Henry Stimson: Statement, August 6,1945."

54. Hunner, *Inventing Los Alamos*, 84-85.

55. Ibid., 121 and 122.

56. Ibid., 116.

57. Ibid., 131.

58. Truslow/Smith, *Manhattan District History*, Volume II, 98.

59. Hunner, *Inventing Los Alamos*, 137/138.

60. The Nuclear Weapon Archive, "Operation Sandstone."

61. armscontrolwonk.com, "Why No One Will Ever Build Another Nagasaki . . . "

62. Atomic Heritage Foundation," Little Boy and Fat Man."

63. Ibid.

64. Denver Post, "Quiz kids-by the dozen."

65. Hunner, "Inventing Los Alamos", 147.

66. Hunner, Inventing *Los Alamos*, 188/189.

67. Michnovicz, Gibson, and Michnovicz, *Los Alamos – 1944-1947*, 19.

68. Buck, Stephanie, *Lustron.*

69. NOVA Online, "The November 12, and September 21,1944 Intercepts".

70. Nova Online. "The February 9, 1944 cable: Klaus Fuchs and Harry Gold."

71. Nova Online. "The September 21, 1944 cable: The Rosenbergs . . ."

72. Declassified Document, "Venona".

73. Pagano, "The Spy Who Stole the Urchin".

74. NOVA Online, "The November 12, and September 21,1944 Intercepts."

75. Atomic Heritage Foundation, "Special Engineer Detachment."

76. The Nuclear Weapon Archive, "Operation Sandstone."

77. Ibid.,

78. atomicheritage.org. "Electronics and Detonators."

79. U.S. Department of Energy, "Bayo Canyon."

80. Whitacre and Belotti, "Native American Heritage."

81. LANL, "Short History of Women," 3.

82. Atomic Heritage Foundation, "Computing and the . . ."

83. Atomic Heritage Foundation, "John von Neuman."

84. Famous Scientists, "John von Neuman."

85. Flank, "Hidden History."

86. Moore, Alan, "Nevada Test Site Overview."

87. Globalsecurity.org, "Weapons of Mass Destruction (WMD)."

## Chapter 12 – Pierce-Eislen and the World Wide Web

1. Berners-Lee, "A Proposal."

2. britannica.com, "Tim Berners-Lee."

3. Ibid., "Tim Berners-Lee."

4. w3.org, "Answers for Young People."

5. webfoundation.org, "History."

6. Ibid.

7. Ibid.

8. docs.microsoft.com, "Cold Fusion and SQL."

# Bibliography

While information was obtained through secondary sources deemed reliable, some that proved to be of questionable quality were discarded, and every effort has been made to cross-check reliability, particularly as related to Los Alamos and Texas's Big Thicket. For both topics, the internet was particularly useful in providing important primary sources or in pointing the way to them.

Important facts relating to both the Big Thicket and Los Alamos relate to events that occurred during fixed periods in time. That condition contrasts with discussions regarding the internet and World Wide Web, which have been notably dynamic, and, consequently, have been subject to more definite revision since the time I experienced working within each.

A bibliography and notes illustrating citations are separated by topic.

## Chapter 1 – The Big Thicket

The Big Thicket and its prior history made reference to several sources of which there was a wealth of information: one was my father's, Eugene Brock's, personal remembrances of a childhood growing up in the Thicket. Those observations are italicized in several parts of the book. The Handbook of Texas Online (TSHA) made available a range of articles on historic activities generated as components of academic research, which, while sometimes of dubious reliability, were, for the most part, of considerable value, and Ancestry.com was an invaluable re-source for confirming histories of the various associated clans.

The following articles were written for the University of North Texas Press in some instances; in others, articles were submitted directly to the handbook.

Published sources included several dedicated to cataloging and preserving history surrounding the Big Thicket:

Abernethy, Francis E., ed. 1986. *Tales From the Big Thicket.* Denton: University of North Texas Press.

Abernethy, Francis E. "Big Thicket." *Handbook of Texas Online.* The Texas State Historical Association. Accessed September 23, 2021. https://www.tshaonline.org/handbook/entries/big-thicket.

Britannica, Editors of Encyclopaedia. "Conquistador." Encyclopedia Britannica. Accessed March 18, 2020. https://www.britannica.com/topic/conquistador-Spanish-history.

Etienne-Gray, Tracé. "Higgins, Pattillo." Handbook of Texas Online. The Texas State Historical Association. https://www.tshaonline.org/handbook/entries/higgins-pattillo.

Hardin, John Wesley. 1973. The Life of John Wesley Hardin. Norman: University of Oklahoma Press.

Hendrix, Don. "Livingston, TX." Handbook of Texas Online. The Texas State Historical Association. 1952 (updated 1995). https://www.tshaonline.org/handbook/entries/livingston-tx.

Isaac, Paul E. "Beaumont, TX." Handbook of Texas Online. The Texas State Historical Association. 1976 (updated 2020). https://www.tshaonline.org/handbook/entries/beaumont-tx.

Kleiner, Diane J. "Batson, TX." Handbook of Texas Online. The Texas State Historical Association. https://www.tshaonline.org/handbook/entries/batson-tx.

Kleiner, Diane J. "Sour Lake, Texas." Handbook of Texas Online. The Texas State Historical Association. https://www.tshaonline.org/handbook/entries/sour-lake-tx.

McCaslin, Richard B. "Polk County." Handbook of Texas Online. The Texas State Historical Association. Accessed September 23, 2021. https://www.tshaonline.org/handbook/entries/polk-county.

National Register of Historic Places. Civil War And Recovery Period 1860-1876. United States Department of the Interior, National Park Service, Section F, Page 3.

"Population History of Counties From 1850-2010." Texas
    Almanac. https://www.texasalmanac.com/drupal-
    backup/images/topics/ctypophistweb2010.pdf.

Smith, Julia Cauble. "Humble Oilfield." Handbook of Texas
    Online. The Texas State Historical Association.
    https://www.tshaonline.org/handbook/entries/humble-
    oilfield.

WeatherForYou. "Big Thicket National Preserve, TX
    Weather." Accessed June 1, 2022.
    https://www.weatherforyou.com/reports/index.php?pan
    ds=Big+Thicket+National+Preserve%2CTexas.

Wooster, Robert. "Leggett, Texas." Handbook of Texas
    Online. The Texas State Historical Association.
    https://www.tshaonline.org/handbook/entries/leggett-
    tx.

Wooster, Robert. "Moscow, Texas." Handbook of Texas
    Online. The Texas State Historical Association.
    https://www.tshaonline.org/handbook/entries/moscow-
    tx.

Wooster, Robert, and Christine Moor Sanders. "Spindletop
    Oilfield." Handbook of Texas Online. The Texas State
    Historical Association.
    https://www.tshaonline.org/handbook/entries/spindleto
    p-oilfield.

## Chapter 2 – Texas Tech, Marriage, and the Depression

Acosta, Teresa Paloma, María-Cristina García, and Cynthia E. Orozco. "Settlement Houses." *Handbook of Texas Online.* The Texas State Historical Association. January 1, 1996 (updated, February 3, 2021). https://www.tshaonline.org/handbook/entries/settlement-houses.

Kever, Jeannie. "Pride lives on in Houston's six historical wards." *Houston Chronicle*, September 7, 2004.

Wagner, Janet K. "Sixth Ward: Carving Out Its Own Place." *Houston History Magazine*, vol. 8, no. 3, pp. 38-41.

Zepeda, Gwendolyn. *The Old Sixth Ward: Carving Out Its Own Place.* Houston: Grand Central Publishing, 2010.

## Chapter 3 – College Station -1941-1948

Butcher, George H. "The Electric Home of the Future." Popular Mechanics Magazine, August 1939, https://blog.coldwellbanker.com/110-years-smart-home-technology-part-one/.

O'Brien, Jay. "Stories From Camp Hearne." KAGS TV. February 22, 2018.

Odintz, Ma Butcher, George H. "The Electric Home of the Future." Popular Mechanics Magazine, August 1939, https://blog.coldwellbanker.com/110-years-smart-home-technology-part-one/rk. "Brazos County." Handbook of Texas Online. The Texas State Historical Association. 1976 (updated September 30, 2020).

https://www.tshaonline.org/handbook/entries/brazos-county.

Texas A&M University. "History of the University." https://www.tamu.edu/about/history.html.

United States Census Bureau. "Census of the Population and Housing."

**Chapter 4 – Los Alamos**

Personal reflections of a time spent in Los Alamos immediately following World War II and the Manhattan Project were in part supplemented by my father, whose participation in the redesign of the original Manhattan Project implosion bomb, Fat Man, made available some anecdotes of interest.

But an important body of work has been developed, including practically every topic imaginable relating to Los Alamos, a substantial portion of which was witnessed by the Manhattan Project scientists. Additional information is available now through the declassification of formerly classified documents as well as documents made available through the various agencies (Atomic Energy Museum, Atomic Heritage Foundation, Atomic Archives, and more) and a few articles written on general interest topics related to life in Los Alamos during the period. Resources referenced in certain specifics known only at the time but not available until recent years include snapshots in time taken from three perspectives:

**As seen through the eight-to-twelve-year-old eyes** that spent some childhood time in Los Alamos during the period immediately post-Manhattan Project. Activities were still secret, and lab employees were barred from discussing their roles in what they were doing.

During our four years in Los Alamos, security was tight—my atomic bomb knowledge remained sketchy. I was aware the Russians had detonated their own version of the atomic bomb, that the US had previously conducted South Pacific tests, that Julius and Ethel Rosenberg had been executed for passing atomic secrets to the Soviets, and that a few spies had been caught.

**As a still school-age student and young adult,** when Dad would occasionally mention a Los Alamos event or circumstance, or when I would examine the goggles he had worn while conducting atomic bomb testing at Yucca Flats, then take them outside to look at the sun.

**As an adult** with research access to formerly classified documents made available after secrecy was lifted and I could look into what had been happening seventy years earlier.

There has been a considerable amount written about the people and activities related to Los Alamos from Manhattan Project times and into the postwar period when Los Alamos laboratories focused on redesigning the original atomic bomb into a more usable format. It was a time when we were there, and Dad was engaged in that activity.

Sources reviewed for the purpose of relating what happened during the critical period following the end of World War II included:

"A short history of women At Los Alamos." Los Alamos
    National Laboratory. March 22, 2018.
    https://www.lanl.gov/discover/science-
    briefs/2018/March/0322-history-of-women.php.

Atomic Archive. "Designs of Two Bombs." Accessed May 13,
    2019. https://www.atomicarchive.com/history/atomic-
    bombing/hiroshima/page-2.html.

"Bayo Canyon, New Mexico, Aggregate Area and Fusrap
    Sites." Energy.gov. Accessed June 2, 2022.
    https://www.energy.gov/lm/bayo-canyon-new-mexico-
    aggregate-area-and-fusrap-sites.

"Electronics and Detonators." Atomic Heritage Foundation,
    July 11, 2017.
    https://www.atomicheritage.org/history/electronics-
    and-detonators.

"Einstein's Letter to President Roosevelt - 1939." Einstein's
    Letter to President Roosevelt - 1939 | Historical
    Documents. Accessed June 3, 2022.
    https://www.atomicarchive.com/resources/documents/b
    eginnings/einstein.html.

Ferenbaugh, Roger W., Thomas E. Buhl, Alan K. Stoker, and
    Wayne R. Hansen. *Environmental Analysis of
    Acid/Middle Pueblo Canyon, Los Alamos, New Mexico.*
    Los Alamos National Laboratory, document number
    LA-9409-MS. August, 1982.

Gibson, Toni Michnovicz and Jon Michnovicz. *Los Alamos: 1944 – 1947*. Charleston: Arcadia Publishing, 2005.

"Glenn Seaborg." Atomic Heritage Foundation. Accessed August 24, 2019. http://www.atomicheritage.org/profile/glenn-seaborg.

Globalsecurity.org - weapons of mass destruction (WMD). Accessed June 8, 2022. https://www.globalsecurity.org/wmd/.

Hales, Peter Bacon. *Atomic Spaces: Living on the Manhattan Project*. Chicago: University of Illinois Press, 1997.

"Harry Daghlian." Atomic Heritage Foundation. https://www.atomicheritage.org/profile/harry-daghlian.

Hawkins, David. "Manhattan District History Project Y The Los Alamos Project Vol. I Inception Until August 1945." United States: N. p., 1961. https://www.osti.gov/biblio/1087644; https://www.osti.gov/servlets/purl/1087644.

Henry Stimson: Statement, August 6,1945. Accessed June 7, 2022. http://www.nuclearfiles.org/menu/library/corresponden ce/stimson-henry/corr_stimson_1945-08-06.htm.

Hosokawa, Bill. Quiz kids-by the dozen. Denver Post, June 19, 1949, 2.

Hunner, Jon. *Inventing Los Alamos: The Growth of an Atomic Community*. Norman: University of Oklahoma Press, 2004.

Jogalekar, Ashutosh. "What John von Neumann really did at Los Alamos." *3 Quarks Daily*, October 26, 2020. https://3quarksdaily.com/3quarksdaily/2020/10/what-john-von-neumann-really-did-at-los-alamos.html.

"John von Neumann." Atomic Heritage Foundation. https://www.atomicheritage.org/profile/john-von-neumann.

"John von Neumann." Famous Scientists. https://www.famousscientists.org/john-von-neumann.

Kelly, Cynthia C., ed. *The Manhattan Project: The Birth of the Atomic Bomb in the Words of Its Creators, Eyewitnesses, and Historians*. New York: Blackdog Press, 2007.

Kiernan, Denise. *The Girls of Atomic City: The Untold Story of the Women Who Helped Win World War II*. New York: Simon & Schuster, Inc., 2013.

"Little Boy and Fat Man." Atomic Heritage Foundation. July 23, 2014. https://www.atomicheritage.org/history/little-boy-and-fat-man.

"Los Alamos, NM." Atomic Heritage Foundation. Accessed 2019. https://www.atomicheritage.org/location/los-alamos-nm.

"Los Alamos Movie Theaters." LOS ALAMOS HISTORY. Accessed June 4, 2022. https://www.losalamoshistory.org/history-blog/los-alamos-movie-theaters.

"Los Alamos." National Parks Service. U.S. Department of the Interior. Accessed June 2, 2022. https://www.nps.gov/mapr/planyourvisit/directions-transportation-los-alamos.htm.

Mason, Katrina R. *Children of Los Alamos: An Oral History of the Town Where the Atomic Age Began.* New York: Twayne Publishers, 1995.

"Computing and the Manhattan Project," Atomic Heritage Foundation, July 18, 2014. https://www.atomicheritage.org/history/computing-and-manhattan-project.

Miller Center. "August 6, 1945: Statement by the President Announcing the Use of the A-Bomb at Hiroshima." https://millercenter.org/the-presidency/presidential-speeches/august-6-1945-statement-president-announcing-use-bomb.

Moore, Alan. "Nevada Test Site Overview." March 18, 2010. https://www.onlinenevada.org/articles/nevada-test-site-overview.

NSA CSS. *Venona.* https://www.nsa.gov/portals/75/documents/news-features/declassified-documents/venona/declass_materials/doc-18.pdf.

"Operation Sandstone." Nuclear Weapons Archive. https://nuclearweaponarchive.org/Usa/Tests/Sandston.html.

Pagano, Owen N. "The Spy Who Stole Urchin: George Koval's Infiltration of the Manhattan Project." PhD diss., The George Washington University, 2014.

"President Roosevelt's Response to Dr. Einstein." President Roosevelt's response to Dr. Einstein | Historical Documents. Accessed June 3, 2022. https://www.atomicarchive.com/resources/documents/beginnings/roosevelt.html.

Seaborg, Glenn T., *The Plutonium Story*. The Journals of Professor Glenn T. Seaborg, 1939 – 1946 New York: Random House, 1995. http://www.atomicheritage.org/profile/glenn-seaborg.

Serber, Robert. *The Los Alamos Primer: The First Lectures on How to Build an Atomic Bomb*. University of California Press, 1992.

"Special Engineer Detachment." Atomic Heritage Foundation. June 4, 2014. https://www.atomicheritage.org/history/special-engineer-detachment.

"Stimson Press Release", Atomic Heritage Foundation., https://www.atomicheritage.org/key-documents/stimson-bomb.

"Tinian Island." Atomic Heritage Foundation. Accessed November 21, 2019. https://www.atomicheritage.org/location/tinian-island.

"Trinity Test – 1945." Atomic Heritage Foundation. June 18, 2014. https://www.atomicheritage.org/history/trinity-test-1945.

Truslow, Edith C., "Manhattan District history. Nonscientific aspects of Los Alamos Project Y, 1942—1946." 1973. United States. https://doi.org/10.2172/4555247. https://www.osti.gov/servlets/purl/4555247.

Truslow, Edith C., and Ralph C. Smith. *Manhattan District History, Project Y, The Los Alamos Project Volume II, August 1945 -December 1946.* Los Alamos: U.S. Atomic Energy Commission (Contract W-7405-ENG). Written in 1947, released in 1961.

United States Nuclear Regulatory Commission, "Fissionable Material,"March 9, 2021 https://www.nrc.gov/reading-rm/basic-ref/glossary/fissionable-material.html.

Venona Intercepts. "The November 12 1944 Cable, and September 21 1941." Nova Online/Secrets, Lies, and Atomic Spies. https://www.pbs.org./wbgh/nova/venona/inte_1944111 2.html.

Venona Intercepts. "The February 9, 1944 cable: Klaus Fuchs and Harry Gold." Nova Online/Secrets, Lies, and Atomic Spies. https://www.pbs.org/wgbh/nova/venona/inte_1944020 9.html.

Venona Intercepts. "The September 21, 1944 cable: The Rosenbergs and the Greenglasses." Nova Online/Secrets, Lies, and Atomic Spies. https://www.pbs.org/wgbh/nova/venona/inte_1944092 1.html.

Whitacre, Madeline, Historian and Belotti, Amy, Archivist, National Security Research Center, "Native American Heritage", Los Alamos National Laboratory, P.O. Box 1663, Los Alamos, New Mexico 87545

Managed By Triad National Security, LLC for the U.S. Dept. of Energy's NNSA. https://discover.lanl.gov/publications/the-vault/2021/native-american-heritage.

Windes, Glenn. "Nuclear Weapons Maintenance in the Early Years – The Mark 5 Bomb." 2002. Global Security.org. https://www.globalsecurity.org/wmd/systems/mk5.htm.

"Why No One Will Ever Build Another Nagasaki Type Bomb." Arms Control Wonk. Accessed June 8, 2022. https://www.armscontrolwonk.com/archive/604623/why-no-one-will-ever-build-another-nagasaki-type-bomb/.

**Chapter 12 – Pierce-Eislen**

Appropriately, some of the information regarding the World Wide Web and its importance as a primary component of the future internet was resourced out of the Web itself. But in the formation of Pierce-Eislen, the majority of information relates to the experiences incurred during the process of developing an internet product from what was first introduced as the World Wide Web and its perceived application potential in the commercial real estate world. Sources accessed included:

"Answers for Young People." Answers for young people - Tim Berners-Lee. Accessed June 3, 2022. https://www.w3.org/People/Berners-Lee/Kids.html.

Berners-Lee, Timothy J. "A Proposal." CERN Document Server, October 28, 1998. https://cds.cern.ch/record/369245?ln=en.

Dennis, M. Aaron. "Tim Berners-Lee." Encyclopedia Britannica, June 4, 2021. https://www.britannica.com/biography/Tim-Berners-Lee.

Gillies, James, and Robert Cailliau. How the Web Was Born: The Story of the World Wide Web. Oxford, New York: Oxford University Press, 2000.

SQL Server Magazine, "Cold Fusion and SQL https://docs.microsoft.com/en-us/previous-

versions/sql/legacy/aa224766(v=sql.80)?redirectedfrom=
    MSDN.

"History of the Web." World Wide Web Foundation.
    https://webfoundation.org/about/vision/history-of-the-
    web/.

Internet Society. "Official Biography: Vint Cerf." Internet Hall
    of Fame, 2022.
    https://www.internethalloffame.org/vint-cerf.

W3C. "Tim Berners-Lee." Accessed June 2, 2022.
    https://www.w3.org/people/Berners-Lee/.

Made in the USA
Las Vegas, NV
21 April 2024

88971267R00236